PATRIOT
AND
PRIEST

MCGILL-QUEEN'S STUDIES IN THE HISTORY OF RELIGION

Volumes in this series have been supported by the Jackman Foundation of Toronto.

SERIES ONE   G.A. RAWLYK, EDITOR

SERIES TWO IN MEMORY OF GEORGE RAWLYK

DONALD HARMAN AKENSON, EDITOR

PATRIOT
AND
PRIEST

Jean-Baptiste Volfius and
the Constitutional Church
in the Côte-d'Or

ANNETTE
CHAPMAN-ADISHO

McGill-Queen's University Press
Montreal & Kingston • London • Chicago

© McGill-Queen's University Press 2019
ISBN 978-0-7735-5870-0 (cloth)
ISBN 978-0-7735-5871-7 (paper)
ISBN 978-0-7735-5987-5 (ePDF)
ISBN 978-0-7735-5988-2 (ePUB)

Legal deposit fourth quarter 2019
Bibliothèque nationale du Québec

Printed in Canada on acid-free paper that is 100% ancient forest free
(100% post-consumer recycled), processed chlorine free

Funded by the   Financé par le
Government   gouvernement
of Canada   du Canada

Canada

Canada Council   Conseil des arts
for the Arts   du Canada

We acknowledge the support of the Canada Council for the Arts.
Nous remercions le Conseil des arts du Canada de son soutien.

Library and Archives Canada Cataloguing in Publication

Title: Patriot and priest : Jean-Baptiste Volfius and the constitutional church
in the Côte-d'Or / Annette Chapman-Adisho.
Other titles: Patriot and priest
Names: Chapman-Adisho, Annette, 1964– author.
Series: McGill-Queen's studies in the history of religion. Series two ; 86.
Description: Series statement: McGill-Queen's studies in the history of religion.
  Series two ; 86 | Includes bibliographical references and index.
Identifiers: Canadiana (print) 20190164891 | Canadiana (ebook) 20190165049
  | ISBN 9780773558717 (paper) | ISBN 9780773558700 (cloth) | ISBN
  9780773559875 (ePDF) | ISBN 9780773559882 (ePUB)
Subjects: LCSH: Volfius, Jean-Baptiste, 1734-1822. | LCSH: Catholic
  Church—France—Côte-d'Or—History—18th century. | LCSH: Catholic
  Church—France—Côte-d'Or—Clergy—History—18th century. | LCSH: Church
  and state—France—Côte-d'Or—History—18th century. | LCSH: France—History
  Revolution, 1789-1799—Religious aspects—Catholic Church. | LCSH: Côte-d'Or
  (France)—Church history—18th century.
Classification: LCC BX1533.C68 C43 2019 | DDC 282.44/4209033—dc23

This book was typeset in 10.5/13 Sabon.

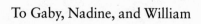

To Gaby, Nadine, and William

Contents

Acknowledgments

Over the course of a long project, one accumulates many debts. I became interested in the experiences of the Catholic Church in revolutionary France in David P. Jordan's seminar at the University of Illinois at Chicago on the Terror. From an initial focus on dechristianization, I moved to this study of Volfius and the Constitutional Church in the Côte-d'Or, landing in this congenial territory through the good offices of David and the late Larry Lee Baker, who proceeded me in the archives in Dijon. Across these many years, David has remained an interested and helpful reader and adviser. His insights into the revolutionaries' complex relationship with Catholicism, and the contributions of Volfius's particular voice, have been invaluable to me. Dale Van Kley provided generous comments at critical stages in this work's production, helping me rethink the study's organization and deepen its argument. I thank the anonymous readers who reviewed this project for McGill-Queen's University Press for their very helpful critiques and commentary. Conversations with Xavier Maréchaux, Gayle V. Fischer, Margo Shea, Josephine Faulk, and the late Betsy Buffington Bates, also proved a great aid in my expansion and revision of this work. In 2010, I had the pleasure of presenting a paper on Volfius in Dijon at a colloquium entitled Religion and Revolution in the Côte-d'Or sponsored by the departmental committee on the history of the revolution. I appreciated the incisive comments my work received there, as well as the gracious hospitality of Christine Lamarre, Claude Farenc, and Frank Laidié. Sébastien Langlois has done a tremendous service to everyone interested in the revolutionary era religious history of northern Burgundy in his organization of the papers of the Abbé Eugène Reinert. He has as well been a most helpful host at the Bibliothèque municipale de Dijon. Archivists, librarians, and reading room staff have been among my greatest allies in this endeavour. I appreciate their knowledge and professionalism as well as the care they take of their aging treasures. In particular, I am indebted to Gérard Moyse, now retired from the Archives départementales de la Côte-d'Or; Fabien Vandemarcq and Valérie Guttienne-Mürger at the Bibliothèque de la Société de Port Royal; and Jacques Rogé, retired archivist of the Archives diocésaines de Dijon. Likewise, I thank the reading room staff of the Archives départementales de la Côte-d'Or, the Newberry Library in Chicago, the Archives nationale Pierrefitte-sur-Seine, and the Philips Reading Room of Widener Library, Harvard University. I would be remiss not to acknowledge the assistance I received from the institutions where I have studied and worked. The interlibrary loan staff at the University of Illinois in Chicago and Salem State University proved time and again that the impossible to obtain was not so. I would like to thank the history departments of both institutions for their financial support at various stages in this project. I also received funding from the College of Arts and Sciences and the School of Graduate Studies at Salem State University. Elizabeth T. Kenney, director of the Center for Research and Creative Activities, and Michele Louro, my colleague in the history department long active in that center, have been steady advocates for university resources to support my work. For her support of this project and steadfast work to see it come into print, I thank Kyla Madden, senior editor at McGill-Queen's University Press. I also thank Barbara Tessman who copyedited this work with great skill and excellent judgment.

Of course, at the end of the day, one returns home. I am most grateful to Gaby Adisho, my partner for all the many years of this endeavour, for his unflagging support, and to my children, Nadine and William, for the joy they have brought me as they grew up with Volfius quietly in the background. Finally, I thank my parents, Joe and Judy Chapman, for their love and encouragement.

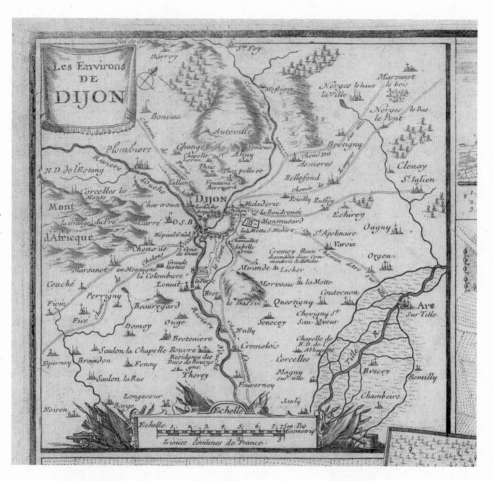

Dijon and surrounding towns, 1770 (detail from map of Dijon, 1770,
Bibliothèque nationale de France).

(*above*) View of Dijon's steeples, 1770 (Bibliothèque nationale de France). This detail from Beaurain's map of Dijon illustrates the importance the mapmaker placed on Dijon's churches. They tower above the city's walls in this image, which places the viewer at ground level.

(*opposite*) René Des Monstiers de Mérinville (Bibliothèque nationale de France).

M. RENÉ DESMONSTIER
DE MERINVILLE.

Evêque de Dijon, Conseiller né du
Parlement dè Bourgogne.

Né dans le Dioe de Limoges le 1er Juille 1742.

Député du Baillage de Dijon.

à l'Assemblée   Nationale de

17   89.

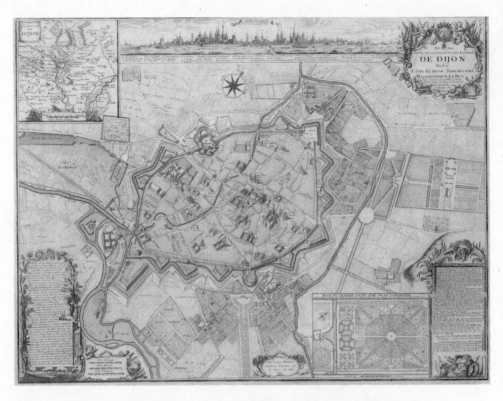

Map of Dijon, 1770 (Bibliothèque nationale de France). This imagined bird's-eye view of Dijon depicts the city principally through its churches, including all the parishes of pre-revolutionary Dijon. It also indicates the faubourgs of Saint-Nicolas and Saint-Pierre, whose parishioners played an active role in petitioning the department to maintain churches more convenient to them in 1791 and 1792 during the struggle over the reduction of parishes in the city.

J.-B. Volfius (Archives diocésaines, Dijon).

Dome of church, Convent of the Bernardines (Bibliothèque municipale de Dijon, L-Est-I 1). In its 1791 plan to reduce Dijon's parishes, the National Assembly proposed an oratory in the chapel of the Bernardine Convent. Both Volfius and the sisters opposed this decision, noting the church's small size.

Saint Jean's Square (Bibliothèque municipale de Dijon, L Est AM-II 11). The refractory priests incarcerated in the spring and summer of 1792 were held in the former seminary located next to Saint Jean's Square.

Views of Saint-Michel and Notre Dame of Dijon (Bibliothèque municipale de Dijon, L Est. AM I-29 and L Est. JE-I 9). In 1791, the National Assembly proposed to reduce Dijon's parishes to four. Among those it proposed to retain were Saint-Michel and Notre-Dame. These wealthy parishes had two of the most ornate churches in the diocese. Parishioners from Saint-Pierre and Saint-Nicolas challenged the assembly's plans, arguing that closing their churches was poor repayment for their support for the revolution.

View of the Cathedral of Saint-Bénigne (Bibliothèque municipale de Dijon, L Est. AH-I 1). Previously the church of the Benedictine monastery in Dijon, Saint-Bénigne became the cathedral of the new diocese of the Côte-d'Or in May 1792.

Map indicating the boundaries of old regime dioceses (1789) within the department and diocese of the Côte-d'Or (from Jean Rigault, *Guide des archives de la Côte-d'Or* [Dijon: Archives départementales de la Côte-d'Or, 1984]. Used with permission of the archives). The diocese of the Côte-d'Or incorporated the former diocese of Dijon in its entirety, as well as portions of the former dioceses of Langres, Autun, Chalon, and Besançon.

LE DÉPARTEMENT EN 1790 : DISTRICTS ET CANTONS .

Autricourt

Villers-Patras
Molesme
Montigny/A

Châtillon / Seine
Laignes
Vanvey

Savoisy
Aisey-le-Duc
Recey / O.

Villaines-en-D.
Aignay-le-Duc
Minot

Grancey-le
-Château
Selongey
Montigny
/V.

Montbard
Bussy
Baigneux-les-Juifs
Salives

Moutier-St-Jean
Saulx-le-D
Fontaine Fr

Flavigny
Frôlois
La Margelle
Is-sur-Tille
Bèze

Epoisses
Semur-en-Auxois
Salmaise
St-Seine-l'Ab.
Gemeaux
Beaumont

Rouvray
Précy-sous-
-Thil
Vitteaux
Messigny
St-Julien

Normier
Lantenay
Plomb.
Mirabeau
Talmay

Saulieu
Mont-
St-J.
Pouilly-en
-A.
Sombernon
Fleurey / O.
Dijon
Longvic
Arc-sur-T
Binges
Pontailler

Quemigny
Gevrey
Rouvres-en-P
Genlis
Pluvault

Liernais
Arconcey
Châteauneuf
Savouges
Aiserey
Auxonne

Marcheseuil
Veuvey
Vergy
Nuits-St-Georges
St-Jean-de
-Losne

Arnay-le-Duc
Bligny / O.
Savigny
Corgoloin
Argilly
Bonnencontre

Viévy
Ivry
Bouze
Beaune
Labergé
Seurre

Nolay
Meursault
Pommard
Meursanges

Corpeau
Merceuil

N

• Chefs-lieux de district

• Chefs-lieux de canton

⁝ Longvic, Pommard : cantons extra-muros

—··— limites de canton

—— limites de district

l.c.u.d.

0   20 km

Map of the department of the Côte-d'Or with districts, cantons, and major
towns (from Jean Rigault, *Guide des archives de la Côte-d'Or* [Dijon: Archives
départementales de la Côte-d'Or, 1984]. Used with permission of
the archives).

PATRIOT
AND
PRIEST

Introduction

On 23 January 1791, Jean-Baptiste Volfius, a priest and professor of eloquence and rhetoric at the Collège des Godrans in Dijon, swore to be faithful to the nation, its laws, and the king, and to maintain "with all my power the constitution decreed by the National Assembly and accepted by the king."[1] By doing so, the fifty-six-year-old Volfius aligned himself with the assembly's vision for a smaller, state-sponsored French Catholic Church. In the revolution's first six months, the National Constituent Assembly divested the church of its wealth, first by abolishing the tithe in August 1789 and then by placing church properties at the disposal of the nation in November of that year. Despite these actions, the revolutionaries pledged to support the former First Estate – the issue was how to do so.

Through its Ecclesiastical Committee, the Constituent Assembly worked out a plan for the reform of the French Catholic Church – the Civil Constitution of the Clergy.[2] Debate opened on the proposed legislation at the end of May 1790. On 12 July, the legislature approved the plan, and, in late August, Louis XVI promulgated it. Its title underscores two important aspects of this new relationship between church and state. First, the plan focused on *civil* or state regulation of the French Catholic Church that was not dependent on the approval of either the French church or the papacy. Although the French Catholic Church had long been a pillar of the French monarchy, the revolution marked a fundamental change in this relationship. The clergy would no longer be a wealthy, well-organized estate in a social order that was divided into three unequal tiers, two (the clergy and the nobility) enjoying most of the privileges and one (the Third Estate) saddled with the most onerous duties. The clergy were now citizens, equal in rights and responsibilities with all others. Second, the assembly defined this new relationship as part of the nation's *constitution*. The assembly proposed to reorganize the former First Estate as part of its plan to address the state's fiscal problems as well as to further its commitment to a society that enshrined the ideals of liberty, equality, and fraternity. The Civil Constitution of the Clergy incorporated France's clergy into the state's political and administrative structures. Regional electors would select parish clergy and bishops, just as they chose other public servants. Further, as public servants, clergy would be compensated by the state. It mattered little that the assembly's work on France's first constitution was not complete when it approved the Civil Constitution of the Clergy in July 1790. This legislation was the first dividend of the promised new order.

As he swore allegiance to the nation, law, and king, Volfius embraced the changes the state proposed for French Catholicism. Beside him were eight of his fellow faculty members from the Collège des Godrans. Not all oath takers in the revolution's second winter were enthusiastic about the assembly's vision for France's Catholic Church. For some, juring, or swearing the oath, simply ensured they would remain in their parish.[3] Volfius, however, had strong revolutionary credentials. In the revolution's first summer, he served as chaplain to Dijon's bourgeois militia, which had been established in response to rumours of unrest in the countryside. The following winter, he became president of city's *Club patriotique*. In addition, Volfius's family was politically active. His younger brother, Alexandre-Eugène, an attorney, played a leading role in Dijon's Third Estate when it met in the spring of 1789 and served as one of its deputies to the Estates-General. The younger Volfius, a member of the Constituent Assembly, remained in Paris as Volfius took the ecclesiastical oath.

Asking clergy to swear an oath of allegiance was not a radical innovation in a revolution characterized by oath taking. The oath required of the clergy was essentially the same as that sworn by General Lafayette and fifty thousand National Guardsmen and troops of the line just six months earlier, in July 1790. Lafayette and his men took their oath as the nation celebrated the first anniversary of the Bastille's fall. What distinguished the ecclesiastical oath from this earlier pledge was the promise to uphold the Civil Constitution of the Clergy. This constitution was the problematic aspect of the oath for many churchmen. France's bishops rejected the oath almost to a man, with only seven jurers among France's 160 archbishops, bishops, and bishops *in partibus*.[4] Response among parish clergy was much higher, but still 47 percent refused to jure.[5] The ecclesiastical oath of 1791 created a schism in the French Catholic Church that persisted for a decade.[6] Unwittingly, by requiring clergy to declare themselves for or against the Civil Constitution of the Clergy, the National Constituent Assembly provided an informal referendum on the revolution. Then, by allowing those who rejected the oath to remain, at least initially, in their parishes, the assembly embedded an important opposition to its efforts.

What was so objectionable about this legislation? To begin with, it decreed a sweeping reorganization of the French Catholic Church, aligning diocesan boundaries with the newly established eighty-three departments. Going forward, local electoral assemblies would select bishops and parish priests, with no special role or weight given to clergy or even to Catholics. Granted, most French men were Catholic (unsurprisingly, women could neither sit as electors nor stand for office), but in some border regions Protestants and Jews were numerous. By October, the thirty bishops sitting in the National Constituent Assembly organized their opposition and published a pamphlet, *Exposition des principes sur la Constitution du clergé*.[7] The bishops argued that the establishment of diocesan councils under the Civil Constitution of the Clergy infringed on episcopal authority. A further objection was the lack of church endorsement for the proposed reforms. As France's bishops made clear, canon law required that either the pope or a church council approve ecclesiastical reforms. Even assuming such an endorsement was forthcoming (and it never was), the bishops rejected the idea that the state could deprive a bishop of his see – a fate faced by 52 titular bishops under the terms of the Civil Constitution, which reduced the number of France's dioceses from 135 to 83. The deputy bishops sought adherents to their position, quickly collecting over 100 signatures and launching a pamphlet war that carried on into the following spring.[8]

Pope Pius VI rejected the revolution's ecclesiastical reforms, including the Civil Constitution. Initially he communicated his objections only to Louis XVI. Despite the pope's warning, the king moved cautiously to enact the legislation, attempting to gain papal support for its most critical provisions. Pius VI's definitive public statement on the revolution's ecclesiastical legislation was slow in coming. Only in the early spring of 1791, after the assembly's decision to require the ecclesiastical oath created a schism in the French church, did the pope issue two bulls, *Quod Aliquantum* and *Charitas*. In the first, he rejected the premise that the church's governance was temporal and not spiritual, and therefore that a secular body could regulate it; in the second, he condemned the newly forming constitutional episcopate and clergy, calling on all who had sworn the ecclesiastical oath to retract it within forty days.[9]

Jean-Baptiste Volfius not only swore the ecclesiastical oath but accepted election as bishop of the diocese of the Côte-d'Or in February 1791. The bishop of Dijon, René Des Monstiers de Mérinville, whose diocese formed the core of the new see, refused to jure the oath, leaving the seat unoccupied, at least from the perspective of the department's administrators. Rejecting the right of the department to elect a new bishop, Des Monstiers de Mérinville left in April for exile. Serving as a deputy to the National Constituent Assembly, Des Monstiers departed from Paris, relating his displeasure with events in his see through pastoral letters. Volfius, newly sanctified as the bishop of the Côte-d'Or, began his effort to govern according to the requirements of the Civil Constitution.

This book, a history of Jean-Baptiste Volfius's episcopacy and the constitutional church in the Côte-d'Or, demonstrates the fortunes and misfortunes of this revolutionary experiment in ecclesiastical reform over its ten-year lifespan. Built out of the archives, this account offers a social and intellectual history of the constitutional church in a provincial setting. Volfius was a thoroughly provincial character. His career did not carry him to Paris. On one opportunity to go to the capital (to lobby for a lycée), he begged off, citing a pressing need to visit the parishes of his diocese.[10] Volfius's career, which he pursued outside of France's political centre, provides an opportunity to see a revolutionary experiment in ecclesiology in a setting that was not driven by national developments or dominated by someone who divided his attention between the local and the national. In its focus on the Côte-d'Or and Volfius, this study expands existing historical work on the constitutional church.

A brief overview of how historians have treated the constitutional church and its clergy is helpful here. After a long history of derision and marginalization by ecclesiastical historians in the nineteenth century, the bishops and clergy of the constitutional church began to find their historians in the twentieth century.[11] By mid-century, studies of the constitutional church expanded from institutional and political concerns to include inquiries into the theological, social, and intellectual facets of this and other aspects of the revolution's religious history.[12] Since the bicentennial in 1989, there has been a further expansion of interest in the constitutional church and the revolution's religious history, including several studies of constitutional bishops.[13] Pride of place belongs to the indomitable Abbé Grégoire. A clergy deputy from Lorraine, Grégoire served in every national legislature from 1789 to 1814, except that of 1791 to 1792 (the Legislative Assembly).[14] He was also a key figure in the reorganization of the constitutional church as the Gallican church in the spring of 1795.[15]

Historians have also examined the careers of several other constitutional clergy active at the national level. One such figure is Adrien Lamourette. Before becoming a constitutional bishop, Lamourette, a Lazarist priest, was a national literary figure engaged in an effort to reconcile the ideas of the French Enlightenment with Catholic theology; with the advent of the revolution, he embraced a theology that united Christianity with the democratic ideals of participatory government.[16] Unlike Volfius's career in the constitutional church, Lamourette's involvement in national politics cut his episcopacy short. In 1791, he went to Paris to serve as a deputy in the Legislative Assembly; his support for Lyon's Girondist revolt, however, resulted in his arrest in September 1793 and his execution early the next year.

Following the Terror, a group of constitutional bishops, clergy, and an activist layman reorganized the constitutional church as the Gallican church. Known as the United Bishops (*Évêques réunis*) this group initially consisted of Augustin-Jean-Charles Clément, constitutional priest and, after 1797, constitutional bishop of the Seine-et-Oise; Jean-Baptiste Royer, constitutional bishop of the Ain and later the Seine; Éléonore-Marie Desbois de Rochefort, constitutional bishop of the Somme; Charles Saillant, a physician and close associate of Clément; and Henri Grégoire, constitutional bishop of Loire-et-Cher. Based in Paris, the group worked tirelessly to revive the revolution's early vision of a national French Catholic Church, but without the financial and administrative relationship to the state decreed by the Civil Constitution of the Clergy. Studies of the challenges, victories, and conflicts of the United Bishops provide important insights into the religious history of the revolution and how a pro-revolutionary Catholicism fared after the National Convention turned away from the Civil Constitution of the Clergy.[17] Other studies expand our knowledge of constitutional clergy and bishops, looking at those active in Paris and in several provincial regions.[18]

In addition to its focus on Volfius, this book presents a regional case study of the constitutional church, supplementing several regional studies of the revolution's religious history that have appeared since the bicentennial. Among these are a study of the struggles between Protestants and Catholics in Languedoc and a study of constitutional and refractory clergy in Lyon.[19] Both of these regions experienced significant religious conflict in the decade from 1791 to 1801. In neither area did the constitutional church have the breathing room to develop its institutions or personnel. Earlier regional studies of Normandy, the Limousin, and Alsace include an examination of both constitutional and refractory clergy.[20] This study joins these earlier works but with a particular interest in the constitutional church and its clergy. With the church judged a schismatic development by Pope Pius VI, historians frequently introduce its history with an assessment of its orthodoxy. While not arguing that, in the lights of Rome, the constitutional church of the Côte-d'Or was orthodox, this study begins with the premise that the clergy who swore the ecclesiastical oath did so believing that the Civil Constitution of the Clergy was not a rejection of Catholic tradition, practice, or theology. Further, they took the oath before Pope Pius VI made his objections known. Once called upon to retract, some did; others, however, persevered, arguing that the reforms implemented by the Civil Constitution returned the church to a purer, more primitive Christianity. That they were mistaken in believing that this revolutionary Catholic Church would prevail is clearer in hindsight than it would have been at the time.

History plays out in both grand and small theatres, and this book looks at the smaller stage, the regional production, not the national one. It addresses questions of the daily experience in the revolution of these constitutional clergy and their bishop. What challenges did they face as they organized themselves and their churches in Dijon, Il-sur-Tille, or Beaune? How did they understand this new church and its relationship to the changes wrought by the revolution? Did the revolutionary rethinking of politics and society extend to theology?

In this book, I address questions that are important for understanding local experience. For example, who took up the effort to build the constitutional church in the Côte-d'Or with Volfius? How did Volfius and the constitutional priests of his diocese interact with each other and with local and national authorities? What was the relationship between the constitutional and the refractory clergy (the term used for those who did not swear the ecclesiastical oath)? What was the response of the laity to this division in the French Catholic church in the Côte-d'Or? And how did all these issues evolve over time? Through the debate between Volfius and Des Monstiers de Mérinville over the legitimacy of the new church and its bishop in the spring of 1791, I look at the underpinning in patristics, church history and doctrine, and biblical studies with reference to the claims of both the proponents and opponents of the constitutional church. I also examine the constitutional church in the Côte-d'Or, and Volfius's continuing leadership, after the Terror, when issues of church discipline and the relationship of this new church, the Gallican Church, to the French state came to the fore.

Regional figures populate the pages of this book, and their story demonstrates the challenges, opportunities, reversals, and changes of heart that made up life in the revolution's first decade. For Catholic clergy, the revolution's developments presented a recurring threat of exile, violence, and, less dramatically, marginalization. Despite the religious reform enacted in the Civil Constitution of the Clergy, the revolutionary assemblies in Paris were never of one mind concerning the French Catholic Church, thus making even clergy who cooperated with their decrees susceptible to harassment and persecution.

Volfius's episcopacy and the experiences of the constitutional clergy of the Côte-d'Or provide important insights into the nature and course of this revolutionary experiment in ecclesiastical reform. Volfius was the only bishop in the department across the ten-year lifespan of the constitutional church. He navigated the challenges of establishing the new church organization, faced its dissolution during the year of the Terror, and returned to his work in its new formulation as the Gallican church after the National Convention upheld the principle of religious liberty in the spring of 1795. Only in October 1801 did Volfius step down as bishop of the Côte-d'Or. He did so adhering to the Concordat reached by Napoleon and Pope Pius VII.

Volfius's ten-year episcopacy is somewhat unusual. Only 33 of the 116 men who served as bishops in the constitutional church remained in place in a single diocese across the decade 1791–1801. Of these 33, 12 spent some portion of the decade in Paris as deputies to France's various revolutionary assemblies. Claude-François-Marie Primat and Jean-Baptiste Royer served as bishops during the entire

decade but did so in two different dioceses. Primat was the constitutional bishop of the Nord before becoming the metropolitan bishop
of Lyon in 1798; Royer, constitutional bishop of the Ain, became
metropolitan of Paris in 1795.

Volfius's career is distinct in other ways as well. While some constitutional clergy, including key leadership in Paris, embraced a
Jansenist ethic and piety, especially after the church's reorganization
in 1795, Volfius was not an adherent of Jansenism. He began his
career as a Jesuit, and it was the order's dissolution in 1763 that
redirected his path toward a position at his secondary school alma
mater, the Collège des Godrans, and as a diocesan priest in Dijon.
As bishop of the Côte-d'Or, Volfius took a charitable view of the
non-juring clergy and sought their reconciliation with the juring
clergy and himself.

The Côte-d'Or presents an interesting location for a study of the
constitutional church. The department had a strong rate of oath taking in the spring of 1791. Sixty-two per cent of parish clergy took
the ecclesiastical oath that year, which was better than the national
average of 52.2 per cent. Juring clergy remained in the majority in
the Côte-d'Or through the early revolution. In the fall of 1792, the
department still had 58 per cent of parish clergy adhering to the ecclesiastical oath.[21] While several factors influenced clergy's responses to
the oath, the constitutional church in the Côte-d'Or began with a
better than average level of support. In exploring northern Burgundy,
this study offers an expansion of regional treatments of the constitutional church and its clergy. In a region located close to the border
with Switzerland, the history of the constitutional clergy in the Côte-
d'Or also sheds light on less well-documented issues such as the
movement in and out of France of refractory clergy and apostolic
vicars, representatives of Catholic bishops or Pope Pius VI. These
envoys worked in various ways to support the refractory clergy.

Historians understand the rupture in the French church and
between Rome and revolutionary France in various ways. Some see
these developments as marking the threshold of the modern era, her-
alding the secularization of European culture in the nineteenth and
twentieth centuries.[22] Others, looking back across the eighteenth
century, point instead to a long-term trend of dechristianization.[23]
Still others understand the revolution's conflicted religious history
as more contingent, less determined by the past or determining of
the future.[24] Volfius and the constitutional clergy in the Côte-d'Or

demonstrate that, while the ecclesiastical oath of 1791 allowed for an initial count of adherents to the Civil Constitution of the Clergy, these priests' oscillated in their support for the revolution and for Volfius. Further, in the perspective of strongly committed constitutional clergy, such as Volfius, the church was never as clearly split as history depicts. Although arguably victims of wishful thinking, Volfius and his colleagues continued to see the possibility of applying the revolution's ecclesiastical reforms across the diocese throughout the ten-year period of the constitutional church's existence.

This book's organization is chronological. The decision to approach this study in a linear manner developed naturally from the ambition to examine the constitutional clergy in the Côte-d'Or across the lifespan of their church. Temporal developments shaped their circumstances. Part of the interest of this study is to trace how the pro-revolutionary ideals of the constitutional clergy fared as the revolution evolved politically and ideologically. The first chapter discusses the establishment of the diocese of Dijon and presents an early modern tale that belies any assumption of rigid hierarchies in church-and-state relations. It also demonstrates that local ecclesiastical authorities wielded considerable influence. Chapter 2 examines the early days of the revolution in the diocese and the responses of its clergy to the call for the estates to meet and write their *cahiers* for the king. Oath taking in the department and the controversies surrounding the election of Jean-Baptiste Volfius as bishop are examined in chapter 3. Then, chapter 4 looks at the agency of national and local actors, including parishioners, in shaping the application of the Civil Constitution of the Clergy's redistricting of parishes in the Côte-d'Or. With chapter 5, the crisis of the French Revolution for Catholic priests accelerates, with a first terror aimed at the refractory clergy in 1792. The experiences in the Côte-d'Or demonstrate the importance of provincial initiatives in this national effort to confront the non-juring clergy. Even as the revolution launched its war against enemies abroad, it came increasingly to worry about enemies at home. Chapter 6 examines the turning of this hostility toward the constitutional clergy in the Terror and the dechristianization movement of 1793 and 1794.

The next three chapters examine the remnants of the constitutional church in the Côte-d'Or that remade itself as part of the Gallican church during the period of Thermidor and the Directory. Chapter 7 examines the constitutional church's efforts to rebuild in the changed atmosphere in church-and-state relations that followed the fall of Robespierre. No longer a partner with the state in the regeneration of the nation, the constitutional clergy of the Côte-d'Or, though few in number, regrouped and considered their future. Chapter 9 looks at the local impact of the Directory's ambivalent policy of religious freedom. Efforts under the Directory to guide citizens to a "rational" religion that included renewed persecution of clergy are the subject of Chapter 9. Chapter 10 examines the conciliar vision of the Gallican Church through its two national councils and especially in its local expression in the synod of the Côte-d'Or, held in 1800. Finally, the Epilogue considers the work of reconciling the clergy in the Côte-d'Or in the years after the Concordat of 1801.

Creating a Diocese: The Case of Dijon

Creating a new diocese was not an ordinary event in the French Catholic Church. In fact, it was exceptional. By the early medieval period, the ecclesiastical provinces and dioceses of France were largely determined.[1] The only period of notable new development came in the fourteenth century, when the second Avignon pope, John XXII, established sixteen new dioceses to combat the heresy of Catharism. All but two of these, as one might expect given the pope's aim, were in southern France. Even after the Concordat of Bologna (1516) gave French kings the right to nominate bishops, they rarely attempted to add dioceses, despite the patronage opportunities this offered. To create a diocese was a complicated affair. It involved negotiating with cathedral chapters and great abbeys that could provide the revenue (*mense épiscopale*) for the diocese. Appealing to abbots and canons to place the wealth of their institutions at the disposal of a new bishop was not easy.[2] Despite a conservative approach to ecclesiastical redistricting, the monarchy did establish four new dioceses in the seventeenth century – Paris (1622), Albi (1675), Blois (1697), and Alais (1697) – and five in the eighteenth century – Dijon (1731), Saint-Claude (1741), Nancy (1777), Saint-Dié (1777), and Moulins (1788).[3] In total, then, on the eve of the revolution, France had 130 dioceses. The city leaders of Dijon had first proposed an episcopal see for their city in the late sixteenth century, and their efforts illustrate the difficulties of redrawing ecclesiastical boundaries as well the complex interplay of parties in both the church and the state whose interests a new diocese affected.

Dijon's growth as a centre for government administration and commerce inspired the overtures to create a bishop's seat in the city. For two centuries, the dukes of Burgundy had made Dijon their capital, spending lavishly to create a refined court culture that rivalled the capitals of Italy and even of France. With the death of Charles the Bold, the last duke of Burgundy in 1477, King Louis XI claimed the duchy. Louis based his title on a century-old agreement that Burgundy would revert to France should the duchy's Valois line end. Louis's land grab did not go unchallenged, and he spent the next six years securing it. In the meantime, to attach the territory ever more firmly to the French state, he established important legal and ennobling institutions within it. Louis placed a sovereign court (*parlement*) in Beaune, and a second peripatetic court (*parlement*) in Dole and Saint-Laurens. The peace of Arras in 1482 settled France's control over Burgundy. Because Beaune had joined the Prince of Orange's challenge to France's claim, Louis XI moved that city's sovereign court to Dijon in 1480.[4] In the century that followed, France's kings favoured Dijon with several more judicial institutions. In the mid-sixteenth century, Francis I established a criminal court (*tournelle)* at Dijon; Henri II added a bureau of forests and waterways (*table de marbre*); and Henry III placed both a chamber of petitions (*chamber des requêtes*) and a bureau of finance in the city. The royal courts and bureaus supported a growing Second Estate of robed nobility who manned the multi-layered legal establishment. For James Farr, these developments in Dijon amounted to a "judicial revolution," that peaked from 1550 to 1650. The growth of Dijon's robed nobility also increased the city's wealth, noticeable in a general shift by the city's artisans to the production of luxury goods. Farr notes that, from 1643 to 1750, the types of luxuries available and the number of artisans involved in these crafts exploded. These included faience makers, carriage makers, painters, sculptors, wigmakers, jewellers, gilders, and more. By 1750, the tax rolls listed 133 luxury artisans, up from forty-nine in 1643.[5] Tax rolls for the era also indicate an increase in individual wealth in Dijon. By the mid-seventeenth century, government ledgers placed an increasing number of individuals in the categories of *bourgeois* and *rentiers*.

STRUGGLE TO ESTABLISH
A NEW DIOCESE AT DIJON

It was in this period of Dijon's growth as a regional administrative centre that the first efforts to secure a bishop for the city occurred. These years overlapped with France's wars of religion. Clouded by the dust of a tumultuous history, the first efforts to establish a diocese in Dijon have been recounted in various ways by historians. Claude Courtépée and Edme Beguillet noted five early efforts by the Dijonnais to secure an episcopal seat: 1575, 1578, 1592, 1597, and 1630.[6] Courtépée and Beguillet provided no details, but their dating is interesting, considering that, from the mid-1570s, Dijon was a centre of the Catholic League, one of the belligerent forces challenging the Crown in the last decade of the wars of religion. The two efforts (1592 and 1597) during Henri IV's reign are also historically curious, as the bishop of Langres, Charles d'Escars, whose territory would be reduced by the creation of a diocese in Dijon, was among the first prelates to support Henri IV, the former protestant leader whose opportunity to reign provided the occasion for his conversion. The order of Henri IV's council supporting the establishment of a diocese at Dijon is one of the archival traces of this early history.[7]

In 1629, Sebastien Zamet, bishop of Langres, made the best-documented effort before the eighteenth century to establish an episcopal seat in Dijon. A reforming bishop involved in both the Catholic Counter-Reformation and the spiritual revival of the Abbey of Port Royal in Paris, Zamet proposed a second seat for his diocese, at La Sainte-Chapelle in Dijon. His attempt to establish this episcopal seat in Dijon provides an interesting window into the complexity of the relationships between church and state in the early modern period and into the competing interests within both.

Born into a family well connected at court, Zamet became bishop of Langres in 1615 at the age of twenty-seven. His ecclesiastical career had begun at the age of three, when Henri IV named the youngster the abbot of Juilly. Zamet's father, an Italian financier attached to the court of France since the 1570s, administered the abbey during his son's minority. Educated at the Sorbonne, Zamet completed a doctorate and served as confessor (*aumônier ordinaire*) to the king. Henri IV remained attentive to Zamet's career and sought to make him the coadjutor to the aged bishop of Langres, Charles d'Escars. However, d'Escars's brother, the Cardinal de Givry, already held the coadjutorship and refused to resign from the lucrative benefice, despite also holding the position of bishop of Metz. In the end, d'Escars survived his brother by two years, and Marie de Medici, Henri IV's widow and regent for the young Louis XIII, named Zamet as coadjutor in 1612.[8] Three years later, upon d'Escars's death, Zamet succeeded to the bishopric.

Young and energetic, Zamet embraced the spirit of the Counter-Reformation. In harmony with the Council of Trent's recommendations, he visited his diocese and worked to improve the clergy's preparation by establishing a seminary at Langres as well as an oratory, a congregation of secular priests devoted to prayer, preaching, and the sacraments, at Dijon. In 1624, he asked Louis XIII to grant him a coadjutor, but the king refused. Five years later, he approached the king again, asking that he support a second episcopal seat at La Sainte-Chapelle in Dijon.[9] La Sainte-Chapelle was an interesting choice. Established in 1172 by Hughes III, duke of Burgundy, following his return from the Holy Land, the chapel enjoyed an exalted position among Dijon's churches. Governed by a dean and initially ten (later twenty-five) canons, the chapel also housed the Holy Host (*la Sainte Hostie*), a gift from Pope Eugene IV in 1433. Imprinted with the figure of a seated Christ, the host purportedly bled at points depicting the wounds of the crucifixion. The dean of la Sainte-Chapelle played a leadership role among Dijon's parishes, presiding over the meetings Dijon's assembly of the clergy.

In his proposal for the second episcopal seat, Zamet carefully delineated the rights the bishop would enjoy at La Sainte-Chapelle, which amounted to officiating at a handful of high feast days. Zamet stated that the second seat would not be used as a first step toward the "dismemberment" of the diocese of Langres, and, to ensure this, his plan required that the bishop and the dean of La Sainte-Chapelle each take an oath never to seek a division of the diocese. Zamet succeeded in getting the endorsement of the king's council, which issued an opinion in favour of his proposal on 19 February 1630.[10] Louis XIII followed the council's pronouncement with a letter to the pope. Thinking all was in order, Zamet dispatched an envoy to Rome with the draft text of a bull the pope might issue.

Opposition came swiftly. The dean of La Sainte-Chapelle asserted that he had not consented to the project, claiming that the church treasurer's endorsement, given in his name, did not represent his views. Joining the dean in the outcry against the second seat were the cathedral canons of Langres, who petitioned the king in early January, as well as the abbots of Dijon's two collegial churches, Saint-Etienne and the Benedictine abbey of Saint-Bénigne. On 21 March, the aggrieved parties dispatched an agent (*procureur*) to Rome to oppose Zamet's project. Besides the ecclesiastical parties, the opposition to Zamet's plan included the mayor and deputies (*échevins*) of Langres. The municipal authorities of Langres were intent on preserving the essential activity the episcopal seat brought to the town, which, unlike Dijon, had not experienced an infusion of governmental offices and the attendant commercial growth. As *mémoires* (public legal briefs) and pamphlets, as well as the coalition of aggrieved parties grew, the Parlement de Paris took up the issue. In early May, the *parlement* annulled the order of the king's council and called upon the Bishop of Langres to explain his project. In the face of this opposition, Zamet withdrew the proposal. Lest the young bishop think again about establishing a seat in Dijon, the canons of Langres commissioned André de Saussay, a popular preacher at court, to write a pamphlet against the project.[11] Priest of the Parisian parishes of Saint-Leu and Saint-Gilles (and, later in his career, bishop of Toul), de Saussay argued that a bishop was "married" to his cathedral church. Zamet's proposal to establish a second cathedral in Dijon was reminiscent, de Saussay opined, of the patriarch Jacob's ingratitude in seeking the beautiful Rachel as a second wife despite already being married to Leah.

The failure of Zamet's proposal is instructive. The second episcopal seat negotiated by Zamet with the canons of La Sainte-Chapelle gave the bishop a very limited scope of activity. Only on a handful of designated occasions would the bishop officiate at La Sainte-Chapelle. When he did so, the proposal carefully defined the prerogatives and position in processions of the canons of La Sainte-Chapelle and the cathedral canons of Langres. Yet even these modest aims provoked strong reaction from ecclesiastical and civil authorities, who found them to be against their interests, and they did not hesitate to turn to Rome and to Paris to make their case against the bishop, and the king who supported him. Following the failure of Zamet's proposal, it would be almost a century before the Dijonnais initiated another effort to establish a diocese in their city.

In 1725, a new effort to establish a diocese in Dijon began. Courtépée and Beguillet credited the success of this initiative to the royal governor of the province, Louis-Henri, prince de Bourbon-Condé.[12] Other historians have likewise emphasized the prince's involvement.[13] Doubtless the support of Henri-Louis, a prince of the blood, was significant for this renewed initiative. We must place Courtépée and Beguillet's assessment in its eighteenth century context, however: in the 1770s, when Courtépée and Beguillet published their work, Henri-Louis's son was governor of Burgundy. Beyond the support of the prince, other important factors aligned in the 1720s to aid the creation of a diocese in Dijon.

The first was the candidate for bishop and his careful positioning. In 1726, Louis XV designated Jean Bouhier, dean of La Sainte-Chapelle, to be bishop, five years before the diocese's creation.[14] By the eighteenth century, the dean of La Sainte-Chapelle was also the vicar general of the archdeaconry of Dijon, and this archdeaconry formed the territory for the new diocese. A further point in his favour was Bouhier's strong connections to Dijon's legal elite. From a family of *parlémentaires*, he began his career as a clerical member (*conseiller clerc*) of the *parlement* of Burgundy and held that position until he became dean of La Sainte-Chapelle in 1703. In 1723, he became as well the first chancellor of Dijon's newly established law school. Bouhier's positioning to be bishop went beyond these important ecclesiastical and legal connections to include the very pragmatic issues of revenue and local church politics. In 1724, the death of Bishop François de Clermont-Tonnerre left the seat of the diocese of Langres vacant. Over the course of the seventeenth century, the bishop of Langres had become the titular head of the Abbey of Saint-Bèze and, in 1721, of Dijon's Saint-Étienne, thus receiving the revenues of these two abbeys.[15] Following Clermont-Tonnerre's death, the king's council issued an order putting the two abbeys under the authority of Bouhier, thus, redirecting the revenue of these abbeys to Bouhier as well as placing him at the head of one traditional centre of opposition to a bishop in Dijon, the Abbey of Saint-Étienne.[16] From that time, the effort to establish the diocese spanned seven years, 1724–31.[17]

Bouhier's candidacy for bishop, even the idea of establishing a bishopric in Dijon, quickly gained opponents, among them the cathedral canons of Langres.[18] The consistorial secretariat of the Vatican also raised concerns requiring clarification. These included the boundaries and parishes of the new diocese; its impact on the episcopal *mense* of Langres; the rights, privileges, and jurisdiction of the canons of Saint-Étienne as well as those of La Sainte-Chapelle and Saint-Bénigne; and the access of the diocese of Langres to the two seminaries in Dijon.[19] Despite the opposition to the new diocese, this time the effort succeeded. On 9 April 1731, Pope Clement XII issued a bull establishing the diocese of Dijon. Louis XV then issued the necessary letters patent, which the *parlement* of Burgundy registered on 8 August. Louis XV justified the new diocese by declaring that it had been sought by several kings and that it would further the faith, because the territory of Langres was too large to be effectively overseen. Further, as the capital of the province of Burgundy, Dijon had the dignity and population necessary for a bishop.[20]

The boundaries of the new diocese conformed to the former archdeaconry of Dijon. No territory was taken from either of the new diocese's large neighbours, Besançon or Autun. In addition, the small diocese of Chalon-sur-Saône retained its holdings within the new diocese's borders. Louis XV partially compensated the bishop of Langres for his financial losses by granting him the *mense abbatiale* of Moutier-Saint-Jean.[21] In addition, the bishop and cathedral chapter of Langres retained the right to appoint the priests of sixteen parishes within the diocese of Dijon.

The continuing authority of Langres over churches in the diocese proved problematic. At mid-century, Claude Bouhier, Dijon's second bishop, partially resolved the difficulties through a swap: his patronage rights (gained due to his title as the successor to the abbots of Saint-Étienne and Saint-Pierre-de-Bèze) over several parishes in Langres for those of the bishop and cathedral chapter of Langres in Dijon's territory. The cathedral canons balked, claiming that the parishes offered were of less value than those they were relinquishing. Yet, after a year's delay, Langres's bishop agreed to the trade. In an ironic coda, Bouhier concluded that he had actually been the loser in the deal, and he spent the last years of his episcopacy unsuccessfully seeking to have the agreement annulled.[22]

The multiple efforts to establish a diocese at Dijon underscore the difficulty of creating new dioceses in early modern France. As John McManners has noted, this fact is too often forgotten when historians discuss the revolution's radical redrawing of ecclesiastical boundaries.[23] Dijon's case highlights the determinative role of local and regional authorities in the effort to create a diocese, as well as in the opposition to it. Not the king, his council, or even a bishop was able to override the interests of the cathedral chapter of Langres or the collegial chapters at La Sainte-Chapelle, Saint-Étienne, and Saint-Bénigne. It was only with the episcopal vacancy in Langres and the consolidation of the leadership of La Sainte-Chapelle and Saint-Étienne under Jean Bouhier, a prominent local figure, that a supportive pope and king could establish the long-desired diocese.

AN EIGHTEENTH-CENTURY DIOCESE

What was the nature of this new diocese? In his study of Dijon, Éric Wenzel details a staid see well integrated into the social and political structures of the region.[24] Carved from the diocese of Langres, Dijon ecclesiastical geography was complete at its creation. The diocese had a dense clerical presence comparable to that of Angers or Chartres. Approximately 500 clergy served parishioners, but most not as parish priests. The diocese had 156 parishes served by 149 curés or parish priests. Forty-one of these priests also had a *binage*, a second chapel or church (*succursale*) linked to their principal sanctuary.[25] The path to priesthood involved two stages, minor orders, which began with first tonsure, and major orders beginning with the subdiaconate (*sous-diaconate*). The diocese of Dijon had strong local recruitment: from 1740 to 1786, over 85 per cent of tonsured clergy came from the diocese. Within the diocese, the city of Dijon held a prominent place in clerical recruitment, with 52 per cent of clergy having their origin in the city over the same period.[26] Almost half of the diocese's tonsured clergy did not proceed to major orders; some acquired benefices without clerical office (cure of souls) such as chaplaincies or a position as a canon or a prebendary. Others took non-beneficed positions within parish churches. To advance to the subdiaconate, the beginning of major orders, one needed either a benefice (not easy to come by) or a *titre clerical* of 100 *livres tournois* or inheritance in property (*biens foncier* or *immeubles*) of equivalent value. Even for those who took major orders, a position as a parish priest remained difficult to obtain. Only 54 per cent of clergy ordained in the diocese between 1740 and 1786 eventually acquired a parish. The average age for new curés was thirty-three.[27]

Below the parish priests was a large clerical underclass distinguished by their lack of a benefice. At the top of the unbeneficed clergy were the vicars, although only about a quarter of Dijon's parishes had vicars. Vicars typically spent almost eight years as chaplains before obtaining their positions. Below vicars, non-beneficed priests held a variety of titles, including *prêtres sociétaires*, *familiers*, *mépartistes*, and *prêtres habituées*. The parish priest chose and compensated these subordinates, and their numbers are difficult to quantify because they do not appear in diocesan registers or the minutes of episcopal visits.

A major controversy relating to the revolution's Civil Constitution of the Clergy was the election of parish priests by the secular assemblies. The opponents of this reform argued that it undermined the authority of bishops. However, when one examines the appointment of priests in the diocese of Dijon, it is clear that the bishop played a limited role, naming only one-third of the diocese's curés before the revolution. Fifty-four per cent of parishes chose their priest, while cathedral or collegial chapters appointed another 9 per cent of the curés. Nobles named the balance.[28] In the diocese of Dijon, acquiring a parish had a lot to do with family connections. The number of parishes was essentially stable across the diocese's existence. On average, seven curial benefices became available each year. Individuals from Dijon tended to dominate the parish clergy, and a number of families maintained control of a benefice through the practice of priests designating a successor, usually uncle to nephew. If the pope concurred, the designation stood without interference from either the bishop or other ecclesiastical benefice holder.[29]

During the diocese's sixty-year existence before the revolutionaries incorporated it into the diocese of the Côte-d'Or, five bishops held the see of Dijon, the first two with strong local connections and the last three owing their appointments to influence at court.[30] The bishop's income in Dijon ranged from 30,000 to 40,000 *livres tournois*, far below the 200,000 of the archbishop of Paris, but above the 20,000 of the bishop of Autun. In comparison with surrounding dioceses, Dijon was modest in size. Langres, even with the loss of Dijon, had almost 500 parishes, while Besançon and Autun had 840 and 708, respectively. The new diocese demonstrated the success of the Counter-Reformation's vision for an educated and professionalized clergy. By the eve of the revolution, the diocese's curés were rural elites that served both parishioner and state. In their parishes, clergy, especially those of long tenure, became well versed in agricultural issues and counselled their parishioners on innovations. In addition, they played a role in medical care for the poor and served as agents of the state in times of crisis.[31]

The diocese also had communities of monks and nuns that were largely stable across the century. In 1700, the *archiprêtre* of Dijon had sixteen female and eighteen male communities. By the time the revolutionaries prohibited the taking of solemn vows and closed male communities in 1790, the number of women's communities had decreased by two, although the male communities remained at eighteen. This consistency in the number of communities is not to suggest that the diocese's religious were static in the eighteenth century. Change just came slowly, with one effort, to close the Ursulines in Saint-Jean-de-Losne, taking the better part of five decades to conclude. Dominique Dinet, a student of the religious in the dioceses of Auxerre, Langres, and Dijon, argues that the monastic orders had far greater viability than is typically attributed to them in a historiography focused on the decline of monastic orders in the eighteenth century. Dinet concludes that it was rare for orders to experience natural extinctions, and that the king's commissions (*commission des secours* in 1727 and *commission des réguliers* in 1765) had limited success in closing houses.[32] In part, this was due to the influence and foot dragging of local interests, as the example of the Ursulines of Saint-Jean-de-Losne demonstrates. In 1732, the *commission de secours* prohibited the convent from receiving new novices. Ten years later, with the support of the mayor, the town deputies (échevins), and the priest, the convent petitioned Cardinal Rohan, who presided over the commission, to reverse this order, arguing that it needed novices to aid the sisters in their work of educating girls. Rohan refused this request, and the convent consented to close in May 1751; nonetheless, it continued to take in students, having twenty-one in 1760. By 1777, it found itself with only six nuns and determined they were unable to continue taking students. The Ursulines of Saint-Jean-de-Losne finally closed their doors in 1789, with two nuns, aged eighty-two and eighty-five, remaining. The tenacity of local interests in this example of one monastic order is reminiscent of that in Dijon's long campaign for a bishop.

The expulsion of the Jesuits from France is one effort against a religious order that stands out for its apparent rapidity and widespread impact.[33] In 1761, the Parlement de Paris issued a judgment against the Jesuits that laid the foundation for their dissolution in France. Paris's action rippled across France, eventually engaging the other eleven *parlements* and two sovereign courts. By February 1763, Louis XV acquiesced to the growing campaign against France's Jesuits, issuing an order effectively endorsing the actions taken by various *parlements*. Central among these was the closing of Jesuit colleges. Dijon's *parlement* stands out for its reluctance to act against the Jesuits. The *parlement* of Burgundy took up the Jesuit's case only on 8 March 1763. Following a pattern well established by other *parlements* in the two-year campaign, it requested the order's constitutions and then issued, in July, a judgment suppressing Jesuit colleges in its jurisdiction. In the city of Dijon, this ruling closed the Collège des Godrans effective 1 October. Students protested the closing of the college, breaking benches and wrecking classrooms. In response, the city blocked the surrounding streets. Despite the protest, the *parlement* expelled the Jesuits from the *collège*, and the city took over its administration, naming the Abbé Merceret, curé of Saint-Nicholas, as principal and the abbé Claude Courtépée as his assistant. The reorganization of the Collège des Godrans required new faculty, and it was at this time that Jean-Baptiste Volfius, future constitutional bishop of the Côte-d'Or, began his career there as professor of rhetoric and eloquence, leaving the Jesuit novitiate to do so.[34]

Today, Courtépée is well known to students of eighteenth-century Burgundy because of the multi-volume *Description générale et particulière du duché de Bourgogne* he wrote with Edme Béguillet, an attorney and *notaire de la province*. Better known of the two to contemporaries, Béguillet worked on the first two volumes only, leaving the project to pursue other studies more focused on civil organization and natural history. Courtépée's interest was the history and organization of towns and parishes. Published from 1775–81, the *Description* ran to five volumes.[35] Courtépée published a new edition on his own a few years later that he intended as a text for students at the Collège des Godrans. This edition omitted topics he believed inappropriate for students, such as court politics. Courtépée's summary of the new diocese's ecclesiastical establishments provides a succinct overview in its final years. On the eve of the revolution, the diocese of Dijon had three abbeys of men and two of women, sixteen priories, three *commanderies* of the Knights of Malta and one of Saint Antoine, three collegial chapters, two seminaries, eleven monasteries of men, six monasteries of women, two *collèges*, five hospitals, and 174 parishes or annexes (a count at slight variance with Éric Wenzel's more recent work).[36]

All politics is local. The creation of the diocese of Dijon underscores that understanding that the local is key to understanding the early modern French church. The hierarchy of the Catholic Church and the accommodations it made with the French monarchy in the sixteenth century suggest that decisions made at the court or endorsed by the papacy triumphed over more local interests. The creation of the diocese of Dijon provides a corrective for this view. Conflicting local

interests managed both to keep alive the ambition of the Dijonnais
to gain a bishop's cap and to prevent their victory. In the end, it was
only by placing key institutions in the hands of one man, Jean Bouhier,
that the diocese's last group of proponents was able to overcome
opposition from the bishop and canons of Langres. Once created,
Dijon was a small but stable diocese that reflected the ambitions of
post-Tridentine Catholicism for an educated, disciplined parish clergy.
Frequently, parish appointments passed conservatively from uncle
to nephew, contributing to the maintaining of the social structure of
the diocese. Below these parish priests laboured a larger and more
tenuously engaged mass of clergy. In addition, secular clergy shared
the field with a regular clergy, monks, and nuns of varied orders and
establishments. The diocese of Dijon was a microcosm of the Catholic
Church and its institutions as they had weathered the storms of recent
centuries. The tempest to come would challenge the entire edifice.

1789: The Diocese of Dijon's Clergy in a Revolutionary Year

In the early part of 1789, the diocese of Dijon's three estates was preparing for the upcoming Estates-General. The previous summer, France's financial crisis had come to a head. Despite almost a decade of effort to reform state expenditures and revenue streams, Louis XVI's government was on the brink of bankruptcy. Bowing to calls for an Estates-General, the king ordered the three estates to convene at Versailles in May 1789. Given that France's Estates-General had not met since 1614, questions quickly arose about how it would be constituted and conducted, leading to demands both for a doubling of the Third Estate and voting by head (not estate). Across the fall of 1788, Jacques Necker, Louis XVI's finance minister, navigated the politics of establishing the Estates-General. By December, Louis XVI issued an edict doubling the representatives of the Third Estate but left undetermined the manner of voting.

THE THREE ESTATES OF DIJON

For the Dijonnais, the calling of the Estates-General was a tremendous political opportunity. Louis XVI called the estates to meet in every judicial district to elect deputies to attend the general meeting at Versailles. In addition, as they met, estates were to write a statement of their concerns, a *cahier des doléances*. The *bailliage* of Dijon was the largest judicial district in northern Burgundy. Its territory overlapped with and exceeded slightly the boundaries of the diocese of Dijon. The Dijonnais prepared energetically for the historic meeting.[1] Before the individual estates met, members of the clergy and the Third Estate advanced their arguments publically. Dijon's Third

Estate, led by a small coterie of lawyers known as the Parti patriote, quickly organized a campaign in support of voting by head and the doubling of the Third Estate, sending two petitions to the king.[2] To add force to their appeal, they sought the support of Dijon's clergy and nobility. Although ultimately frustrated in this desire, they did find steady allies in the lower clergy of the *bailliage*.

Dijon's lower clergy also organized early to advance their agenda, presenting their concerns in two unsigned pamphlets. In the first, produced in the early months of 1789, individuals who identified themselves only as country priests (*curés de campagne*) published their fiscal and social demands.[3] They called for a living wage for clergy, arguing that the *portion congrue*, the salary granted to clerics without a benefice, was not adequate to meet their needs. They urged the abolition of *binages*, a practice in which the same priest served two parishes, and called for the representation of the lower clergy in ecclesiastical governance. To obtain these reforms, they appealed to the king and to the nation. They followed this anonymous pamphlet with a second, which outlined, not the grievances of the cures, but those of their parishioners.[4] Arguing that they were in a unique position to witness the misery of the people, these clergy identified the causes of popular destitution: the *taille*, the *corvée*, military conscription, the high price of salt, labour services and rents due to lords of manors, and the expense of legal cases.

In both of these pamphlets, the anonymous priests called for a more just system of taxation. They argued that clergy should pay taxes because they too enjoyed the benefits of good government and military protection.[5] For the people, the most onerous of taxes was the *taille*, a direct tax imposed on either persons or property. It placed an enormous weight on the peasantry, a burden that was not shared by either the nobility or the clergy.[6] The *corvée* served as a further example of the people's exploitation. Although Louis XVI abolished this labour tax, which had required peasants to work several days annually to maintain roads, the Estates of Burgundy merely transformed it into a fiscal tax, raising the *taille* to finance highway maintenance. Increasing the bitterness of the response to this action was their subsequent failure to repair the roads. The highways, the clerics argued, were public works that a general tax paid by all should support.[7] The call of Dijon's clergy for equal liability for taxation mirrored sentiments widespread in France on the eve of the revolution. As Philippe Grateau found in his study of rural *cahiers*, two-thirds of the concerns raised related to equality in taxation.[8] Despite their arguments for more equitable taxation and the end of seigneurial dues, the curés did not advocate eliminating social distinctions. They judged inequality of rank as established by God and necessary for political and moral tranquility.[9]

The spirit of the curés' pamphlets continued in the official *cahier* of the clergy in the *bailliage* of Dijon.[10] Meeting at the end of April, the clergy called for extensive and aggressive changes in taxation, the administration of justice, and the prerogatives of the monarchy. They also sought specific ecclesiastical reforms. As the first order of business, the clerics called for a general and fundamental law that would guarantee the principal rights of citizens, provinces, the nation, and the different social orders. Citizens required freedom from arbitrary detention, freedom of speech (within limits), and the right to property. They also needed equality before the law, and equal opportunity and compensation in ecclesiastical, civil, and military positions.[11] Although the clergy opened their discussion with the rights of individuals, they recognized as well the corporate rights of orders, provinces, and the nation. Provinces should keep their laws and customs, particular courts and estates, if they had them. The nation's rights included maintaining the monarchy and regulating its succession, preserving Catholicism as the national religion, and having an account from the king's ministers of the nation's income from taxes and loans. The three orders, the curés argued, had a right to deliberate separately and to express their distinctive voices in the Estates-General. No order – clergy, nobility, or commons – should be forced into a unanimous decision by the other two. They called on the Estates-General to suppress direct taxes that were based on estate, such as the *taille*, and to establish instead new taxes applicable to all citizens.[12] Among the ecclesiastical reforms they proposed was an increase in the *portion congrue* to 1200 *livres* for curés and 600 *livres* for vicars.

The clergy's progressive agenda for the Estates-General is most apparent when compared with the restrained proposals presented by Dijon's nobles. Meeting at the end of 1788 in La Sainte-Chapelle, the Second Estate proposed modest changes in taxation. Addressing the taxes known as *additionnels*, which were paid only by the Third Estate, they proposed that these be split between the Second and Third Estates by the Estates-General. These *additionnels*, they were quick to specify, did not include the *taille*.[13] Second, noting that most mayors were not elected, they urged that the Third Estate be allowed to choose their representatives for the Estates-General. They supported voting by order and suggested only one change in this practice, namely, that any one of the three orders have the right to veto legislation dealing with taxation.[14] They urged that the province not be divided. In closing, the nobles expressed disappointment that so few of Dijon's clergy accepted their invitation to unite with them. They sought "the most indissoluble union with the other two orders."[15] To further this aim, they proposed an assembly to allow commissioners from the three estates to work together on a common *cahier*.[16] Dijon's nobles sought from the Estates-General reforms that guaranteed their privilege and that returned political prerogatives they had lost to the Crown during the seventeenth century.[17]

In many respects, the aspirations of Dijon's Third Estate paralleled those of its lower clergy. Meeting in March to draft its *cahier*, Dijon's Third Estate called for an end to feudal rights, protested the abuses of the upper clergy, demanded fiscal equality, and underscored the need for a constitution.[18] On 31 March, the Third Estate asked the clergy to support them in a call to end the financial privileges of the First Estate and in a demand for voting by head at the upcoming meeting of the Estates-General. Des Monstiers de Mérinville, Dijon's bishop, refused to submit the propositions to a vote, and four days later the clergy sent their regrets to the Third Estate, reporting that they could not agree to give up their financial privileges and that they preferred to leave the decision on the manner of voting to the Estates-General itself.[19]

The Estates-General convened at Versailles in early May. It took only six weeks for the Third Estate and its allies from the clergy and the nobility to overturn the political scaffolding of absolutism. By the middle of June, the Third Estate had transformed itself into the National Assembly and proclaimed its sovereignty. As quickly, social order disintegrated in the countryside. Peasants rioted, rumour filled the marketplace, and a general unease spread across the nation. In Dijon, a travelling Englishman, Arthur Young, witnessed the impassioned summer of 1789. Spending only three days in the city, Young commented on a range of developments, including the flight of the intendant, Amelot de Chaillou, and of the governor, the prince of Condé, both threatened with violence should they return. Unrest in the countryside led Dijon's bourgeoisie to form a 300-man militia that possessed six cannons.[20] In the heat of July, the old order collapsed.

JEAN-BAPTISTE VOLFIUS, REVOLUTIONARY ABBÉ

The bourgeois militia of Dijon was among the city's first revolutionary organizations. A mass at the church of Saint-Michel soon integrated it into the city's life. To preside over this service, Dijon's municipal assembly turned to the abbé Jean-Baptiste Volfius, a fifty-five-year-old professor of rhetoric and eloquence at the city's Collège des Godrans.

Volfius was an interesting choice. Although he was a priest, his career and interests were scholarly. Before the revolution, he had presented several public addresses. At the Collège des Godrans, he had spoken on the usefulness of history and the methods for its study. From 1774, he was a member of Dijon's Académie des sciences, arts, et belles lettres, delivering an address in 1779 on how one judges matters of taste. Almost a decade later, he spoke on the education of women. He was also the author of a manual on rhetoric that enjoyed some success, with a second edition in 1781 and a final edition in 1814.[21]

Volfius came from a family well connected to Dijon's world of lawyers and magistrates. Born on 7 April 1734, he was the eldest son of Jean-François Volfius, a Westphalian immigrant to Dijon, and Marie Pélissonier, daughter of the royal notary of Blaisy-Bas. The elder Volfius had moved to Dijon in 1719 at the end of his studies in his native city of Essen. After serving for a decade as clerk to several procurators of the *parlement* of Dijon and in the *bailliage* of Autun, he became a procurator of the *parlement* in 1729. A year earlier, he received letters of naturalization from Louis XV. The senior Volfius married Pélissonier in 1733, and the couple had seven children, all baptized at the church of Notre-Dame in Dijon. Jean-Baptiste, their eldest, studied at the Jesuit Collège des Godrans, and at fifteen continued his education at the Jesuit seminary in Reims followed by university in Pont-à-Mousson in preparation for a vocation with the order.[22] Although the normal course was two years at both Reims and Pont-à-Mousson, Volfius did not finish his fourth year. It is possible that the expulsion of the Jesuits from France ended his studies. In August 1762, the Parlement de Paris ordered the Jesuit *collèges* closed, an action that was completed the following April. Volfius's final year of study was 1762.[23] Two years later, Louis XV issued a royal declaration dissolving the Jesuit order in France and forcing its members into exile.[24] Volfius could have continued his studies, because the Jesuit university at Pont-à-Mousson enjoyed a reprieve from the Parlement de Paris's actions due to its location in Lorraine, territory governed by Louis XV's father-in-law, Stanislas Leszczyński, until his death in 1766. Following Stanislas's death, the territory reverted to France, and the king transferred the university to Nancy, suppressing the Lorraine Jesuits.[25] Whatever influence the order's troubles had on young Volfius, he decided to pursue a clerical career outside of the Jesuits, becoming a diocesan priest and applying for a position at the reorganized Collège des Godrans. With the closing of the Jesuit *collèges*, Dijon's Collège des Godrans became a royal secondary school (*collège*) and hired new faculty. Volfius applied for one of two chairs in rhetoric and eloquence and received the position over eight other applicants at the end of September 1763. Like Volfius, several of the new faculty were former students of the *collège*, and, despite the change of its administration, the curriculum remained largely the same. The focus continued to be Latin and religious culture, with some instruction in mathematics, physics, and logic.[26]

During the revolutionary summer of 1789, Volfius's speech before the assembled militia focused on the fall of the old order. He used his address to give the Dijonnais a theological interpretation of the nation's new political direction. Previously the king's authority had derived from his role as the intermediary between God (the father) and the French people (his children). Now, the king enjoyed greater authority because he was bound to his people and therefore stood on an unshakeable foundation. United, the nation suffered from none of the rivalries or divisions of the three orders.[27] As Volfius explained to the gathered militiamen, the king moved from a position above the people but below God to a position beside the people, united with them. The newly unified nation presented the world with a model of equality. Volfius cautioned that the dissolution of orders did not create individual equality, which he characterized as an idle fantasy. Through the National Assembly, the French had established *political* equality.[28] Although applauding the end of orders as good for all three former estates, Volfius expressed sympathy for the nobility's claim of service to the state. He cautioned his listeners against attacking those members of the first two estates who continued to have pretensions, the natural result of eight centuries of privilege. Yet he also called upon the clergy and the nobility to lay down their "sad prerogatives ... monuments of the barbarous centuries" and recognize the "onerous" burden of these prerogatives for the people.[29]

Volfius's speech was prepared on short notice: The municipal assembly had asked him to give the address only the evening before the event. That it pleased its sponsors is apparent from their decision to publish it.[30] With this speech, Volfius began his career as a representative for the revolution in Dijon and of the church's role in it. Presenting the church as the temple of the nation, Volfius believed that priests had a responsibility to lead the way, renouncing their privilege and setting an example for the National Assembly.[31]

Although Paul Pisani, writing at the beginning of the twentieth century, interpreted Volfius's entry into revolutionary politics as motivated by family pressure, there is ample evidence of his enthusiasm for the new order.[32] Like his younger brother, Alexandre-Eugène, Volfius aligned with the revolution.[33] A founding member of the city's Club patriotique, the elder Volfius became its president in January 1790. The following summer, he stepped down to become the confessor (*aumonier*) for the city's National Guard.[34] In the year following the address at Saint-Michel, he delivered and published three more speeches that interpreted events in the revolution's first year. In each, he gave attention to the role of religion in the new political and social order. True religion, he maintained, was patriotic and embraced the changes coming from Paris.

In early December 1789, Volfius again interpreted events, speaking to the city's National Guard, this time focusing on the National Assembly's support for the monarchy and religion. Volfius's message was clear: the new-found liberty of the French did not threaten either institution. That some perceived a danger in the actions of the National Assembly was understandable, given the far-reaching reforms being enacted. Among those affecting the church were the abolition of the tithe and the nationalization of church properties.[35]

Rejecting the idea that the National Assembly was building France's liberty on the "ruins of religion," Volfius asserted that the wealth of the church was destined to serve the nation during public calamities.[36] And, he asked, what crisis could be greater than the present, when the state faced dissolution? Volfius also refuted the idea that an impoverished clergy commanded less respect. To make such a claim scandalized the church fathers and the centuries of virtuous clergy who had dedicated their lives to serving the people.[37] Volfius's address emphasized the servant nature of the church and interpreted the church's duty as being to both the state and its parishioners. In this call for the church to place its resources at the disposal of the nation, Volfius echoed the national discussion among leading French clergy. His awareness of this larger discussion is apparent in his citations to François de Bonal, bishop of Clermont.

Volfius then turned his attention to the monarchy. Echoing his speech before the militiamen, he countered claims that the assembly's actions diminished the king, arguing that the sovereign was more distinguished than ever because he now ruled over free men. United with the nation, the king enjoyed an inviolable authority and an enhanced majesty that reflected not just one man but the nation as a whole.[38]

As he spoke, Volfius flattered his audience. They were educated, successful men, learned in law and the arts and sciences, or young men yet to begin their careers. He commended them for their service to the nation and assured them that the National Assembly's reforms would make industry freer and allow local men to open enterprises. He urged his audience to reassure those suffering hardship as the nation reformed that their troubles would pass. With some citizens choosing to leave the city and the nation, emigration was a concern for Volfius. Yet, the most appalling emigration, Volfius warned, was that of wealth, gold and silver, because it brought an end to commerce and industry.[39]

THE POLITICAL CLUBS OF DIJON IN 1790

In Dijon, the new year 1790 brought significant political reorganization as a result of the National Assembly's division of France into departments. Dijon became the seat of the new department of the Côte-d'Or. Established on 9 February 1790, the Côte-d'Or had slightly fewer than 350,000 inhabitants. The assembly's plan divided the department into seven districts, eighty-six cantons, and 762 communes.[40] André Rémy-Arnoult, an attorney at the *parlement* of Dijon and a deputy to the National Assembly, suggested the name Côte-d'Or, which invoked the rich vineyards of the territory's southern districts. The department, the districts, and the communes held elections for council members in January and February. Across the Côte-d'Or, these elections largely legalized actions taken during the crisis of July 1789, when citizen militias in various towns put new councilmen into place to counter urban and rural unrest. In Dijon, the municipal elections reversed the revolutionary developments of the previous summer. The Parti patriote, which had forced the addition of twelve non-noble commissioners on the city's council, lost in the winter elections.[41] Dijon's electorate, a small number of wealthy citizens, chose a group of aristocrats hostile to the revolutionary reforms emanating from Paris.[42] The upset resulted from a poor economy. By their vote, Dijon's electorate adopted the position being argued in the city's pamphlet literature, that only the rich "were capable of restoring the prosperity of the city."[43] Despite its defeat, the Parti patriote maintained its influence at the departmental level. In part, the party's influence over public opinion was the result of its journal, *Le journal patriotique de Bourgogne*, established in January 1790.[44]

By the spring of 1790, both the supporters and opponents of the revolution had organized political clubs in Dijon. The Parti patriote had transformed itself into the Club patriotique in early August 1789. Initially, this club intended to provide the Dijonnais with access to national newspapers and with a place to discuss current events. Soon, however, it undertook philanthropic work, raising 40,000 *livres* by October to buy bread for the needy. In May 1790, it renamed itself the Société des amis de la Constitution, affiliating loosely with the Parisian society of the same name, better known as the Jacobins.[45] Dijon was one of the earliest provincial cities to establish a Jacobin club. Although modelled after the Parisian club, it focused on local issues.[46] In response to the political activities of the Parti patriote and its later incarnations, Dijon's aristocrats established a club called the Amis de la Paix in March 1790. Its activities quickly aroused the suspicions of the Club patriotique, and, on April 20, its members invaded the new group's meeting and put an end to the club.[47] This action did not end the tension between Dijon's aristocrats and the Club patriotique. In the summer, the aristocratic party again organized itself in a club, this time calling their organization the Amis du Roi. The city closed this club in November after being ordered to do so by the department's directory. In December, Dijon's aristocrats aligned with wealthier members of the bourgeoisie and even some artisans who were suffering economically to establish the Société Tussat. Its goal was to establish an armed force that could counter the National Guard, which supported the revolution. Working through the district of Dijon's directory, the Société des amis de la Constitution managed to have the meeting of the Société Tussat forbidden. Despite such conflict, alliances remained fluid in the tumultuous times in which the Dijonnais found themselves. Louis-Bernard Guyton de Morveau, for instance, a celebrated chemist and attorney who served as the first president of the Club patriotique in August 1789, had so shifted his alliances that he was a founding member of the Société Tussat in December 1790.[48]

THE FESTIVAL OF FEDERATION IN DIJON

The tension between the supporters and opponents of the revolution in Dijon is apparent in two speeches given by Abbé Volfius in the late spring of 1790. On 18 May 1790, Volfius addressed the city's National Guard unit at a ceremony of federation with similar units in other departments. Two weeks later, he spoke before the closing session of the district of Dijon's electoral assembly. In both speeches, he argued for the merit of the revolution's reforms, which established equality based on citizenship rather than privileges based upon one's birth or position.

Dijon's federation ceremony followed in the wake of a national movement. Throughout the fall and winter, local militias across France had met together and declared their unity.[49] In Dijon, the ceremony of federation brought together the National Guard units of northern Burgundy. These included units from the department of the Côte-d'Or, the Ain, the Yonne, and the Saône-et-Loire.[50] Six thousand armed men assembled on the Cours du Parc under the command of Georges-Louis-Marie de Buffon, the son of the naturalist. They swore on the altar of the nation "to maintain with all their power the constitution of the realm, to be faithful to the nation, to the law and to the king and to execute the decrees of the National Assembly sanctioned or accepted by the king."[51] The controversial ecclesiastical oath demanded of the clergy six months later would repeat much of this formula.

Volfius opened his address by invoking the image of the Maccabean revolt (175–141 BCE), in which rebels in Judea wrested control from the Seleucid Empire. Led by Judas Maccabeus, the Maccabees fought the troops of Antiochus IV as well as their own co-religionists who controlled the Temple in Jerusalem and were cooperating with the Seleucid ruler. The rebels refused to sacrifice to Antiochus, declaring that to do so would defile their religion. Like the Maccabees, Volfius declared, the gathered militiamen were few in number and faced external and internal enemies. However, they too fought a righteous battle for God and country.[52]

Volfius emphasized the link between religion and patriotism. Integral to patriotism was respect for religion; integral to religion was the love of *la patrie*. For Volfius, one's *patrie* was not the soil that constituted an inheritance or the village of one's birth. Instead, it was one's *nation*, a community joined together to protect its natural rights. Like other revolutionary writers, Volfius used *patrie* to indicate an intentional political unit formed by citizens.[53] Liberty was essential to the nation, and it was the ancien régime's lack of liberty that precluded it from developing a true nation.[54] Referring to the National Assembly's Declaration of the Rights of Man and of the Citizen, Volfius underscored that these rights came from God's "eternal charter" and preceded the action of any assembly.[55] As the nation's civilian militia, the first duty of the assembled men was to law. Religion, the state's natural ally in the regeneration of its citizens, supplemented the law. Turning his attention to members of the former First and Second Estates, Volfius urged them to seek the dignity of citizenship and to weigh the advantages of the revolution against their losses.[56]

Two weeks after the ceremony of federation, Volfius spoke at the closing session of the district of Dijon's electoral assembly. Having served as president of the assembly, Volfius noted that he spoke not as a priest but as a friend of the revolution.[57] In his speech, he addressed the divisions created by the year's revolutionary developments. Reiterating his support for the end of orders, Volfius declared the former distinctions to be the "inventions of despotism" and an "insult to reason." The French, he affirmed, were "more than a family of brothers"; they were citizens with "an equal influence in public affairs."[58] Volfius especially urged the peasantry to judge for themselves if the revolution was good. Previously, he argued, they had "counted for nothing." Now, they were "men equal in rights with all men." Formerly, they had been "harassed in all parts and in all senses" by the militias, by the *gabelle*, the *corvées*, and so on. Now, "[their] homes ... lands ... and persons [were] free from all debasing claims."[59] He called on peasants to return home and respect property rights. Violence, he warned, only aided their enemies; free men obeyed laws and did not take justice into their own hands.[60]

By appealing to the peasantry to cooperate with the revolution, Volfius tacitly acknowledged that political participation was not open to everyone. His status as an elector marked him as one of a small number of citizens able to pay the requisite taxes, equivalent to three days' wages.[61] In devoting nearly half of his speech to an appeal for the peasantry's support, he underscored the significant questions being raised about the revolution and its benefits.

For Volfius, the revolution was the beginning of a new and better order. Free from burdensome obligations, the peasants could view themselves as equal with all people. To those at the other end of the social and economic spectrum who missed their former privileges, he urged patience and willingness to sacrifice in the present. The future would more than compensate them, as industry and agriculture thrived under a freer, more rational administration. In August 1789, being a member, or at least an intimate associate, of the city's Parti patriote, Volfius publicly aligned himself with the revolution. By January, he was president of Club patriotique. His support for the revolution did not waver, even as the deputies in Paris significantly reconstituted the Catholic Church in France. Volfius interpreted the end of orders, the abolition of the tithe, the confiscation of church properties, and the closing of monasteries as reforms warranted in a state remaking itself. France would lead Europe into a new age.

The Dijonnais, inhabiting a city of modest proportions, a *ville parlémentaire* and ancient provincial capital, led quiet lives and conducted business as usual as the eighteenth century entered its final decades. The tensions and divisions beneath this calm surface revealed themselves as the city's Third Estate, joined by its lower clergy, engaged with the controversies and promises of the revolution. For the city's Parti patriote, the Estates-General of 1789 and the subsequent revolution presented the opportunity to establish a more equitable political and fiscal order. Although rising to municipal leadership in the chaotic summer of 1789, the Parti patriote was swept out of office by the elections of 1790. However, its influence remained strong in the new district and departmental councils as well as in the city's National Guard. From these bases of power, it challenged those who would slow or reverse the revolution. In his addresses, Volfius supported the patriots of Dijon and celebrated the National Assembly's reordering of France's society, even its legislation impacting the church. The assembly's actions, Volfius argued, returned the church to its earliest and noblest practices. Religion and patriotism, God and nation, were intertwined, representing humanity's loftiest ideals. Like the nation's representatives in Paris, Dijon's patriots were creating a new and ideal community, a *patrie* sanctioned by God and claiming the loyalty of all.

As a spokesman for the revolution, Volfius was enthusiastic and undaunted by the radical nature of the changes occurring around him. He applauded the end of privileged orders and declared France a new state that was regenerating itself. The temple of religion was the temple of the nation, and the new liberty of the French people was good. It was not a threat to religion or to the monarchy. In asking Abbé Volfius to bless its new citizen militia, and to speak for the revolutionary changes underway, Dijon's Parti patriote initiated his revolutionary career. He not only endorsed efforts to maintain order locally but also embraced the reforms in church and state emanating from Paris. A new age had dawned, and, in Volfius's vision, it was good.

A Bishop for the Côte-d'Or

The department of the Côte d'Or encompassed the old regime diocese of Dijon and part of the former diocese of Langres. Neither
René Des Monstiers de Mérinville, bishop of Dijon, nor Cardinal
César Guillaume de la Luzerne, bishop of Langres, swore the oath
required by the Civil Constitution of the Clergy. Both bishops were
members of the Constituent Assembly; Des Monstiers de Mérinville
was among the thirty deputy-bishops who issued the *Exposition
des principes*, a pamphlet critical of the Civil Constitution of the
Clergy, the previous fall. The refusal of both bishops to take the
oath left the newly created see of the Côte-d'Or empty, at least in
the eyes of departmental authorities. In contrast to the bishops, the
department's parish clergy took the oath in good number. Initially,
62 per cent took the oath, but this proportion declined slightly to 58
following the publication of Pius VI's brief *Caritas quae* calling for
clergy to refuse to jure or to retract their pledge.[1] In the district of
Dijon, the percentage of oath-taking clergy was even higher at 67.5
per cent. Distinct from its district, however, was the city of Dijon,
where the priests of the city's seven parishes refused to take the oath,
explaining their position as an expression of solidarity with their
bishop. At the Collège des Godrans, ten clergy did take the oath,
among them Jean-Baptiste Volfius.[2]

In the Civil Constitution of the Clergy, Volfius found a new and better link between the church and the nation. He carefully distinguished
the church's spiritual realm, with which the nation could not inter-
fere, from the exterior realm, which was open to negotiation with the
political order. Volfius's advocacy of the Civil Constitution included
pragmatic as well as philosophical arguments. In his first pastoral

letter following his election as bishop, he urged the clergy of the Côte-d'Or to take the ecclesiastical oath and to place their vocation and future firmly in France's new political and ecclesiastical order.

In that letter, Volfius argued that the legislation represented a higher form of Catholicism because it broke the link between the church and despotism. It made the "destiny of the Catholic religion inseparable from that of the Nation," establishing an eternal alliance between the two.[3] For Volfius, there had long been two disciplines in the church, the spiritual and "the police" or the external. Initially, during its early centuries of persecution, the church had both policed itself and cultivated its spiritual life. Following the conversion of Constantine, the church became part of the political order and complied in its exterior regime with the wishes of the sovereign. As Volfius wrote, citing the fourth century St. Optatus of Milevis, "the church was in the state, and not the state in the church."[4]

For Volfius, clergy who refused to take the ecclesiastical oath were promoting civil disorder. The Civil Constitution of the Clergy was part of the state's constitution and a factor in the success of the revolution. Appealing to those who rejected the legislation, Volfius urged them to join its supporters in the temple of religion and of the nation. As he closed his letter he declared, "These are propitious and salutary days ... Let us place at the foot of the Cross all sentiments contrary to peace and admonished by God, so that concord is re-established among all citizens favouring the development of this new order which purifies and regenerates all."[5]

In the Côte-d'Or, Volfius was not alone in his advocacy of the Civil Constitution of the Clergy. Local political clubs also supported the Constituent Assembly's vision for the French church.[6] The Société des amis de la Constitution of Beaune offered its support in a variety of ways. In the spring of 1791, it reported to the department about the continuing activity of the canons of Beaune who, according to the Civil Constitution of the Clergy, should have disbanded.[7] Yet, as Beaune's Société des amis noted, the canons continued to proceed daily to the church of Saint-Nicolas dressed in ecclesiastical garb. Once there, they celebrated mass.[8] The department responded with a stiffly worded rebuke denouncing the canons for continuing to wear their habits after the suppression of their order.[9] The Beaune society also published and circulated an open letter written by the abbé Jean-Louis Gouttes, a clergy deputy of the Constituent Assembly and the consti-tutional bishop-elect of the department of the Saône-et-Loire.[10]

Gouttes's letter is among the traces of the local campaign for the Civil Constitution of the Clergy that remain in the departmental archives in Dijon. It rests filed alongside Volfius's speeches, enthusiastic declarations of support by local clergy, and correspondence from Paris.[11] Gouttes entered national politics in 1789 as a deputy to the Estates-General from Languedoc. Early in his life, he served in a dragoon regiment but left it to return to his studies and an ecclesiastical career. In 1791, the fifty-two-year-old Gouttes, by then a deputy in the Constituent Assembly, was a strong advocate of economic reform and a supporter of the nationalization of church properties. As constitutional bishop-elect of the Saône-et-Loire, he replaced Talleyrand, formerly prelate of the region, as the bishop of Autun.[12]

In his defence of the Civil Constitution of the Clergy, Gouttes cast the legislation as a return to the historic practices of the church. In an imaginative church history, he declared that, following the Pragmatic Sanction of 1438, the people named their pastors. He also noted that this was the practice of St. Ambrose (bishop of Milan in the fourth century, but with origins in Gaul). The French church deviated from this tradition with the Concordat of Bologna signed by François I and Pope Leo X in 1516, an agreement that interfered with the French church's self-regulation. To those demanding that the pope be consulted on the new legislation, Gouttes responded that this had never been the practice of the French church. Like the African church of antiquity, the French church had governed itself. The Concordat between François I and Leo X was a self-serving pact between the king, who gained a new avenue for patronage, and the pope, who profited from a sizeable increase in revenue.[13] The agreement amounted to a gross abuse of power. To illustrate his point, Gouttes referred his reader to the case of the duke of Sully, a protestant who had held three abbeys at the death of Henri IV.[14] The Parlement de Paris had attempted to challenge the king's authority and make ecclesiastical appointments itself, but the situation remained unchanged. Powerful men still made all the appointments to the highest positions of the French church.[15] Given the corruption of the past, only the Constituent Assembly could effect change and restore to the people the liberty denied them by force and violence over the years. A national church council composed of those who profited from the previous abuses would never result in reform.[16]

Gouttes's description of the French clergy as an elected corps prior to the machinations of François I and Leo X in the early sixteenth century is fanciful at best. The Pragmatic Sanction of Bourges provided for major benefices such as bishoprics, abbeys, and priories to be filled by election, but smaller ones, such as curés, continued to be appointed. In the case of parish clergy, it was the bishop or other benefice holder who controlled the appointment. Majority vote did not decide elections; rather, they were determined by the principle of competent authority. Thus, while the people might participate in an election, their role was limited to acclamation, and eventually, the authority to choose a bishop devolved to the cathedral chapter alone. The monarchy's influence remained strong despite the sanction's provision for elections. Between 1483 and 1515, 79 of the 109 bishops in the French church were royal councillors or members of their families.[17] Whatever problems Gouttes may have had with historical accuracy, his impulse to turn to church history to support his arguments concerning the Civil Constitution of the Clergy was widely shared, among both its supporters and detractors.

THE ECCLESIASTICAL OATH IN THE CÔTE-D'OR

In mid-November 1790, René Des Monstiers de Mérinville wrote to the district of Dijon's directory informing them that he intended to remain the bishop of Dijon.[18] He meant, of course, the diocese of Dijon, which was established in 1731 and had been under his care since 1787. He informed the district's administrators that he would continue to exercise episcopal authority over the territory entrusted to him until the pope ruled on the new organization of the clergy. Des Monstiers de Mérinville's position could not have come as a surprise to the district administrators. A member of the Constituent Assembly, Des Monstiers de Mérinville joined the other bishops serving in the assembly in issuing a pamphlet critical of the Civil Constitution of the Clergy.

The dean and canons of the cathedral in Dijon joined Des Monstiers de Mérinville in his opposition to the new law. In another pamphlet published in late November, the canons declared their opposition to the legislation.[19] As the leaders of the principal church in the diocese, they declared themselves the model for its faithful and for other churches in these dangerous and difficult times. Given this role, they felt compelled to assert the church's true principles concerning its organization and jurisdiction.[20] They also felt obliged to highlight the errors of the Civil Constitution of the Clergy. Principal

among these was the elimination of their positions. Noting that
church councils and papal bulls had established the special functions
of canons, they declared that their work was not superfluous. They
were the bishop's eyes and the head of the *tribunal de conscience*.
Further, as theologians, they taught and preached. Their duties were
similar to those of other clergy, with additional responsibilities for
public prayer, worship, and the administration of foundations. As
the crypts of the church of Saint-Bénigne bore witness, the cathedral canons had carried out their duties even before there was a
French monarchy.[21] Endorsing the bishop-deputies' pamphlet, the
canons argued that all faithful and good Catholics should await the
pope's judgment before complying with the Civil Constitution of the
Clergy. Comparing themselves to the Maccabees (see Volfius's use of
the same images in Chapter 2), they concluded that, although they
found themselves surrounded by contempt, affliction, and persecution, they would "submit with the same resignation to the Decrees of
Providence" knowing that "only in the breast of God and of Religion"
could they lament their losses.[22] Yet Des Monstiers de Mérinville's
intransigence and the opposition of the cathedral's dean and canons did little to slow the implementation of the Civil Constitution
of the Clergy in the department. Armed in late December with the
authority to require clergy to take the ecclesiastical oath, the civil
administrators began to organize the department's diocese.

The majority of the Côte-d'Or's parish clergy took the oath, with
most doing so between late January and mid-February 1791. Some
enthusiastically embraced the new church order. In early December,
even before the king promulgated the law requiring the ecclesiastical
oath, the abbé Louis-Antoine Alotte, a member of Dijon's Société
des amis de la Constitution, wrote twice to inform departmental
administrators of his compliance. Declaring "a person who, in the
old regime, received the letters of nobility did not feel a joy more
lively than that which I felt in seeing the present witness of your
bounty toward me."[23] Girardot, deacon in Dijon's Saint-Pierre's parish, took the oath on 23 January before four municipal delegates.[24]
An eager supporter of the new church order, Girardot wrote to the
district administrators in early March to declare that nothing – not
a decrepit and dying aristocracy, not fanaticism with all its satel-
lites – would detach him from it. Thinking his sentiments possibly
instructive for others, he invited the city to print his letter in the
Journal patriotique.[25] Soon afterwards, he wrote again, this time

sharing a letter he had sent to Volfius, the bishop-elect of the new diocese. In this letter, Girardot attributed to God the selection of Volfius as the new bishop. Volfius was the new David, long destined to succeed Saul, who was refractory to the law of the Lord. Indeed, Girardot asserted, Volfius was greater than David, having all his strengths without his weaknesses.[26]

Not all clergy took the oath so enthusiastically. Eugène Reinert, priest and local historian, concluded from his study of the department's oath taking that while some, such as Alotte and Girardot, were eager to jure, others at the opposite end of the spectrum jured because they felt they must, being reluctant to leave their parishioners to an uncertain fate. Reinert noted, however, that most juring clergy in the diocese fell between these two extremes.[27] His research allows a window into the complexity of the issue for the priests of the department. Many sought to take the oath with restrictions, the most common restrictions being objections to the election of parish priests and to the Civil Constitution of the Clergy's new ecclesiastical jurisdictions. Juring with these restrictions, Reinert judged, represented the most limited adherence possible. The other popular restriction was to add to one's oath Jesus's admonition in Matthew 22:21 to render unto Caesar that which is Caesar's and to God that which is God's. Some municipalities accepted these restrictive oaths, sending them forward to their districts. Reinert found that some areas were more influenced by Des Monstiers de Mérinville's opposition to the Civil Constitution of the Clergy than others. Particularly supportive of the bishop were Dijon and the towns bordering the Burgundy canal then under construction: Bessey, Izeure, Aiserey, Longcourt, Toulon, Fenay, Breteniers, and Ouges. Other areas, including Mirebeau, Nuits-Saint-Georges, and Genlis, were strong centres for oath taking.[28]

The administration of the oath did not prove to be a simple matter. District and municipal authorities monitored and reported on clergy compliance, and, at times, clerics retook the oath to more precisely fulfil decrees emanating from Paris or Dijon. Two examples demonstrate the multiple administrative responses the occasion of the oath generated in the Côte-d'Or. In January, the administrators of the district of Saint-Jean-de-Losne reported that the chief vicar, L.M.J. François of the village of Saint-Seine-en-Bache, had taken the oath.[29] Three weeks later, the city council of Saint-Seine-en-Bache sent a second communication confirming that L.M.J. François had

indeed sworn to be faithful to nation, law, and king in compliance
with the decree of the National Assembly. In this communication,
the village officials described the ceremony, noting that the mayor
and municipal officers were in attendance and that, in addition to
the oath, François gave a speech on the need to obey the laws and
decrees of the National Assembly. They also noted in this second
correspondence that François renewed his oath on 6 February.[30] In
the village of Combertaut in the district of Beaune, the curé François
Sivry took the oath before mass on 23 January and then again on 13
February. The second oath followed the mass, as instructed by the
National Assembly on 9 January 1791.[31] These duplicate ceremonies
demonstrate the efforts both clergy and civil administrators took to
comply precisely with the varied directives they received.

The abbé Louis-Antoine Alotte, the vicar L.M.J. François, and
the curé François Sivry are only three individuals out of 421 who
took the oath in the spring of 1791 in the Côte-d'Or.[32] François and
Sivry are unusual because, nine years later, they were still part of
the department's constitutional clergy, a group whose number had
dwindled considerably.[33] In taking the oath in 1791, however, they
were not embracing a fringe position, but one that more than half of
their colleagues in parish ministry were choosing as well.

Among the clergy who refused to take the oath were five professors from the Collège des Godran. Writing to the department's
directory on 21 January 1791, these professors informed the directory of their intention to resign their positions rather than take an
oath that violated their consciences.[34] All offered to remain at their
posts until their successors could be found. Two professors of theology related that, should they be permitted to take the oath with
the same reservations offered by the theologians of the Sorbonne
and the University of Paris's Collège de Navarre, they would gladly
continue in their positions.[35] The department's civil authorities
were not inclined to accept reservations and acted on the letters
of resignation without hesitation, naming successors for three of
the professors the same day.[36] The department replaced the other
two, who were professors of theology, two months later, following the recommendation of the diocese's new bishop, Jean-Baptiste
Volfius. The departing theology professors made clear how difficult
the decision to resign had been as well as their hope to continue in
their positions for a time. In the end, ten professors at the Collège
des Godran took the oath.[37]

ELECTING A NEW BISHOP

In late January 1791, the departmental administrators of the Côte-d'Or moved to elect a new bishop. They did this through a printed circular, distributed by the *procureur-syndics* of each district, that declared the see of Dijon vacant and announced a mass to nominate a new bishop.[38] The date for the mass was Sunday, 13 February.[39] As might be expected, word of the impending election reached Des Monstiers de Mérinville, who continued to reside in Paris, and he quickly penned a letter addressed to the electors of the Côte-d'Or.[40] In this letter, he warned clergy against accepting the nomination for bishop, and he instructed lay electors on the error of believing that they could elect their pastors. The church, Des Monstiers de Mérinville argued, was built upon the rock of Peter, the apostle, and not upon the people. Although the people at times had chosen the early church's leadership, they long ago had ceded that role. Further, the church retained the right to modify or suppress movements extolling the simplicity of the church's early practices. The idea that the people could elect a bishop was illegitimate because it came from a political assembly that allowed even heretics and infidels to act as electors. Furthermore, Des Monstiers de Mérinville reminded the electors that his seat was not vacant. He had not died, resigned, or committed a crime. Without one of these three conditions, he remained bishop of Dijon. Should they believe that his failure to take the oath justified the department's declaring his seat vacant, he pointed out that he had taken two previous oaths that guaranteed his submission to temporal authority. Closing his letter, he warned the electors that, in naming a new bishop, they placed a usurper on his episcopal seat. The new bishop's absolutions would be invalid, and anathemas were sure to rain down on all who participated in his appointment.[41]

It is difficult to judge the effect of Des Monstiers de Mérinville's letter on the electors of the Côte-d'Or. Eugène Reinert noted that Des Monstiers de Mérinville had supporters in the electoral assembly, naming four individuals – Messieurs Surenais, Sizugne, Cottin, and Maltête – who insisted that his letter be read publicly. These electors had copies for distribution, but the assembly refused to circulate the letter to the parishes.[42] Claude-Bernard Navier, president of the electoral assembly, reported that Des Monstiers de Mérinville's letter was met with indignation and did not have its intended effect of dividing the electors. Rather, it increased their zeal, and they chose the new bishop, Volfius, on the first vote. Out of 564 electors, there were 125 absences.[43] For a handful of those who stayed away, letters remain explaining their absence. The reasons offered for not participating are varied. One man begged off because of an injury. As proof of his claim, he offered his mayor as a witness.[44] Others were kept away by death or illness in their families.[45] In addition, the election was held in February, a month when weather could make travel difficult.[46] It is likely that some of the electors who failed to attend did so in support of Des Monstiers de Mérinville. The mayor of Auxonne wrote to inform the authorities that, despite great interest in the bishop's election, the town lacked two electors for the proposed assembly because its curé was among the non-juring clergy. Continuing, the mayor noted that he hoped soon to replace the priest and to hold primary assemblies to choose new electors.[47] Explicit support for Des Monstiers de Mérinville is found in three letters from the curé Claudon, priest of Saint-Médard, a parish church that shared the cathedral of Saint-Étienne in Dijon. Writing the Friday before the opening of the electoral assembly, Claudon explained that the election was against his principles and sentiments and that, therefore, he had no clergy or musicians to offer for the service.[48] In a second letter, dated the same day, he offered what he termed a clearer explanation. The problem was timing: his church, Saint-Médard, celebrated its mass at 10:00 on Sunday mornings, preventing him from attending the election.[49] His resolution not to attend was firm, and the next day he wrote yet another letter informing the authorities that neither he nor his vicar were available.[50] In response, the directory of the Côte-d'Or authorized the city's *procureur général* to make the necessary arrangements for the service with the cooperation of the church wardens and asked a delegation of clergy to invite Claudon, the organist, and the master of music to participate.[51] Despite these instances of dissent, it is striking that the overwhelming majority of electors participated in this assembly to choose the new bishop. In the final count, Volfius received 342 votes out of 439, easily surpassing curé Guy Bouillotte, priest at Arnay-le-Duc and a deputy to the Constituent Assembly, who was also in the running.[52]

The proclamation of Volfius as bishop was a distinguished event. The electors, members of the district court and National Guard, as well as a large crowd of Dijonnais packed the cathedral early on Wednesday morning to hear Claude Bernard Navier, president of the electoral assembly, proclaim Volfius's victory.[53] Following mass, the electors dedicated a bust of a citizen soldier who had been killed near Nancy and joined the gathered citizens in taking the oath pledging allegiance to nation, law, and king. Only the mayor of Dijon, Chartraire de Montigny, refused to swear the oath, initially seeking to promise only to die for the king and the nation. Yet he quickly reversed himself when the crowd denounced him.[54]

Volfius used the occasion of his election to highlight how the Civil Constitution of the Clergy restored the ancient church's practice of allowing the people to name their pastors. Although protesting his unworthiness, Volfius declared himself ready to take up the challenge in order to counter the malevolent arguments pitting religion against country. Volfius declared man, and presumably woman, naturally Christian and the Civil Constitution a regeneration and purification of the social pact.[55]

The divisions created by Volfius's election, which was part of the department's effort to enforce the Civil Constitution of the Clergy, left some traces in popular culture. Reinert collected two rhymes that circulated after Volfius's election. They underscore the varied reactions to his election and the changes it portended. The first, attributed to Dragonneau, commander of the National Guard in Bussey-le-Grand, praised the new bishop.

> Vous avez l'onction, les mœurs, la science,
> Vous éclairez l'esprit, le cœur, la conscience,
> L'agricole entête revient au sûr espoir
> Jus le bon grain maître pour un nouveau semoir.[56]

> You have the blessing, the morality, the science,
> You enlighten the spirit, the heart, the conscience,
> Stubborn agriculture recovers a sure hope
> Juice the good seed master for a new sower

The second, anonymous, rhyme issued a dire warning:

> Mon promis courit [sic] à la potence
> Mon secours est un terme de mépris
> Mon troisième le nom d'un impie sectair [sic]
> Nous tout sera bientot exommunis [sic]

My betrothed runs to the gallows
My help is a term of contempt
My third the name of an impious sectarian
We all will soon be excommunicated[57]

Having elected Volfius, the department now had the problem of installing him. The legislation called for three bishops – the metropolitan and two from neighboring dioceses – to participate in the consecration of a newly elected prelate.[58] The officials in the Côte-d'Or sought to assemble the necessary clerics by writing to one of the few higher clergy to swear the ecclesiastical oath, Étienne Charles de Loménie de Brienne, a French cardinal and archbishop of Sens, and to Claude-Antoine Valdec Delessart, the minister of the interior. Neither provided any help. De Loménie de Brienne declined to consecrate Volfius, despite praising the electors' choice.[59] His reasons were personal: he could not participate in the "spoliation" of Des Monstiers de Mérinville, a good friend. Delessart replied that he did not know whether the bishops in the departments surrounding the Côte-d'Or had a taken the oath or not, and suggested that the department write to each directory.[60] The authorities in Dijon then wrote to the departments of the Haute-Saône, the Vosges, the Jura, the Haut-Rhin, and the Haut-Marne.[61] None of these departments had a consecrated, juring bishop they could offer. The *procureur-général* of the Jura noted that the electors in Besançon had chosen a metropolitan, Philippe-Charles-François Séguin, but unfortunately, he had not yet accepted the honour.[62] The officials in the Haut-Rhin had no bishop to offer but expressed the hope that Volfius might be consecrated in time to participate in the installation of their new bishop.[63] The administrators in the Haute-Marne responded late, but in the affirmative, noting that, once he was consecrated, their bishop, Antoine-Hubert Wandelaincourt, could assist.[64] Wandelaincourt's assistance was not needed. By the time the response from the Haute-Marne arrived, Volfius's consecration was half a month behind him. In the end, Jean-Baptiste Gobel, the metropolitan of Paris, consecrated Volfius at the Congregation of the Oratory on Sunday, 13 March assisted by Jean-Baptiste Massieu and Jean-Baptiste Aubry, the newly elected bishops of the Oise and the Meuse, respectively.[65] On 20 March, Volfius returned to Dijon to a celebrity's welcome. The *Journal patriotique de la Côte-d'Or* reported that "the crowd surrounded his modest carriage crying: *long live the nation, the law, the King and M. Volfius our good* bishop ... [A]dministrators ... National Guard units ... and citizens of all professions, forming one family, filling the house, the courtyards and the street, they celebrated him as the most respectable minister of religion, the head of the pastors of the department, the father and the friend of all its citizens."[66] The celebrations concluded with fireworks and the pealing of bells. Two days later, Volfius took possession of his diocese in a ceremony at the cathedral church in Dijon.[67]

Despite the enthusiasm reported by the *Journal patriotique*, Volfius's first months as bishop were not easy. He had trouble filling the parishes of the Côte-d'Or with juring clergy. In April, the administrators of the district of Is-sur-Tille wrote requesting assistants (*desservans*) for several parishes. Volfius replied that, at the moment, he had no priests to spare, as he could not even find priests for all the parishes in Dijon. After Easter, he hoped to assist them.[68] In an effort to sort out the situation, he requested that the administrators make a table of all the parishes and succursal churches in the district, indicating their former curés and vicars and whether or not these individuals took the ecclesiastical oath.[69] The district replied that it was already gathering this data; however, there is no further information about this project, so it seems likely that Is-sur-Tille's census of its clergy was absorbed into the general redistricting of parishes that occurred in the spring and summer of 1791.[70]

A second illustration of the troubles Volfius faced was his struggle to secure the items necessary for the masses of Holy Week that first Easter. On 19 April, he wrote to the departmental directory requesting their assistance in acquiring the liturgical and sacramental items needed for the masses of Maundy Thursday and Easter Sunday. Several items were missing from the cathedral, including the mitre and a silver candlestick and basin. Volfius believed that the Ursulines had the missing silver and were refusing to hand it over. He also had only rough robes to wear and needed more refined ones befitting the occasion. These he believed might be obtainable from the abbey of Cîteaux. In addition to these material needs, he wrote that he needed a bailiff, as it was unbecoming for a bishop to have to part the crowd to enter the cathedral. Finally, the cathedral itself needed to be organized. It lacked sufficient confessionals, and he did not yet have the keys to the tabernacle, the sacristy, or the existing confessionals. Further, the cathedral's staff was in disarray; the soloists, members of the children's choir, and lower choir (*bas-chœur*), as well

as the sacristan all needed to know, at least provisionally, their salaries.[71] The department passed Volfius's laundry list of issues down
the chain to the directory of the district of Dijon. That directory
responded by sending one of their members to obtain the necessary
objects and to open all the cabinets.[72]

In his first months as bishop, Volfius struggled for legitimacy. In his
everyday public life, he sought to place juring priests in the parishes
of Dijon. He worked to gain control of the cathedral, its liturgical items, physical space, and staff. Beyond these practical struggles,
Volfius also soon engaged in a war of words, fought through pamphlets, to win the confidence of his new diocese.

THE BATTLE FOR LEGITIMACY

Volfius issued his first pastoral letter at the beginning of April. Warning the faithful that a party of ministers was preparing to create
a schism, Volfius argued that the Civil Constitution of the Clergy
did not abolish religion but, rather, represented a higher expression
of it. Further, he noted that, in allying with the church rather than
attacking it, the French revolutionaries were demonstrating their
enlightenment.[73] In this letter, Volfius appealed both to the faithful and the clergy of his diocese. Reiterating his position that the
Civil Constitution merely returned the church to traditional practices from when it was a primitive institution, he further argued that
bishops had never derived their authority from the pope but always
from Jesus Christ. Second, he noted that the Constituent Assembly was succeeding in reforming the church where bishops, synods,
and general councils had failed. Along with returning to the people
their ancient right to name their pastors, the Constituent Assembly
had established a more equitable division of dioceses and parishes.
These new ecclesiastical jurisdictions served the people better. The
election of pastors was an example of the return to the church's
early practices, and was supported, Volfius argued, by the report of
St. Cyprian, the third-century bishop of Carthage, concerning the
people's involvement in the election of Pope Cornelius and by the
Council of Chalcedon's judgment that election by the people was
the most canonical and legitimate means to choose a pastor. Allowing the people to choose their pastors did not diminish the church's
authority, because the church sanctified the candidate and conferred
upon him spiritual authority. Only in requiring clergy to swear an

oath did Volfius believe the assembly overstepped its bounds. This indiscretion, however, was not a concern, since it merely required clergy to submit to the primitive discipline of the church. To those clergy who rejected the legislation, Volfius warned that the success of the revolution was at stake. Resistance to the new order created an intolerable disorder in the diocese.[74]

Des Monstiers de Mérinville answered Volfius's first pastoral letter in short order. The abbé Henri Dillon, vicar-general of the former diocese of Dijon and dean of La Sainte-Chapelle in the city, also responded.[75] They took different tactics in their refutation of Volfius: Des Monstiers de Mérinville condemned Volfius's election and subsequent usurpation of his diocese; Dillon refuted Volfius's defence of the Civil Constitution of the Clergy.

Writing from Paris, Des Monstiers de Mérinville declared Volfius's election void because the diocese was not vacant. Additionally, the new boundary established by the Constituent Assembly was not legitimate, as neither the pope nor a church council had endorsed it.[76] By taking their positions, he argued, the new constitutional bishops had created a schism separating the French church from the universal Catholic Church. The Council of Trent explicitly granted the pope the authority to institute bishops. Consecrated by individuals who lacked the authority to do so, Volfius's ordination was void; further, all absolutions granted by him, with the exception of the last rite, were without effect. Des Monstiers de Mérinville called on the clergy of the diocese to refuse to obey Volfius. He instructed the faithful not to recognize him as bishop and not to take sacraments or attend a mass celebrated by a constitutional priest. Any cleric who took over the parish of a non-juring priest was a schismatic. Declaring himself the one true bishop of Dijon, Des Monstiers de Mérinville reminded his flock that there could be only one bishop in a diocese, and, as St. Cyprian had argued, all bishops were linked to the chair of St. Peter.[77]

Following Des Monstiers de Mérinville's missive, Henri Dillon published an open letter to Volfius. Dillon rejected the idea that merely writing to inform the pope of one's election constituted communion with the pontiff. Even heretics such as Novatian, Arius, and Eusebius had written to the pope.[78] Further, because the Civil Constitution of the Clergy violated Catholic teachings, the sacraments performed by constitutional clergy, while they might appear the same, would be of a different essence and would not have the authority of sacraments and instruction offered by legitimate pastors. The Civil Constitution destroyed the pope's jurisdiction, establishing a new equality between bishops and priests and placing real authority in the episcopal councils – an aberration contrary to all the church's councils.[79] Refuting Volfius's arguments supporting the new dioceses and the election of pastors, Dillon declared that the Council of Chalcedon had never decreed that ecclesiastical jurisdictions were to follow civil ones; rather, it had called on the emperor to correct a territorial division establishing two metropolitans in one province. Further, he held that Volfius misconstrued St. Cyprian's report on the election of Pope Cornelius. The bishops elected Cornelius; the people only gave their opinion. Summarizing his argument, Dillon wrote that the councils of the church held that pastors had to be elected by clergy. Explicitly, in 869 the Council of Constantinople held the clergy without the laity elected bishops, patriarchs, and metropolitans. The idea of electing pastors was a complete innovation, as they had never been elected in the ancient church. The bishop was responsible for the entire diocese and needed to have confidence in its clergy. Such confidence would not be possible if the people foisted priests upon bishops.[80]

Volfius and Dillon present conflicting readings of ecclesiastical history. While this is not the place to sort out the accuracy of each cleric's claim, that they made these claims is noteworthy. They turned to a common set of sources – the scriptures, acts of various church councils, and prominent seventeenth-century church historians to build their case for and against the Civil Constitution of the Clergy. In their recourse to church historians, Dillon took his cue from Louis Sébastien le Nain de Tillemont, while Volfius relied upon Bossuet and Louis d'Eynac Thomassin. With respect to ancient authorities, St. Cyprian figured prominently in the letters of both men, his ecclesiology including elements that were helpful to both sides in the controversy over the Civil Constitution. For Volfius and the other constitutional clergy, St. Cyprian's support of a role for the people in choosing their leadership was important. At the same time, Cyprian's position on the unity of the church and on the importance of Peter to apostolic succession were useful to opponents of the Civil Constitution because both emphasize the pre-eminence of the pope.[81]

The pamphlet war between Volfius, Des Monstiers de Mérinville, and Henri Dillon highlights the efforts by both sides to use church history to legitimate their position. This reference to ancient history was, in some ways, parallel to the appeal by French revolutionaries, in the secular realm, to the example of the Roman Republic. There was, however, a significant difference in these two appeals.[82] The revolutionaries were in general agreement about what happened in the early Roman Republic and why it was significant as they remade the French nation. If their vision of the ancient republic was not always consistent with historical reality, they at least agreed on that vision. By contrast, the nature of the early Christian Church engendered more disagreement.

The need to appeal to church history to justify opposition to the Civil Constitution of the Clergy quickly disappeared for Des Monstiers de Mérinville and the other non-juring clergy. After a delay of nearly a year, Pope Pius VI issued a brief on the Civil Constitution on 10 March 1791.[83] Although it was intended to be public, France's bishops kept the pope's unqualified condemnation of the legislation secret for nearly six weeks. For its part, the Constituent Assembly sought to negotiate with the pope before the release of the brief. The bishops, likewise, hoped an agreement might be reached. The Constituent Assembly sent Philippe de Ségur as ambassador to Rome, recalling the Cardinal de Bernis after he refused to take the ecclesiastical oath. Aware that the French bishops had not publish his brief, Pius VI issued a second one on 13 April, giving juring clergy forty days to retract their oaths. He also refused Ségur an audience because he had himself taken the oath. Informed of the pontiff's intransigence, the Constituent Assembly broke diplomatic relations with the papacy in early May. Backed into a corner, the bishops published the pope's briefs on 4 May.

In early June, Des Monstiers de Mérinville issued a second pastoral letter and order (*ordonnance*), attaching them to Pius VI's April brief.[84] His letter echoed the pope's position: the Civil Constitution of the Clergy was a heresy and its adherents guilty of schism.[85] Borrowing a metaphor from St. Cyprian, Des Monstiers de Mérinville argued that, as the successor of all bishops governing the church since Jesus Christ, he was the last link in a long chain. Volfius, on the other hand, was the first link in a new chain. His very newness was evidence of his illegitimacy.[86] That Volfius was part of the heresy of the Civil Constitution was more forgivable than his participation in the schism occurring throughout the French church.[87] Des Monstiers de Mérinville called on the faithful to reject Volfius and challenged the closing of parishes and dismissal of pastors. The claim that the

church had no interest in the boundaries of dioceses and parishes was
specious, he argued. Further, the church exclusively held the right to
install and remove its ministers.[88] In his order, attached to the pope's
letter, Des Monstiers de Mérinville instructed the faithful to adhere
to the pontiff's judgment with respect to the Civil Constitution of
the clergy reminding them of Pope Innocent XII's stance against the
Gallican liberties declared by the French Assembly of the Clergy in
1682. Innocent had held that, although the French church remained
"zealous for its liberty, and rightly so," it had a duty to be faithful to
"the mother of the churches," the "church chosen by God."[89]

The central issue in the pamphlet war between Des Monstiers de Mérinville, aided by his episcopal vicar Henri Dillon, and Volfius in the
spring of 1791 was legitimacy. For Volfius, the revolution returned the
church to its ancient practices and a truer Christianity. He appealed
to the people of the Côte-d'Or to recognize the legitimacy of these
reforms and his authority as bishop. Arguing that the constitutional
church was essential to the revolution, Volfius developed ideas in
his first pastoral letter that he had expressed earlier in speeches celebrating the establishment of Dijon's bourgeois militia and, later, its
National Guard. For Volfius, religion was necessary to the revolution
and to the new order because it provided a foundation for the nation.
The revolution was helpful to religion because, through its reforms, it
returned the church to the simplicity of its first days.

On the other side, Des Monstiers de Mérinville and Dillon judged
Volfius's claims of authority baseless. Only established canonical
procedures could reform the church, and the Civil Constitution of
the Clergy had no such sanction. It had the support of neither a
church council nor the pope. Further, Pius VI confirmed its illicit
nature in his briefs of March and April 1791. The borders of dioceses
as well as the installation of bishops and priests were not matters for
civil authority. The Civil Constitution was a heresy and had created
a schism in the church. Volfius's appeal to ancient church practices
failed to acknowledge that the church had legitimately changed its
procedures over the course of its history.

Mired in controversy, the constitutional church in the Côte-d'Or
began to organize itself. For its new bishop, the first months presented challenges both practical and theological. Volfius embraced
both, moving forward to help create a new order in church and state.

4

Organizing the Constitutional Church
in the Côte-d'Or

In June 1791, neither Des Monstiers de Mérinville nor Volfius could claim victory in the Côte-d'Or. While Volfius worked to establish the new constitutional church, Des Monstiers de Mérinville called on the diocese's priests to resist the reorganization of the diocese. We know that only 4 per cent of the department's priests renounced their oath.[1] But such precise statistics were not available to contemporaries, and it was anything but apparent from Dijon that the juring clergy were in the majority. In part, this was because even those who took the ecclesiastical oath were not always eager to cooperate with the new church organization. Volfius did not find it easy to fill parishes with juring clergy or to convince clergy in the countryside, even those who had taken the oath, to read his pastoral letters to their parishioners.[2]

For one observer, M. Gros, *procureur-syndic* of the commune of Dijon, the fortunes of the constitutional church looked anything but promising. In a letter to the president of the Chambres des Comptes de Bourgogne, who was living as an émigré in Fribourg, Switzerland, Gros reported on the constitutional clergy active in the city: "We have here only nine juring [priests] two of whom are public officials, the abbé Volfius and the abbé Melchoir, both professors at the *collège*, three *mépartistes*, one from Saint-Michel, M. Beaudet, the second from Saint-Jean, M. Tarnière, and the third from Saint-Philibert, plus at Saint-Jean the abbé Nouvellier, a bad lot, and a defrocked monk from [the Abbey of] Citeaux, at Saint-Philibert a Benedictine, Dom Champagne, and at Saint-Pierre the abbé Girardot, a simple deacon who was denied the priesthood in the last ordination."[3] Gros also noted that initially oath taking was greater in the countryside, as the clergy there were less hostile to the orders of the department than were those in Dijon. However, he reported, as priests realized their error, they retracted their oaths or refused to read Volfius's pastoral letters.

RATIONALIZING AND REDUCING
THE PARISHES OF THE CÔTE-D'OR

Despite Gros's critical assessment, departmental and district authorities began to reorganize the church in their jurisdictions. Archival evidence of these efforts is fragmentary but shows clear intent and consistent effort in carrying forward the requirements of the Civil Constitution of the Clergy. Districts held elections to fill parishes where priests had refused the oath.

As early as February 1791, the district of Arnay-le-Duc replaced sixteen refractory clergy with those who had taken the oath, and put a seventeenth juror in a parish left vacant by the death of its priest.[4] In March, the district of Dijon nominated twenty-five individuals to parishes, three to serve in the city of Dijon, and twenty-two others for towns and villages.[5] Sixteen of these priests replaced individuals who had taken the oath with restrictions, a practice rejected by the Constituent Assembly. The constitutional clergy nominated in Dijon, with only two exceptions, came from the lower ranks of the parish clergy. Nineteen were vicars, two *mépartistes*, and two *desservants*. Those not coming from the lower ranks of the parish clergy were a curé and an oratorian who had been a professor of theology. One individual is listed only as a priest from Auxonne, without the exact position he held noted. This list suggests that, in the district of Dijon, the new constitutional church provided career advancement for a number of priests. Other districts also held elections to fill their parishes in March. Saint-Jean-de-Losne elected clergy to thirteen parishes. Beaune filled fourteen positions with constitutionals. The effort to place juring clergy in parishes continued into the fall with three districts, Saint-Jean-de-Losne, Is-sur-Tille, and Châtillon-sur-Seine convening electoral assemblies to elect clergy.[6] Election results do not offer a full picture for any of the department's districts. The district of Arnay-le-Duc provided the most extensive list of its parishes in its work to redraw diocesan boundaries.

The ecclesiastical reforms of the new law went beyond clerical oath taking, electing parish priests, and installing a new bishop.

They also reduced the number of parishes in each diocese. In the Côte-d'Or, the process of ecclesiastical redistricting, which was no less contentious than the election of Volfius, began even before the new bishop was in place.

On the evening of 3 December 1790 seven women interrupted a meeting of the directory of the district of Dijon. Claiming to represent many others, the women pressed into the district directory's chamber. A handwritten report signed by the vice-president and secretary of the directory describes the women and their demands that evening.[7] Concerned about rumours of parish closings, they came as deputies of religion. The delegation consisted of two married women (the wives of a bookbinder and an invalid), two widows – one self-declared to avoid being beaten – and three single women, including a fruit merchant. The demoiselle Florimond served as the group's spokeswoman and demanded to know if the administration planned to close the parishes of Saint-Jean and La Sainte-Chapelle. Whatever the cost, she asserted on the women's behalf, they would keep those parishes open. The nation could sell the goods of monks – to that they were indifferent – but it could not close their parishes.

The apparently surprised administrators dealt with the women's interruption by appealing to procedure. Having heard their concerns, they informed them that they could not respond until the women presented a formal petition. To write a petition, they needed to ask the city for permission to meet and deliberate. The directory's brief report on the delegation of women indicates only that they accepted the administrators' response and left. Did they write a petition following the procedures outlined? The archives provide no answer. Their demands, however, are interesting, appearing as they did in early December 1790. The Civil Constitution of the Clergy called for a radical rationalization of the Catholic Church in France; that this process required the closing of many parishes was not lost on France's laity, nor did they accept it passively.

In the Côte-d'Or, the rationalization of parishes began in March 1791, in the same month electors chose the department's new bishop. The most complete plan for redistricting came from Arnay-le-Duc, located southwest of Dijon.[8] That district's administrators reported that, when Des Monstiers de Mérinville failed to implement the reduction of parishes called for in the Civil Constitution of the Clergy, they began to reorganize the parishes of their region. Combining small churches or absorbing them into larger ones, they

established forty-five parishes and organized them into nine cantons. Following their work, parishes in the district ranged from 456
parishioners at Savigny-sous-Malain to 1,350 in Nievy. The district
also established ten succursals – free-standing chapels dependent on
larger parish churches – that had between 305 and 420 parishioners.
In reorganizing the parish, Arnay-le-Duc's authorities used several
criteria: the location and condition of roads, the position of rivers,
population distribution, the interests of commerce and agriculture,
and the possible objections of rural parishioners, especially to the
distance of the parish church from their homes. They noted that they
granted larger towns succursal churches. Sixteen of the parishes they
closed contained fewer than a hundred parishioners, with nine of
these having fewer than fifty. In some instances, they joined parishes
of 200–400 parishioners to create larger ones with 500–600 individuals. In all, the district closed thirty-seven parishes.

For the priests and people of Arnay-le-Duc, this reorganization
meant significant change. Some villages began to anticipate the sale
of church properties, including the parish rectories. According to
the provisions of the Civil Constitution of the Clergy, a priest whose
parish closed could be elected as the pastor of a new parish.[9] Yet this
provision was largely unutilized because many clergy in the district
refused to take the ecclesiastical oath.[10]

Despite the efforts of local authorities to comply with the regulations coming from Paris, they faced many priests and parishioners who
resisted the new church order. The *Journal patriotique du département de la Côte-d'Or*, a weekly newspaper printed in Dijon, reported
some of the protests. In Flavigny, a village sixty kilometres northwest
of Dijon, the captain of the National Guard said in April that his
men could not come to Dijon to swear the required oath of loyalty to
nation, law, and king.[11] Part of the problem was the distance between
Flavigny and Dijon and the need for many of the militia's members,
mostly farmers, to attend to their fields, but an additional factor was
the presence of three refractory priests who were disturbing public
tranquility. The captain wrote that the guardsmen were needed to
maintain order and prevent further trouble.

The journal reported opposition to the new church order in Dijon
as well. A short untitled item in late May recounted an attack on the
rogations, processions on the three days before Ascension Thursday.
The niece of the former vicar of Saint-Nicolas threw water on the
faithful as they followed Volfius and several of his priests. Although

she was arrested and jailed, the authorities judged the young woman not culpable because she received false counsel to do what she did.[12]

NATIONAL VERSUS LOCAL VISIONS
FOR THE PARISHES OF DIJON

The most contested development of Volfius's first year as bishop was the reduction of the parishes of Dijon. In mid-May 1791, the Constituent Assembly issued a decree reorganizing the city's parishes.[13] It reduced Dijon's seven parishes to four, establishing the cathedral at Saint-Étienne and retaining the churches of Saint-Bénigne, Saint-Michel, and Notre-Dame. It established two oratories, one at Saint-Nicolas and the other in the chapel of the former Bernardine convent.[14] The Constituent Assembly's plan slated three churches for closure: Saint-Pierre, Saint-Jean, and Saint-Philibert. The parish of Saint-Médard met in the church of Saint-Étienne. Saint-Bénigne, not previously a parish church, had been part of the city's Benedictine monastery, which had by then been closed. The Constituent Assembly also closed La Sainte-Chapelle, a wealthy collegiate chapel with a rich medieval history.[15] As a collegial church, La Sainte-Chapelle had become an anomaly in France because the Civil Constitution of the Clergy had eliminated the office of canon.

Parishioners from Saint-Nicolas and Saint-Pierre responded immediately to the proposed church closings by petitioning the department.[16] The crux of the parishioners' argument was that the Constituent Assembly's plan maintained the churches in the city's more affluent centre at the expense of it poorer suburbs. Architectural importance apparently guided the assembly's plan. Volfius lent his support to the petitions from Saint-Nicolas and Saint-Pierre. Writing in July to departmental administrators, he argued that it made more sense to establish a succursal at Saint-Nicolas, rather than to have the two proposed oratories.[17] The succursal could serve the suburb around Saint-Nicolas, and the chapel of the Bernardines could be closed and the property sold. If the concern was economy, Volfius noted, it would be less expensive for the department to maintain one vicar at Saint-Nicolas than to maintain two chapels. Following his letter to the department, Volfius wrote to the Ecclesiastical Committee of the Constituent Assembly.[18] Aware of a petition from Saint-Pierre's parishioners asking for a succursal, he lent some support to their request, but wrote that he viewed Saint-Nicolas as the more necessary parish.

Like Volfius, the department's directory took the petitions from Saint-Nicolas and Saint-Pierre seriously. In early August, they wrote to the minister of the interior about the local proposal that Dijon have two succursals rather than two oratories. The response from Paris was unbending. Whatever merits the petitions might have, they insisted that the directory enforce the May decree.[19] In early September, the Ecclesiastical Committee addressed a form letter to the department echoing the interior minister's decision. As a whole, they noted that departments were using succursals far more frequently than chapels or oratories,[20] and they observed that this practice was creating divisions at a time when unity was essential. Oratories, the committee believed, were preferable because they served the people on festivals and Sundays but did not create a separate allegiance.

As the correspondence from the Côte-d'Or indicates, reorganizing the parishes in France's larger cities was a matter of both local and national interest. In September, the Ecclesiastical Committee instructed the departments to send departmental and district orders as well as letters from the bishop with plans for ecclesiastical redistricting. The Côte-d'Or's directory carefully followed these instructions, making note of the committee's preference for oratories in a draft of their response.[21]

Dijon's Catholic parishioners were not as easily silenced, and the petition campaign begun in the summer continued into the fall. In early September, the parishioners of Saint-Nicolas addressed a petition to their deputies in the newly elected Legislative Assembly.[22] The petition from Saint-Nicolas is noteworthy because, among the several circulated, it is the most explicit in its social and political critique of the redistricting plan. Signed by thirty-four individuals, sixteen of whom indicated the assent of their spouses, the petition argued that the redistricting of Dijon's parishes should reflect the values of the nation's new constitution.[23] They reminded the deputies that the four parishes to remain open were located in the city's more affluent interior. Only Saint-Bénigne sat on the city's periphery in a position to serve poorer citizens living there and in the suburbs. They argued that providing three parishes for the wealthy was illogical as well as unjust, because the rich had little need of the church's ministry, enjoying as they did the necessities of life. Further, as the whole citizenry contributed equally to the public weal, it was only fair that the people's convenience determine the city's parishes. Pointing to the constitution, the petitioners noted that it destroyed old inequities.

Further, their parish stood steadfast with the revolution in its first six months, in stark contrast to the hostility of the city's more centrally located churches. Closing Saint-Nicolas was poor repayment for their patriotism. A more natural redistricting would maintain the parishes of Saint-Michel, Saint-Bénigne, and Saint-Nicolas, and put an additional parish in the former church of the Cordeliers. Although some might object to closing the beautiful church of Notre-Dame, aesthetic considerations should not deter the deputies, because, the petitioners argued, buildings were not ends in themselves, but were intended for public usefulness. In closing, the parishioners suggested that personal interest had dictated the proposed redistricting.

In a further appeal for social justice, Saint-Nicolas's petitioners argued that priests serving the poor should be paid higher salaries than those serving the rich. Saint-Nicolas merited an episcopal vicar because of its many impoverished parishioners. Only an episcopal vicar would earn an honest salary of 2000 *livres* and have a permanent residence in the parish. The two simple vicars proposed by the National Assembly's plan would receive half that salary.

The parishioners of Saint-Nicolas were aware of – if slightly misinformed about – the Civil Constitution of the Clergy's provisions and the plan from Paris for redistricting Dijon's urban parishes.[24] In upholding the values of public utility and equality, they highlighted the revolution's inclusive rhetoric and vision for society. Importantly, the petition did not reject the assembly's right to reform the church's institutions; however, it did call for the assembly to live up to revolutionary ideals.

Saint-Nicolas's parishioners were not the only Dijonnais to petition the Legislative Assembly in the fall of 1791. In October and November, two groups of citizens, neither specifically identified as parishioners of a particular parish, submitted petitions to departmental administrators suggesting changes to the proposed parish structure for Dijon. One hundred seventy individuals signed the October petition. They largely agreed with the assembly's plan but suggested making Saint-Bénigne the cathedral parish.[25] Further, they proposed an oratory in the church of the Carmelites rather than in the chapel of the Bernardines, arguing that the latter was too small and isolated. The November petitioners, declaring themselves "active citizens" and thus asserting their ability to participate in the new order, suggested several revisions to the assembly's plan, arguing that it was inconvenient for the public.[26] Because Saint-Étienne and Saint-Michel were side by side, they proposed closing Saint-Étienne and placing the cathedral in the centrally located and beautiful Saint-Michel. Constructed from the late fifteenth to the mid-sixteenth century, Saint-Michel's façade was an ornate mix of both Gothic and Renaissance elements. It was also adjacent to the diocese's seminary and the bishop's residence. Their plan suggested that the former church of the Cordeliers, Saint-Bénigne, and Notre-Dame serve as Dijon's other three parishes. They suggested maintaining Saint-Nicolas as a succursal of Notre-Dame. The church of the Cordeliers was convenient for the parishioners of Saint-Pierre, removing their concerns about travelling to the city's centre. In their petition, the active citizens, about 150 in all, rejected the idea of placing the cathedral at Saint-Bénigne because the church was on the edge of the city, and the former monastery buildings proposed for the bishop's residence and seminary needed costly repairs.

The Bernardines also weighed in on the assembly's proposed plan.[27] Writing to the department's directory, they noted that their church was too small to serve the suburb of Saint-Pierre for Sunday mass. The inhabitants would not fit into the chapel even if they utilized the bell tower. They suggested instead the larger church of the Cordeliers.

In late November, Saint-Pierre's parishioners sent a second petition to the department, advocating for the people of the city's southeast suburb. They observed that the proposed redistricting demonstrated a lack of familiarity with local conditions. Closing their parish presented a special hardship in the winter, because women, children, the elderly, and the infirm would have difficulty walking to Saint-Michel. The redistricting plan placed them in the position of either "exposing their lives" or "missing their spiritual aid." Interestingly, retaining the church of Saint-Pierre was not their concern. Instead they sought to preserve the *parish* as a community of people. They suggest that their parish be placed in the former church of the Cordeliers as a succursal to Saint-Michel.[28]

Six months after the National Assembly's decree, the reorganization of Dijon's parishes remained unresolved and a matter of significant public interest. In late November, Volfius wrote to the department's *procureur-général-syndic* and urged him to respond to the concerns of Saint-Nicolas's and Saint-Pierre's parishioners.[29] Warning that "an ugly explosion was threatening to erupt," he related two recent encounters. Several men, women, and children from Saint-Nicolas had forced their way into his home, and it was only with difficulty that he had appeased them. On a separate occasion, as he passed close to the suburb of Saint-Pierre, stone workers threatened to give him a "petition in stones." Rumours were circulating that he supported the redistricting decreed the previous May. As this was not the case, he wrote that he would be forced to publish his position if the department did not act quickly.[30] In appealing for action, Volfius noted that the department had not suffered the religious troubles plaguing other areas. He attributed the relative freedom from religious disturbances to his efforts, pointing out that he had placed a number of good priests in its parishes. In addition, the diocese had thirty seminarians, more, he claimed, than any other department in the kingdom.

The petitioners from Dijon's parishes contested the national government's authority to decide the matter of Dijon's urban parishes.[31] While accepting that some churches would close, they rejected a plan they judged contrary to the revolution's ideals of the end of privilege and a rational organization of society. A plan that maintained wealthy central parishes at the expense of the workers in the suburbs was unacceptable. The Civil Constitution of the Clergy was not the issue. Dijon's laity opposed the government's effort to apply the law's provisions contrary to the spirit of the new order.

In May 1792, the Legislative Assembly issued a decree revising the redistricting plan for the parishes of Dijon.[32] For the parishioners of Saint-Pierre and Saint-Nicolas, the new decree represented a victory. Dijon was to have three parishes: Saint-Michel, Notre-Dame, Saint-Bénigne, which would be the cathedral. It would also have two succursals, one at Saint-Nicolas and the other in the church of the Cordeliers, but no oratories. The assembly's decree followed the department's recommendation made in late December. In the end, redistricting Dijon's parishes was a joint effort of the city's parishioners, departmental authorities, and the new bishop. The city's laity made the parish closings an issue that neither the department's directory nor its new bishop could ignore. Further, in their rejection of the May 1791 plan, the parishioners had offered both a practical and ideological critique of Paris's directive.

It was the department's directory, and not Volfius, who supported the idea of placing the new cathedral and seminary at Saint-Bénigne. Previously an abbey church, it was in poor repair, as were the buildings adjacent to it. In November 1791, Volfius advised the department to assess the cost repairing Saint-Bénigne before moving the cathedral,

seminary, and bishop's residence from Saint- Étienne.[33] Both Saint-
Étienne and Saint-Bénigne were ancient churches in the diocese,
being established in the fifth and sixth centuries, respectively.[34]

Once the decision to place the cathedral in Saint-Bénigne was firm,
Volfius moved quickly to tackle the issue of the church's restoration.
In early June 1792, he wrote to departmental officials and requested
they take Saint-Étienne's paving stones immediately after the Octave
of the Holy Sacrament and install them in Saint-Bénigne.[35] Because
the department planned to close and sell Saint-Étienne, Volfius felt
some urgency to acquire the paving stones before civil authorities
took possession of the church. In a second letter, Volfius requested
that the churches of Saint-Jean and Saint-Philibert, also scheduled to
be closed and sold, remain open and serve the cathedral's parishioners during Saint-Bénigne's restoration.[36]

A year and a half after the first clergy swore the ecclesiastical oath
and Volfius accepted the position of bishop, a decree from the Legislative Assembly settled the cathedral and parish organization of
Dijon. It was a negotiated settlement coming after dogged argument
on the part of Dijon's parishioners and careful diplomacy by the
new bishop. It demonstrated that, while civil authorities could initiate the reforms envisioned in the Civil Constitution of the Clergy,
they could not control their implementation. Making the Civil Constitution a reality required negotiation with the people who saw
their parishes and clergy as a community interest. The redrawing of
Dijon's urban parishes also indicated a broad degree of support for
the Civil Constitution's vision of a leaner, more rationally organized
Catholic Church.

The contested beginning of the constitutional church in the Côte-
d'Or was not limited to parish boundaries or the recruitment of juring
priests. Because the Constituent Assembly determined in May 1791
that non-juring clergy could remain temporarily in their parishes,
Volfius and the constitutional clergy began their efforts to organize
a new church that had an embedded opposition. This divided clergy,
and growing tensions as the Legislative Assembly debated the possibility of war with Austria, created a fraught atmosphere as the
constitutional church entered its second year.

The First Terror against the Clergy, 1792

The winter and spring of 1792 were difficult in the Côte-d'Or. A drought the previous summer made vegetables scarce and expensive – so much so that Bishop Volfius relaxed the dietary restrictions for Lent, allowing the faithful to consume meat and fat four days of the week.[1] An incident in the village of Longchamp, some twenty-five kilometres southeast of Dijon, indicates the desperation citizens felt. Late in the evening of 26 March, a crowd of twenty men armed with cudgels and accompanied by the mayor, the *procureur*, and a municipal officer descended on the rectory. Having already emptied the municipal till, the rioters demanded the parish council's funds. Stalling, Alexandre Chamberland, the long-serving vicar and by then the constitutional priest of Longchamp, told the villagers that the church had only five hundred *livres*.[2] Undeterred, the municipal officer ordered Chamberland to have the money ready the next day. Did Chamberland surrender the church's cash? We do not know. The account of the riot in Longchamp comes from a letter written by Marpault, a member of Longchamp's National Guard. Having been forced to join the rioters, Marpault wrote some four days later to the National Guard gendarmerie in Auxonne to submit his resignation. Neighbours looting local cashboxes and threatening fellow citizens were not individuals Marpault desired either to join or to confront. In response to Marpault's letter, the district of Saint-Jean-de-Losne ordered an investigation, observing that Longchamp's officials had not reported any unrest. In its minutes that March, however, Longchamp's council did note great need among the village's poor.[3]

The revolution's third year found the Côte-d'Or burdened by economic and social tensions. In Dijon, the town's wealthiest citizens emigrated, eroding the local economy.[4] Adding to the strain was the growing threat of war. Concerns about the revolution's enemies, both external and internal, increased after the king's flight from Paris the previous June. The recalcitrance of the non-juring clergy, as well as Austria's and Prussia's support, albeit conditional, for the king in the Declaration of Pillnitz, seemed further evidence of the dangers facing the revolutionaries. The Legislative Assembly, elected in September, increasingly turned its attention to the question of war, with the public debate coming to a head in late December and January.

CONCERNS ABOUT REFRACTORY CLERGY

In this period of hardship and heightened tensions, the department of the Côte-d'Or took its first actions against the non-juring, refractory clergy. On 11 March 1792, the department ordered all refractory clergy to reside in Dijon. Although free to live where they chose, they had to inform the authorities of their domicile.[5] Abbé Guérin, a late nineteenth-century historian, explained the department's action as an attempt to redirect parishioners to the constitutional clergy.[6] To explain its action, however, the department's order pointed to the disruptive influence of the refractory clergy and the uncertainty of the times. Religion, the department maintained, served as a pretext for agitation in the countryside. Guérin reported that four hundred refractory priests came to live in the city. Undoubtedly, this figure is exaggerated. As a whole, historian Marcel Henriot estimated that the department only had 270 refractory clergy.[7] Guillaume Gros, the department's *procureur-syndic* in 1792 wrote that 160 to 180 refractory clergy resided in the town.[8]

The administrators in the Côte-d'Or were not alone in their concern about the activities of refractory clergy. By the end of April, forty-two departments either exiled or interned their non-juring clergy, taking action after the Legislative Assembly's effort to suppress the refractory clergy failed. In November, the assembly passed a decree requiring non-juring clergy to take an oath of loyalty or forfeit their pensions. However, Louis XVI vetoed the law.[9]

Even among clergy who swore the oath, there was lackluster support for Volfius and the constitutional church. The directory of the district of Is-sur-Tille reported that four or five clerics refused to read Volfius's recently issued pastoral letter.[10] One priest, noting that he had taken the oath to the Civil Constitution of the Clergy, declared he would be faithful to the law as soon as it was "illuminated by a legitimate authority." A vicar assured authorities that he would read Volfius's pastoral letter, but privately, not at mass. A newly elected parish priest, his superior, rejected the vicar's plan as disobedience to the Civil Constitution. For the district authorities in Is-sur-Tille, such refusals to read Volfius's letter left them with the problem of what action to take. Was it necessary to replace these priests?

A year and a half after its passage, the Civil Constitution of the Clergy, the revolution's major legislative initiative for the former First Estate, remained only partially implemented. Departments boasted newly elected constitutional bishops and at times a considerable number of clergy who swore the required oath, yet there remained those who actively or passively resisted the revolution's religious reforms. In 1792, the departments and then the Legislative Assembly turned their attention to the refractory clergy, a perceived fifth column that they judged as too disruptive to local populations to ignore any longer. Like the dechristianization movement that characterized the Terror of 1793 and 1794, the effort to suppress refractories in 1792 began in the departments. Scholars of the revolution's religious history characterize the actions taken against the non-juring priests as the beginning of a "long Terror" for France's clergy that stretched from 1792 to 1794.[11] Events in the Côte-d'Or affirm this historical judgment.

In the Côte-d'Or, the struggle to confront the non-juring clergy continued into the late spring of 1792. In April, Volfius refused the city's request that he lobby the Legislative Assembly for a lycée because the stay in Paris would keep him away from the department all summer. Pointing to the recent declaration of war on Austria (20 April) and to the increasing activity of the refractory clergy, he suggested that he could best contribute to public order and peace by making his planned pastoral visits.[12] A reminder of the agitation in the countryside came again in May as the district of Arnay-le-Duc reported concern about the activities of non-juring priests. In the village of Arnay-sur-Perroux, the public prosecutor stated that he suspected three priests of instigating unrest. One in particular, the abbé Pounelle, preyed on "feeble women" and was the "singular cause of domestic troubles in the countryside." Responding to the prosecutor's concerns, the district directory ordered Pounelle escorted to Dijon to be deported.[13]

THE IMPRISONMENT OF
REFRACTORY CLERGY IN DIJON

In June, the antipathy felt by Dijon's patriots toward the refractory priests exploded in the department's most significant episode
of religious repression before the Terror. Briefly stated, the Jacobin
Club of Dijon organized the arrest of over one hundred refractory
clergy resident in Dijon and then held them for two weeks while
local authorities remained largely passive, intervening only to ensure
the security of the priests in their extra-legal detention. The priests'
imprisonment ended after the minister of the interior demanded
that the department secure the priests' liberty and property rights
as guaranteed by the constitution. Standing outside of these official
bodies, the club members of Dijon, aided by crowds that included
women and children, claimed the right to secure the nation against
its enemies, in this case embodied in the refactory priests.

At the end of the nineteenth century, the abbé Guérin published
an account of this episode written by a refractory priest, the Abbé
Leprince, former canon of La Sainte-Chapelle.[14] Leprince escaped
imprisonment in June 1792 by going into hiding. According to him,
on Sunday, 17 June, a speaker at Dijon's Jacobin Club gave a speech
against the enemies of the country –specifically émigrés, their families, and non-juring priests. The speech followed the club's receipt
of sad news. Lieutenant colonel Cazotte, serving in the second battalion of volunteers from the Côte-d'Or, and thirty of his men had
been killed during combat at Gliswelle, a small hamlet in northeast-
ern France. Among the enemy dead – the speaker claimed – were
priests carrying arms.[15] For the Dijonnais gathered in June 1792,
the heroism of their volunteers was self-evident, as was the danger
facing the nation. Leaving the meeting, the crowd went to the Place
Royale, removed the cannons, and moved them to the gates of the city.
The next day, the leaders of the city's Jacobin Club met and decided
to imprison all non-juring priests. They compiled a list of names and
appealed to a "horde of sans-culottes, women and children" to carry
out the arrests, promising five francs for each priest detained.[16]

On the second day of these developments – after the Jacobin Club
ordered the arrests of the priests – the city council became involved.
Although receiving a petition that morning to disarm the nation's
enemies, the councillors ignored it, believing that to act would lead
to violence. As Dijonnais rounded up and detained clergy, however,

the city council dispatched two commissioners and the public prosecutor to investigate. The commissioners' report echoes the claims
made by Leprince. Suspicious of the refractory priests, the people
called for their deportation; the news of Cazotte's death and reports
of developments in Paris further fuelled the unrest. In the commissioners' report, it is clear that the crowds knew of the king's refusal
(repeated with a second veto in May) to support the Legislative
Assembly's efforts to sanction refractory clergy. The commissioners
also reported that the crowd believed the king had dissolved the constitutional cabinet in Paris.[17] Although the cabinet was still in place,
the king had reshuffled his ministers, dismissing Jean-Marie Roland
and other recently appointed Girondin members following Roland's
criticism of his veto of the legislation against the refractories. While
not a formal party, the Girondins were a faction within the Jacobin
Club that increasingly defined their interests in opposition to that
of Robespierre and other Jacobins. They rose to influence in the
Legislative Assembly.[18]

The night of 18–19 June was a long one for the city's council members. Dispatching two members to check on the detained priests, they
concluded their session at one o'clock in the morning. Reconvening
a few hours later, they learned of the department's decision (made on
the recommendation of the district directory) to move the priests to
the former seminary adjacent to the church and Saint Jean square.[19]

The municipal, district, and departmental authorities in this affair
worked to secure the safety of the priests, but they took no actions to
confront the crowd's usurpation of police authority. In their reports,
the authorities in Dijon vaguely described those acting against the
priests, identifying them only as "the crowd" or "citizens." More
pointed, Leprince's account clearly identifies Dijon's Jacobin-
affiliated political club as the instigator of these arrests and notes
the National Guard's role in moving the priests to the seminary.

On 19 June, the crowd went to houses of the Sisters of the Good
Shepherd, the Carmelites, and the Dames du Refuge and removed
their members. They attempted to arrest the Dames de la Visitation,
but their superior sent an urgent request for assistance to the city's
directory. In response to the attacks on the women's orders, the
municipal directory sent National Guardsmen to stop the arrests and
escort the women back to their houses.[20] Nevertheless, the actions in
Dijon inspired arrests in surrounding villages. In Plombières, the people detained their chaplain, an elderly man of eighty. At Marsannay,

villagers arrested the former *prieur curé* and the canon of Champlitte, both of whom had taken refuge in the chateau of Arcelot.[21]

Watching developments with alarm, Volfius and his episcopal council petitioned the department to release the captives to their supervision. Although acknowledging that some dissident pastors had disturbed the peace of the people, the petition asked the department to free the very elderly, the ill, and those guilty only of "erroneous opinions." Further, Volfius and his council proposed that those clergy not "denounced by public opinion" be supervised by the constitutional clergy, arguing that their example might bring the refractory clergy around to the "defence of the nation, the maintenance of the constitution, and the re-establishment of peace in the Realm." The department applauded the generosity of the constitutional priests but declined their offer. Writing that, considering the "infraction of the law" the non-juring priests had committed, the department decided to secure their personal safety by keeping them under guard until they could be released without danger.[22] Volfius appealed to the department to print the episcopal council's petition in order to stop rumours attributing the arrests to the constitutional clergy.[23]

On 21 June, three days into the crisis, the city ordered the National Guard, the national gendarmes, and the police to enforce the constitution, which protected persons and property; anyone attacking either was to be arrested and taken before a justice of the peace. The city published the order as a large broadside, including on it the signatures of the mayor and the municipal council's secretary.[24] Unlike the city, the department took no official action in the early days of the crisis, although it wrote to the Legislative Assembly. On 23 June, Guyton de Morveau, a deputy for the Côte-d'Or in the assembly, read the department's letter. While acknowledging the extra-legal nature of the arrests, the department lent them some credibility by describing the priests as "unfortunate victims of blind fanaticism" and "impious superstition." Guyton de Morveau added his support for the arrests by asking whether the state should act against the people who had risen up in defence of the constitution.[25]

Louis XVI did not share the department's hesitance to act against those detaining the refractory clergy. The king communicated his displeasure to the department through his minister of the interior, the marquis de Terrier, demanding that the department secure for the refractory clergy the constitution's protection of citizens and their property.[26] Under pressure from Paris to intervene on behalf of the refractory priests, the departmental and municipal authorities attempted to free the priests on 2 July but failed when a large crowd gathered and the priests refused to leave. Two days later, during the night of 4–5 July, with the assistance of three cannoneers, the department and the city released the priests. At this time, the department also revoked its earlier order requiring non-juring priests to reside in Dijon and declared them at liberty to reside where "it seemed good to them."[27]

The arrest of the non-juring priests in June 1792 lives in the history of Dijon as the revolution's greatest outrage against religion. It was certainly the most dramatic action taken by pro-revolutionary individuals against the non-juring priests. Several details of these events are interesting. First, the mobs that arrested the priests included women. Dijon's patriotic women formed a club parallel to the male Jacobin-affiliated club in 1791. Initially known as Société des Amies de la Constitution (like the male club), they changed their name to the Société des Amies de la République after the fall of the Monarchy in August 1792. The women's club was an active presence in Dijon's patriot political activities until the National Convention suppressed women's clubs in October 1793.[28] In this incident, the opposition of women to the non-juring priests is important. Normally, the revolution's religious history has highlighted women's support for refractory priests.[29] Here, however, a number of women, enough to constitute a "mob," acted based upon their political allegiance to the revolution and defined the refractory priests as enemies of the state.

A second point of interest in this account is the autonomy of Dijon's population in carrying out this insurrection against local authority. The opposition of the authorities to this seizure of public police power is evident in the first reports. However, neither the city council nor the councils of the district or the department intervened, except to secure the safety and humane treatment of the priests. Guyton de Moreau's account of the department's letter to the Legislative Assembly suggested that departmental officials had some sympathy for the leaders of this action. In contrast to the department's complicity, the city ordered those with police authority to enforce the law, although to no effect. In accounts of the revolution, we are accustomed to the crowds of Paris carrying the day and changing the direction of events through insurrection and violence. With the arrests of the refractory priests in Dijon, we see this revolutionary fervour displayed in a provincial setting. That it took National Guardsmen reinforced by three cannoneers to overcome the people demonstrates the strength of the popular revolt in Dijon.

Another important matter to notice is the perception of the patriots in Dijon that the refractory clergy were a danger to the nation. This was a perception that they shared with forty-two other departments, which renders it some weight. The Civil Constitution of the Clergy, enforced by the ecclesiastical oath in 1791, had a troubled start. By May 1791, the Constituent Assembly backpedalled on the requirement that all priests either take the oath or resign from their position, permitting non-juring, refractory priests to remain in their parishes as long as their services did not conflict with those of the constitutional curé, provided one was in place. On the ground, the new constitutional bishops and local electoral assemblies struggled to fill parishes with juring clergy. Along with this effort, district directories began to redistrict the parishes in their region to comply with the Civil Constitution of the Clergy's guidelines.

For local parishes, 1791 and 1792 were years of dramatic change. Priests uncooperative with these changes embodied for the local patriots the growing counter-revolutionary danger. One should not hastily dismiss the sympathy of Volfius and his episcopal council for the imprisoned refractory clergy. While hindsight allows a seemingly neat definition of the "constitutional" and the "refractory" clergy, the lived experience was fluid. Some jured and refused to cooperate; some did not jure but, in the opinion of the patriot priests, might come around with time. Volfius and his colleagues did not see themselves as completely separate from their fellow clergymen who had not sworn to uphold the Civil Constitution. Further, they believed that, just as they were building a new church order for the nation, they might lend a hand in addressing the misguided convictions of the non-juring clergy. The political tensions that erupted in the Côte-d'Or between Dijon's patriots and the refractory clergy soon exploded with even greater volatility at the national level.

THE FALL OF THE MONARCHY
AND ITS CONSEQUENCES FOR CLERGY

The war was not going well for the French. Within a month of its declaration, the Legislative Assembly passed emergency legislation to secure Paris and the nation. Among these provisions was a law to deport any non-juring priest denounced by at least twenty citizens. A second provision called for 20,000 National Guard troops from the provinces, to aid in the defence of Paris. The king refused both measures, vetoing them on 19 June. The next day, the Cordeliers club and several radical sections organized a large demonstration at the Tuileries Palace. Finding a way into the palace, the demonstrators harangued the king for hours, forcing him to don the Phrygian cap and to toast the nation. While this day passed without bloodshed, its challenge to the monarchy alarmed revolutionary leaders, among them General Lafayette, who returned to Paris from the front the following week and made appeals to the Legislative Assembly to protect the monarchy and appeals to the king to move to a more secure position outside Paris. Lafayette also tried to rally Paris's National Guard to march on the Jacobin Club, which he believed to be behind the recent disturbances. Lafayette's entreaties fell on deaf ears all around.

The military situation continued to deteriorate and, in early July, the Legislative Assembly called on all administrative bodies to meet daily in permanent session. It also pressured the king to accept the 20,000 National Guardsmen sought earlier. Louis consented to allow the guardsmen to gather, as they had the past two years, to mark the Bastille's fall, but he directed that the provincial companies should then move on to Soissons, 110 kilometres northeast of Paris. Provincial guardsmen arrived in the capital throughout July. The forty-eight sections of Paris, the city's local government units, moved to an emergency footing in response to the Legislative Assembly's order, broadening the membership of their assemblies to include citizens with less means. The section assemblies had been restricted to active citizens but were now open to passive citizens as well. As Prussian forces advanced across the border and toward Paris, the provincial militias issued the first calls to abolish the monarchy. By the beginning of August, some of Paris's sections joined this critical chorus. Two developments heightened the sense of danger animating the city. At the end of July, Robespierre made a speech at the Jacobin Club demanding the abolition of the monarchy. Robespierre's speech followed two key developments: first, the abortive attempt of General Lafayette to turn the Army of the North on Paris against the Legislative Assembly, and second, the publication of the Brunswick Manifesto, which promised retribution to any who harmed France's royal family.

The night of 9–10 August, the Cordelier Club and the sections of Saint-Antoine and Saint-Marcel, both heavily populated by artisans, workers, and the urban poor, along with sections from the Left Bank, organized an attack on the Tuileries Palace, resulting in one of the bloodiest insurrections of the revolution. The artillery units assigned to the king's guard joined the rioters in the early hours of 10 August, prompting Louis XVI and his family to flee across the palace gardens to the Legislative Assembly. The battle at the palace continued, leaving nearly a thousand dead – six hundred of the king's Swiss Guard, and nearly four hundred insurgents. Now the king's keeper, the Legislative Assembly suspended the monarchy that day and placed Louis in protective custody, eventually imprisoning him and the royal family in the Temple, the old fortress of the Knights Templar in central Paris. The following month, on 22 September, the newly elected National Convention, successor to the Legislative Assembly, declared France a republic.

Following the fall of the monarchy, the Legislative Assembly took aim at the enemies of the revolution, among them the refractory clergy. In August 1792, the assembly – by then essentially a rump parliament with fewer than a hundred members following the departure of conservative and royalists deputies –passed a new oath for the clergy, known as the oath of liberty and equality. It required anyone receiving a state salary or pension to swear "to be faithful to the Nation and to maintain liberty and equality or to die defending it."[30] Refractory clergy could swear the oath of liberty and equality without swearing the ecclesiastical oath requiring them to uphold the constitution. Ironically, once again, the assembly created a means by which refractory clergy could remain in the nation, although as persecution in Paris intensified many non-juring clergy chose to leave France in the fall of 1792.

The wealth and activities of the church and its personnel led to several other decrees in August 1792. The Legislative Assembly ordered the church's bronze melted for cannons, and it requisitioned its gold and silver for coin. Further, the assembly dissolved the remaining monastic congregations and followed the commune of Paris in ordering the suppression of the *casuel*, the special fees paid to priests for ceremonies such as baptisms, marriages, and funerals. Finally, again following the Parisian commune, it prohibited clergy from wearing ecclesiastical dress outside of exercising their official functions.[31]

THE SEPTEMBER MASSACRES AND THE
DEPORTATION OF THE REFRACTORY CLERGY

Non-juring priests were of particular concern. Initially, the rump assembly merely put into effect a decree first passed on 27 May 1792, but not enacted because of the royal veto. That law, as noted above, opened denounced priests to deportation. On 23 August, the assembly strengthened the state's hand by adopting a new law that required the immediate deportation or internment of all refractory clergy. This law, which went into effect three days later, required all refractory priests functioning publicly to leave the country within fifteen days. The Legislative Assembly enacted this new law because of concerns about the influence of refractory priests on the electoral assemblies scheduled for 2 September that would select deputies for the National Convention, which would write a new constitution for France.[32]

The deportation of the refractory clergy was an ambitious project. Local governments issued passports and gave priests a travel allowance equivalent to three *livres* for every ten leagues they needed to travel to reach the border or nearest point of embarkation. The legislation exempted from deportation those who were over sixty years of age or infirm, but required them to live communally in the departmental seat. National figures for the number of priests deported do not exist.[33] For the department of the Côte-d'Or, 151 priests received passports following the decree. Of these, only 101 were actually refractories required by the law to emigrate. The other fifty priests were canons, *méparatists*, chaplains, and other clergy. In addition, the department deported twenty priests without passports, and ten others left the department after being deposed by constitutional clergy, receiving their passports in their new department of residence. Fifteen priests over the age of sixty went to live in a common house. In all, 146 refractory priests in the Côte-d'Or obeyed the edict.[34] Generally, in Dijon, the refractory clergy saw the new law as a safeguard because it allowed them to emigrate without the fear of losing their property.

Compliance with the new law was fuelled by news of massacres in Paris. For six days, from 2 to 7 September, mobs, which included National Guardsmen from Paris and the provinces, went to each prison, monastery, and seminary in Paris and killed inmates and residents. In all, they massacred 1,100 to 1,400 people, approximately

50 per cent of the prison population. The victims included many priests arrested in the weeks immediately preceding the massacre, their names provided to the Parisian sections by the new insurrectional Paris commune.[35] In the district of Dijon, only three priests had presented themselves for passports on 3 September. The following three days, however, a crowd of non-juring priests turned out. On 14 September, three days before the deadline, the last priest registered his passport,s the one hundredth priest in the district to do so. The district of Semur registered only five passport requests. In other districts, priests frequently obtained a passport from their village, and the department recorded these passports only later, in the spring of 1793.[36]

Most of the Côte-d'Or's emigrating priests went to Switzerland, although a few went to Freiburg.[37] Contemporaries believed that several refractory priests never left the department, a conviction supported by the discovery of two unlucky individuals, Honoré Fréjacques, a vicar of Notre-Dame, and François Thuillier, curé of Chassey. Found hiding in the woods of Flavigny in May 1793, they were shot by National Guardsmen.[38] By December 1792, priests began attempting to return. Most of these were *non-fonctionnaires,* priests not required by the law of 26 August to emigrate. Appealing to return, they claimed to have misunderstood the law when they left, and the department's debate about imposing seals on the property of those who had emigrated unnecessarily appears to have motivated some to return. Also, the peril of staying and, likewise, of returning had lessened significantly by year's end.[39]

With the law of 26 August 1792, did the state overcome the opposition of the refractory clergy? In the department of the Côte-d'Or, the answer is largely yes. The law forced into hiding the refractories who did not emigrate. A few chose to take an eleventh-hour oath and assimilate, at least publicly, to the new political climate.[40] Nationally, the law was a success for those concerned about the activities of the refractory clergy. For the most part, districts deported their troublesome clerics, and the few refractories that remained faced increased surveillance following the oath of liberty and equality.[41]

The deportation of the refractory clergy and the massacres of early September were the first expression of the Terror against France's clergy.[42] Though initially aimed at refractory priests, the state's repressive actions turned the following year toward the constitutional clergy. The second Terror, which occurred in the fall and winter of 1793–4, required clergy, even those long aligned with the revolution, to renounce their ordinations and abandon their practice of Catholicism.

VOLFIUS ADAPTS TO CHANGING TIMES

Volfius and his colleagues in the constitutional church slipped into the background as authorities set their sights on the refractory clergy. On 20 September, Volfius issued a pastoral letter on the war that offered tacit support for the state's crackdown on the refractory clergy.[43] Portraying the French as a nation betrayed, and as the object of envy for other monarchs, he argued that internal intrigue supported France's enemies. Yet, despite these challenges, the state had united and moved forward, holding elections for the new National Convention. The French, he opined, now placed their hope in the new legislature and in God. For Volfius, the French held the cause of humanity in their hands. He called on his listeners not to follow those sowing dissension. Behind the mask of an exaggerated patriotism, these "bloodthirsty men" spread mistrust, suspicion, and hatred that could lead only to anarchy and end in slavery. This critical time "when the eyes of the universe were on the French" would decide "the health of the empire, our happiness, and the fate of future generations."[44] He urged the country to aspire to greatness: "In this solemn and grand era, when all the universe has its eyes on us, let us show ourselves worthy of the protection of heaven, and of the esteem of foreign nations."[45]

Four months later, at the end of January 1793, Volfius wrote his next pastoral letter.[46] In it, he urged the faithful to unite and overcome the divisions present in the diocese since the beginning of his administration. The Civil Constitution of the Clergy had returned the Catholic Church to its ancient canons and responded to the new needs of the state. These two goals were unimpeachable. No ancient church authority objected to the destruction of abuses in the exterior discipline of the church. In addition, most people in the diocese recognized the validity of the Civil Constitution and followed "the vow of religion and of the nation." The church's gains in this new revolutionary order would be for naught, however, if there was not a parallel improvement in moral conduct.[47] In the days leading up to Lent, he urged his flock to take as their model the early Christian community discussed in the Acts of the Apostles. In his description of this ideal church, Volfius stressed order, hierarchy, and a mystical unity. He underscored the central role and authority of the bishop and stressed that the early Christians were good citizens as well as good Christians. Quoting Tertullian's *Apologie*, he wrote "we carry arms ..., we cultivate the earth, we administer justice, we fill the towns..., the assemblies of people, the senate, the palace.[48]

Concerns about the war receded in this letter but did not disappear entirely: at the end, Volfius reminded his listeners that France's army carried liberty and constitutional government with them. Religion supported both; it also purified French morals and supplemented the state's laws. Liberty united with the gospel was renewing France and, through France, Europe.[49]

Also in January 1793, Volfius issued a letter instructing the priests of the diocese concerning a law of 20 September 1792 regarding the creation of a civil registry for births, marriages, and deaths. He wrote in response to priests' requests for instructions on how to conduct themselves in relation to baptisms, marriages, and funerals. He underscored that his directives were provisional until the church fully understood the will of "all our cooperators." Despite the change in procedure, he emphasized that the secularization of birth, marriage, and death records did not remove the church from these affairs, as some "malevolent spirits" suggested.[50] Taking the example of marriage, Volfius noted that it remained a sacrament for Christians. Although no longer involved in guaranteeing the legality of marriages and the legitimacy of children, the church retained a role in consecrating unions as "a grand sacrament in Christ ... representing the celestial union of Jesus Christ with his Church."[51] He urged his colleagues to support the law and to use his guidelines to aid them to carry it out. With respect to each rite, the priest should act only after the civil authorities had done so. Thus, a baptism should follow the magistrate's civil record of the birth.[52] The law of 20 September also legalized divorce, a subject about which Volfius is silent in his pastoral instructions.

Many, like the "malevolent spirits" castigated by Volfius, have seen the law of 20 September as a first step toward the separation of church and state. This interpretation ignores the conditions that created the law.[53] With the deportation of the refractory clergy from France, many departments found that they had no clergy available to register births, marriages, and deaths. In some areas, a general state of anarchy in the legal registration existed. As early as January 1792, the Legislative

Assembly began to receive requests that something be done about such registrations. With the law of 20 September, the revolutionaries did not separate church and state but rather fused them. Through this law, the state reformed Catholic doctrine and insisted that the constitutional clergy obey its commands above those of the church. The National Convention condemned bishops who spoke out against the nation's laws, such as Fauchet in the department of Calvados and Gratien in the department of Seine-Inférieure, who wrote pamphlets instructing clergy to adhere to orthodox Catholic practices regarding divorce and marriage. One outcome of the law of 20 September was that it allowed French couples to be married without a priest but did not allow priests to refuse to marry a couple.[54]

Volfius's interpretation of the law was less strict than Fauchet's and Gratien's. In addressing the church's prohibition on marriages during Advent and Lent, Volfius argued that a general dispensation applied, in effect allowing such marriages.[55] Further, with respect to traditional impediments to marriage, Volfius noted that the opinions of the canonists varied, and bishops were normally allowed to establish ecclesiastical law in their dioceses. Because of the diocese's size, curés should give dispensations as they deemed them appropriate, working always to maintain morals. In doubtful cases, of course, they could refer the couple to the bishop.[56]

Volfius's January letter also dealt with issues other than the new law. At the end of his missive, Volfius offered a few guidelines for Lent. Scarcity again restricted the Lenten fast, and he allowed meat and fat on Mondays, Tuesdays, Thursdays, and Sundays, with the exception of Easter Sunday.[57] The war also found its way into his closing remarks. Noting the fall of two villages and others under siege, he wrote that, although France faced enemies both within its borders and outside of them, the republic would prevail. Its armies awakened "seeds of liberty that reside in the hearts of all peoples" and ended all tyrannies. He encouraged priests not to despair. God stood with France and gave courage to her warriors and wisdom to her people. They need only redouble their prayers. Praising their love of country and of religion, Volfius urged them to lead their flock with such devotion that even their detractors would respect them.[58]

Although commenting on the war, Volfius's pastoral letters in late January 1793 are silent on a particularly momentous event of that month, the sentencing and execution of Louis XVI. This silence is surprising. From the start of the revolution, Volfius had endorsed

and supported every major revolutionary development. He incorporated the end of orders, the nationalization of church properties, the
Civil Constitution of the Clergy, and the establishment of the republic into a larger scheme that linked the nation and religion. Breaking
his usual pattern, Volfius passed over the trial, sentencing, and death
of the king without published comment.

One explanation for this silence was the changed political climate.
The monarchy was no more, a fact Minister of the Interior Jean-
Marie Roland underscored for France's constitutional clergy with an
order prohibiting prayers for the monarchy. Religious practice, the
minister instructed, was not free from civil authority, and the state
had an interest in maintaining public order. Clergy were not to pray
for an authority abolished by the "sovereign Nation."[59] The spring
following the king's execution brought further indications of an
increasingly strained relationship between the constitutional church
and civil authorities. On 6 April, the department of the Côte-d'Or
ordered Volfius to return to the district of Dijon's treasury the 962
livres and 9 *sous* granted to him a little over a year earlier to create a bishop's chapel. The department ordered the money returned
after the National Convention disallowed expenses for a bishop's
chapel.[60] In early May, the department issued an order that prohibited ministers of any faith from leading public processions because
they disrupted citizens engaged in their daily business. Formerly, the
department wrote, the state recognized a single religion, now the law
allowed all faiths without preference, and thus each faith needed to
remove itself from the public arena.[61]

The strain of war led the revolutionaries to confront the refractory
clergy's rejection of the revolution's religious reforms. France's provinces led this effort, with Dijon's Jacobin Club taking the bold measure of arresting over one hundred refractory clergy in June 1792.
On the national level, Louis XVI used the royal veto to block the
Legislative Assembly's efforts to address the refractory clergy. Only
after the fall of the monarchy did the assembly successfully moved
against the non-juring clergy. For the constitutional clergy in the
Côte-d'Or, the crisis of the clergy arrests provided an opportunity
to seek greater authority over those who rejected the new church
organization. By offering to assume responsibility for the refractories, Volfius and his episcopal council voiced their conviction that,
through example, they might bring around those who refused the

revolution's vision. Volfius's indirect support for the deportation of refractory priests three months later signals the beginning of an important shift in the revolution's relationship with the constitutional church. Strategic silences mark Volfius's pastoral letters in the first months of the republic: he did not object to the state's actions against the refractories; he made no comment on Louis XVI's trial and execution; he omitted any discussion of the state's endorsement of divorce as he instructed his clergy on how to respond to the new civil registry for birth, marriage, and death. The revolution initiated four years earlier had sought to remake France and its institutions, including the church. Armed and radicalized by the emergency of the war, the republic's leaders soon judged even the constitutional clergy suspect.

6

Battling Fanaticism:
Dechristianization in the Côte-d'Or

In 1793, the revolutionaries in Paris faced two significant challenges to their authority. In March, a counter-revolutionary civil war broke out in the Vendée, a region south of Brittany on France's Atlantic seaboard. The National Convention's call for the conscription of 300,000 men had provoked the uprising: this demand was the last straw for a region long lukewarm about the revolution. Among the rebels were several refractory priests. Their presence in the revolt confirmed for France's patriots the inherent unreliability of the non-juring clergy.[1]

The second challenge, which began in June, differed from that of the Vendée. Known as the federalist uprisings, these protests followed the National Convention's purge of the Girondins.[2] Urban, bourgeois, pro-revolutionary republicans in several of France's largest cities – Lyon, Bordeaux, Marseille, and Toulon – rose up in revolt following the purge. They objected not to the revolution but to the arrest of the Girondins, who were elected representatives of the people. As in the Vendée, priests joined the fray on the side of the National Convention's opponents. However, this time, the priests involved were constitutional clergy.[3]

Following the outbreak of civil war, the National Convention decreed death to any priest found in France who should have left during the deportation ordered in August 1792. By September, it expanded the earlier order to include priests acting as accomplices of France's enemies, whether within the nation or outside of it. In addition, it declared that the state would deport clergy who had been denounced by at least six citizens, and not twenty, as in the law of the previous year.[4]

The civil war in the Vendée and the federalist revolts heightened the general suspicion surrounding the clergy and their commitment to the state. In the fall of 1793 and the winter of 1794, patriots acting in the name of the revolution took aim at the clergy, and especially the constitutional clergy who had not been targeted by the previous year's deportation order. Historians later named the various anti-clerical efforts of 1793–4 the dechristianization movement. Occurring simultaneously with the Terror of year 2, this movement had its first manifestations in the provinces under the guidance of the National Convention's *représentants en mission*, deputies dispatched across France to oversee military and civilian affairs in specific regions. Dechristianization was also spread by detachments of the *armée révolutionnaire*, a citizen's army composed of ordinary Parisians who went into the countryside ostensibly to secure provisions for the city.

LIMITING THE PUBLIC EXPRESSION OF RELIGION

In the Côte-d'Or, restrictions on religious expression began in November 1793 with an order issued by J.B. Milhaud and Louis Guyardin, representatives on mission attached to the Army of the Rhine. As the National Convention's representatives, they had broad authority. Thirty-five years old and a deputy from the Haute-Marne, Guyardin undertook several missions to the Army of the Rhine. Twenty-seven-year-old Milhaud, a career military officer elected to the convention from the department of Cantal in south-central France, served on missions to the Armies of the Rhine and the Ardennes.[5] In the Côte-d'Or, Milhaud and Guyardin limited religious services and prohibited the display of religious symbols.[6] In addition, they ordered a collection of the church's gold and silver ornaments, declaring that these riches had too long insulted the misery of the people. They instructed departments to establish a commission that included members of the popular societies to inventory and report on these spoils. They also called for departments to celebrate married priests as apostles of humanity and to deport clergy who slowed the "triumph of reason and the destruction of prejudices." To provide a check on local officials, Milhaud and Guyardin advised committees of surveillance to denounce public officials and others who failed to comply with their order. Issued from Strasbourg on 7 November 1793, the order appeared in the Côte-d'Or nine days later. The department added its own instructions to reinforce the decree.[7] Placing the onus on local authorities to guarantee compliance, the department ordered the removal of all crosses, ornaments, tableaux, busts, and other pious monuments on the outside of religious buildings. It also called on local administrators to enforce the restriction on ecclesiastical garb in public. Citizen committees formed the previous summer to grant certificates of good citizenship (*certificat de civisme*) became commissions to research the spoils of *fanatisme* (that is, items taken from churches). These commissions received and inventoried items taken from churches. Dechristianization in the Côte-d'Or also involved renaming some towns and villages. Those named after saints or royalty were encouraged to take revolutionary names. In Dijon, the *faubourg* Saint-Pierre adopted the name Marat, as did the place des Cordeliers.[8] Priests, municipal officers, or others opposing the order were subject to arrest. The department printed the two orders together and sent them to each town, village, and *société populaire*.

Despite the department's efforts to eliminate the public expression of religion, the faithful persisted, as Beaune's *société populaire* reported in mid-November.[9] The Beaune society wrote to inform departmental authorities that Catholic ministers continued to appear in the streets in ecclesiastical dress for burials and other ceremonies. What was needed, they declared, was for the department to raise the flame of reason and increase the people's love for the nation. With their letter dated the day after the department's order, Beaune's *société populaire* had probably not seen the new instructions from Dijon. Its report provides an indication of the loose enforcement of earlier departmental orders and the law of 18 August 1793 prohibiting ecclesiastical dress and public processions.

In November, the department ordered churches to end offerings of consecrated bread.[10] It justified this intervention into religious affairs on economic grounds by claiming that the practice involved 200,000 *livres* of bread each year, offending a public concerned with their own subsistence. This was bread that nourished no one and that the department could ill afford to lose. The department's claim here is clearly hyperbole: the churches of the Côte-d'Or, reduced in number and divided in alliance between the constitutional and refractory clergy, could not have utilized so much bread for the Eucharist.

DECHRISTIANIZATION

It was in November as well that two priests, Jean-Augustin Alteyrac and Charles Chaisneau, publicly resigned the priesthood in order to align themselves more strongly with the revolution.[11] Submitting his letters of ordination to the district of Châtillon-sur-Seine, Alteyrac asked that the district send them to the National Convention as "a proof of the progress of philosophy in the party of the republic." Ordained in 1768, Alteyrac had been a priest for twenty-five years,[12] although he had only recently arrived in the district of Châtillon-sur-Seine. Before the Civil Constitution of the Clergy, he had been a professor of eloquence at Cambray. He came to the parish of Brion in the district of Châtillon-sur-Seine in 1791 to replace the curé, Pierre Le Gros, who had been ill for several years. Alteyrac's brother was a farmer (*propriétaire cultivateur*) in the parish.[13] Following his resignation, the district forwarded Alteyrac's letters of ordination to the president of the National Convention and reported the case to the department. The department decided to publicize Alteyrac's resignation and that of Charles Chaisneau, curé of Plombières, in the hopes that they would inspire others.[14] The department did this by issuing a small pamphlet about Alteyrac's resignation and a statement written by Chaisneau renouncing his ordination.

Although a curé for several years, Chaisneau had arrived in Plombières only three years earlier. Several publications demonstrate his support for the revolution.[15] By renouncing his vows, he hoped to prove his patriotism. The republic, he reasoned, could not have two altars: "All altars must fall and disappear in front of the altar of the nation, the altar of the god of liberty and of equality."[16] In renouncing the priesthood, Chaisneau wrote that he was leaving not only his profession but also his livelihood. Having ceded his modest inheritance to his family, he announced that he left the priesthood with nothing. He asked that he be allowed to buy the rectory of Plombières where he was residing for 1000 *écus*, to be paid over time. The department's pamphlet noted that it had forwarded Chaisneau's request to the National Convention. In the meantime, he would continue to live in the rectory.[17] In closing, the pamphlet included an offer from P. Causse, the printer, to take as an apprentice any priest between the age of twenty-five and thirty who left the priesthood. Causse wrote that he would accept, without asking payment, all who would abandon their useless functions, and that he would teach them the art of printing to ensure them an honest existence.[18]

Alteyrac's and Chaisneau's resignations, accompanied by total renunciations of their former positions as priests, exactly caught the spirit of the day.[19] Throughout the fall of 1793, the National Convention's representatives on mission laboured to end what they deemed superstition and fanaticism. A national leader in this effort was Joseph Fouché, deputy from Loire-Inférieure, who had taken minor orders with the Oratorians. Fouché pursued various highly publicized and widely imitated strategies to rid the nation of religious sophisms. At Nevers, he ordered celibate clergy to marry, adopt a child, or take into their homes an indigent elderly person. At the cathedral of Moulins, he held a parade of patriots dressed in clerical robes that ended in an *auto-da-fé* of the robes, sculptures, and other items from the cathedral. The Paris commune, the city's municipal government, was slow to engage in the anti-clerical and anti-Catholic violence pursued by Fouché. However, with the return of Pierre-Gaspard Chaumette, who briefly served as a representative on mission with Fouché in Nevers, it too took up the dechristianization campaign. On the night of 6 November, a group of patriots including Anacharsis Cloots and Léonard Bourdon went to the home of the constitutional metropolitan of Paris, Jean-Baptiste Gobel, and urged him to resign. The next day, Gobel, joined by eleven of his episcopal vicars, resigned his position before the National Convention.[20] Like the refractory priests, constitutional clergy were now suspect.

In the two years since Volfius' Lenten message of January 1792, the position of the revolutionary leaders in Paris with respect to France's Catholic clergy had shifted radically, as had the leaders themselves. The Civil Constitution of the Clergy had proved to be an unpopular and divisive plan for forging a new relationship with the former First Estate. Although the deportation of refractory clergy in the fall of 1792 was an attempt to resolve the division in favour of the constitutional clergy, it too failed to produce a Catholic Church that was both loyal to the state and popularly supported. The uprising in the Vendée demonstrated that deportation had not removed the threat of refractory clergy, while the federalist rebellions three months later revealed a new danger, the constitutional clergy. It was in the months following these domestic crises that the Terror unfolded as representatives on mission and local patriots sought to *défanatiser* the people.[21] At the beginning of the twentieth century, Alphonse Aulard and Albert Mathiez used the term *dechristianization* to describe this revolutionary project.[22]

The problem of the Terror is significant for historians of the French Revolution. Nineteenth-century republicans and twentieth-century Marxists have argued that the special circumstances of foreign and civil war explained the excesses of the year: the Terror was necessary.[23] Robespierre made the same claim.[24] The argument that circumstances forced the revolutionaries' hand is troubled by the reality, perhaps more apparent in hindsight than at the time, that the most acute period of crisis was over. By September 1793, the nation was advancing against its internal and external challengers. For Robespierre, the Terror was also a means of regeneration. By smiting its enemies, the revolution would establish "the imagined and desired republic."[25] François Furet presented a significant challenge to the thesis of circumstance with his argument that terror was inherent in the revolution from its first days. The policy of terror relied on the idea that the people were the indivisible sovereign of the republic. This unity ruled out dissent and fuelled the Terror's search for factions.[26] A more moderate understanding of the Terror argues that it was a repressive police action and an effort to remake the political culture of France. This new political culture included the revolutionary calendar; the renaming of streets, towns, and even citizens to reflect revolutionary values; and the adoption of forms of address (*citoyen*) and of dress that reflected the imagined egalitarianism of the *sans-culottes*.[27] Still, the problem of the Terror's violence remains. If the revolutionaries were not driven by necessity or ideology, what propelled them to the violent repressions of year 2? Marisa Linton has presented a compelling argument for contingency – for a Terror and an official ideal of Terror that grew out of the revolution's course and the choices of individuals.[28] The campaign against the church was unique among the activities of the Terror, because of its wide reach. Indeed, for most ordinary French men and women, dechristianization was, as Donald Sutherland has argued, the face of the Terror.[29]

The effort to dechristianize republican France encompassed a range of activities. At its most benign, it involved decrees that stripped churches of metal plate and coin to fuel the war machine and restricted the public display of religious symbols and dress. In addition to these acts promulgated by the National Convention, the commune of Paris, and the departments, the autumn of 1793 witnessed a virulent and widespread iconoclasm and anti-clericalism. Representatives on mission and divisions of the *armée révolution-naire* turned churches into stables, barracks, and even arsenals.[30] They compelled priests to resign and occasionally to marry; they led iconoclastic processions with dechristianizers dressed in ecclesiastical garb and concluding *auto-da-fés* of the faith's symbols. It should be noted that dechristianizers carried out their actions without authorization from the National Convention: deputies as prominent as Robespierre opposed their activities. Perhaps surprisingly, local authorities, including many former priests, quickly took up the battle against the church.

Some reject the idea that dechristianization can be explained by the contingencies of the revolution.[31] Dale Van Kley and Michel Vovelle have stressed the long process of dechristianization across the eighteenth century.[32] Vovelle argued that the dechristianizers of year 2 "simply brought to light the true state of indifference which had already begun," and he attributed this development to "philosophical propaganda during the Enlightenment."[33] Richard Cobb, viewing the phenomenon through the actions of the revolutionary army, argued that it was not a systematic movement, except with respect to the few matters addressed by the National Convention's decrees, such as the removal of bells and silver and the destruction of external signs of religion. In its most violent actions, Cobb argued, dechristianization was an act of anarchy. Some dechristianizers – the ones Cobb found most optimistic – were simply atheists who believed that what they labelled religious fanaticism could be overthrown. Others were Catholics in disguise or "more likely disciples of Jean-Jacques [Rousseau]" who sought to establish a civil religion.[34] Donald Sutherland, pointing to the political crises of 1793, judged the movement first and foremost a break with the constitutional church. Because they had failed to be the "first line of defense against 'fanaticism,'" the state attacked the constitutional clergy. For Sutherland, the dechristianization movement was yet another strategy in the struggle against a popular counter-revolution, and the constitutional church a victim of the Vendée.[35] Bernard Plongeron has argued that dechristianization, like the Terror itself, occurred in the absence of a "state of law." For him, the violence of 1793–4 destroyed both politics and religion. This destruction was the result of an exceptional climate, and so we return to those circumstances.[36]

DECHRISTIANIZATION IN THE CÔTE-D'OR

In the Côte-d'Or, the battle against *fanatisme* was both ideological and practical. The ideological effort to lead people out of superstition came through speeches in the Temple of Reason, pamphlets such as the one celebrating the resignations of Aleytrac and Chaisneau, and short columns titled "Instruction républicaine" printed in the weekly journal *Le Nécessaire*.[37] The practical effort involved the closing of the department's churches, the destruction or confiscation of its religious art, and a campaign in support of clerical resignations.

Dechristianization in the Côte-d'Or owed a lot to the efforts of the representatives on mission assigned to the department, especially André-Antoine "Pioche-Fer" Bernard de Saintes. Bernard de Saintes was a deputy from the department of the Charente-Inférieur on France's Atlantic coast. In August 1793, the National Convention sent him to six departments in eastern France to secure the frontier and to implement the *levée en masse*.[38] Bernard de Saintes established his general headquarters in Besançon, the former capital of the Franche-Comté. Strategically located in a horseshoe-shaped bend of the Doubs River, Besançon is dominated by its imposing citadel, enlarged and redesigned in the seventeenth century by Louis XIV's military architect, Sébastien de Vauban. Adopting the revolutionary name Pioche-Fer (Pick-axe), Bernard de Saintes built his reputation on brutality. In October 1793, he wrote to the Committee of Public Safety requesting more guillotines.[39] In the area under his authority, he reorganized departmental and district directories, removing personnel whom he viewed as too moderate and replacing them with true *montagnards*, supporters of the Jacobin agenda in the National Convention.[40] He also encouraged the effort to *défanatiser* the people. However, he did not undertake this work alone; rather, he found enthusiastic local patriots willing to aid him in his efforts.

One expression of dechristianization was the cult of reason. Like other aspects of dechristianization, it began without legislative decree. On 10 November, the commune of Paris celebrated a festival of reason in the cathedral of Notre-Dame. The cathedral then became the Temple of Reason. Before the ceremony in Paris, Clermont held a festival with a goddess, and Le Havre established a *fête décadaire* in honour of reason. Other towns, including Dijon, quickly imitated Paris's example.[41] Dijon established a Temple of Reason on 30 November 1793 (10 *frimaire l'an 2* in the revolutionary calendar) in the cathedral of Saint-Bénigne but moved it later to the church of Saint-Michel. To transform Saint-Michel, François Devosges, sculptor, artist, and founder of Dijon's school of design, removed the bas-reliefs and gilded bronzes from the church's altar and constructed a platform to hold the musicians, the people's magistrates, and the speakers.[42]

The dechristianization movement in the Côte-d'Or accelerated in February 1794. Early in the month, a member of Dijon's *société populaire* gave a speech at the Temple of Reason announcing the central themes of the effort. Calling on the Dijonnais to turn away from the fallacy of a supernatural religion and a corrupt morality, the speaker urged them to embrace reason and liberty. Only these could produce good citizens and true republicans. Published anonymously, the speech offers few clues to the identity of its author.[43] It is a sophisticated speech in its use of both theology and history. Opening his address by quoting from Corneille, the speaker begins by asserting that traditional religion served only to hold the people captive:

> Peut-être qu'après tout [*sic*] ces croyances publiques
> Ne sont qu'inventions de sages politiques,
> Pour contenir un peuple ou bien pour l'émouvoir,
> Et dessus sa foiblesse [*sic*] affermir leur pouvoir.[44]

> Perhaps after all these public beliefs
> Are only the inventions of wise politics,
> To contain a people or better to move them
> And above its weakness strengthen their power.

In the speaker's estimation, government and priests conspired to keep people ignorant, but liberty and reason defeated them.[45] Despite his attack on religion, much of his argument reflected the ideals of eighteenth-century deism. Through the study of nature, its harmony and regularity, one found God, the author of all order who intended humanity to live in community.[46] Those who oppressed their brothers were monsters deserving destruction. All religions were true, and all religions were false. In a pointed attack on Christianity, the speaker declared as false any religion that claimed God speaks and sends messengers who ask individuals to believe in him. Returning to his initial claim that the church and state had colluded to delude the people, the speaker argued that, since the time of Constantine, priests had lived privileged lives at the expense of the people. The alliance between church and state had brought discord and civil war. Concluding, the speaker called on citizens to examine religion dispassionately.[47] For something to be virtuous, it had to be useful to human society and based in the civic order.

The speaker advocated a morality based on utility. The point was to act morally in one's home, and to teach one's children the republican virtues of good manners, frugalness, honesty, and love of one's country and its laws. Liberty was the source of all good. Despite his call to turn away from superstition and priests, he warned his listeners not to judge all priests as charlatans and imposters, noting that many enlightened and celebrated men had been believers, including Pascal, Racine, the great men of Port-Royal abbey, Fénélon, Massillon, and Fleury. Further, he called on his listeners to believe in the honesty of most constitutional clergy and not to reproach them for their faith, commenting, "their departure is sad enough, without increasing the bitterness of it."[48]

In concluding his speech, the speaker reminded his listeners of France's victories over its external and internal enemies. While the rest of Europe conscripted its army by force, in France citizens volunteered to serve. Further, those not on the front lines were busy in the background supplying the army. A new day had dawned, and it was not possible for the French to return to their childhood. The task at hand was to let liberty and reason reign by converting the superstitious into citizens of the republic.[49]

The speaker's image of a morally superior revolution is not to be trusted, although it may be excused, as he had not yet witnessed the worst of either the Terror or the dechristianization movement in the department. In the course of the Terror, there were 23 executions in Dijon, while, 104 people perished in the department as a whole.[50] Among the earliest victims was Lazare Fondard, executed for allegedly instigating a riot of 100 to 150 young men in opposition to the conscription ordered by the National Convention in March 1793.[51]

At the end of February, Joly, Bernard de Saintes's secretary, reported in a brief article in the paper Le Nécessaire that "fanaticism" was in dire straits. Bernard de Saintes, Joly wrote, was using all means possible to enlighten the people and lead them toward a sane morality and away from the hypocrisy and lies of the priests. As part of this effort, Le Nécessaire, a paper initially edited by the attorney Gabet, a member of Dijon's *Société des amis de la constitution* or Jacobin Club, would publish the names of the citizens who resigned their functions as priests. Those who did not do so, he made clear, did not wish to be citizens.[52]

The first report of the *déprêtrisés* – that is, priests who had resigned from their positions and handed over their letters of ordination to the department – appeared the following week. It listed fifteen priests, along with the parishes they had served. In a brief commentary, the journal chided those who had yet to resign: "Oh, you who believe because one told you, become men! Make use, finally, of your reason; look, by its help, to know with us if that which you have learned from religion carries a sacred imprint, or if one discovers there only some absurdities advanced without foundation."[53] The list of resignations published on 5 March (15 *ventôse*) was to be the first of many. For the next three months, through the first week of June, the journal published the names of 141 individuals who had resigned. Leaving the priesthood in the spring of 1794 was a public event, and the pressure on priests to renounce their vows was considerable.

Representatives on mission also used posters to publicize clerical resignations. Antoine-Louis Albitte, sent by the National Convention to the departments of Ain and Mont-Blanc, published and distributed posters that listed the names of former priests.[54] The administrators of the Côte-d'Or received Albitte's posters, but it is not possible to know if they followed the instructions that urged them to widely publicize these resignations as a way of encouraging others. The posters certainly enabled them to be aware of the events in these neighbouring departments and something of the manner in which these resignations occurred. On one poster, Albitte included the text of the *Acte d'abdication de prêtrise* as well as a speech by one priest explaining his reasons for resigning and renouncing his beliefs. Jean-Louis Peysson, formerly curé at Belley, wrote that, although he recognized the prejudice, errors, and charlatanism of the Christian faith, he had remained a priest to avoid dissension in his parish.[55] In large tables on each poster, Albitte printed the names of the priests who resigned, as well as their age, place of birth, year of ordination, and previous position. The statement signed by the priests declared that they recognized the error of their previous beliefs and the duplicity of their former positions. Renouncing their previous life, the priests promised to live or to die for the republic.

In total, on thirteen posters, covering six districts for the department of Mont-Blanc and nine districts for the department of Ain, Albitte published the names of 500 priests.[56]

Among the priests who resigned in the Côte-d'Or during the spring of 1794 was the constitutional bishop, Jean-Baptiste Volfius. *Le Nécessaire* noted Volfius's resignation on 15 March (25 *ventôse*).[57] Below his name a brief note explained that the bishop resigned his functions as of 21 February (3 *ventôse*), but, because he had not submitted his letters of ordination, the department had questioned his sincerity. At a practical level, this meant that the department was recommending that Volfius not receive the pension the law provided for former priests.[58] Volfius, the journal noted, wrote a second letter on 4 March (14 *ventôse*) renouncing his functions and declaring his intention to submit his letters of ordination to the department as soon as possible. Ultimately, Volfius did get his letters of ordination to the department. In a file copy of a letter dated 17 *germinal l'an* 2 (6 April 1794), the bureau of police wrote that it was forwarding Volfius's letters of ordination as well as those of nineteen other former priests to the National Convention's Committee of Public Instruction.[59] The *Affiches de Dijon ou Journal du department de la Côte-D'Or* published Volfius's initial resignation on 21 February 21 (3 *ventôse*).[60]

Volfius's resignation came after a difficult period of persecution that he described after the Terror in a letter to the abbé Grégoire.[61] In the winter of 1794, the department imprisoned then released Volfius but threatened to detain him again if he did not resign. Although he initially resisted the demands that he resign, he relented after he saw the department's churches closing and its priests surrendering their letters of ordination. Further, he wrote Grégoire, colleagues urged him to surrender his letters of ordination, arguing that in themselves they represented nothing. His family and friends also prevailed upon him to resign, fearing confiscation of their property if he were arrested again. According to Volfius, Bernard de Saintes was the driving force behind the dechristianization of the Côte-d'Or, and it was with him that he negotiated his statement of resignation. For the most part, Volfius found the representative's revisions of his statement to be inconsequential. Only one was unacceptable to the bishop: Bernard de Saintes had wanted Volfius to state that religion was an invention of politics, but Volfius refused, arguing that to do so would compromise his beliefs.[62]

Volfius's published statement summarized the path of the constitutional clergy from the application of the Civil Constitution of the
Clergy in the winter of 1791 to its demise in the winter of 1794,
its content influenced, of course, by the political atmosphere of
the Terror. First, he noted that it was the people who had elected
him bishop. Then, he added that he had accepted the post only to
contribute to the success of the revolution, which, he reminded his
readers, he enthusiastically embraced. Poor health, age, and other
preoccupations forced him to resign. In leaving his post, Volfius
declared that "like Fénelon ... I detest hypocrisy, superstition and
fanaticism."[63] Continuing, he wrote that the religion of the Gospel
was one of equality and fraternity and that he had "preached only
union, kindness, love of the laws, and all the virtues that make for
the happiness of men."[64] In leaving his position, he noted with satisfaction that no religious trouble had dishonuored the department
and that his efforts had contributed to its tranquility.

IMPRISONMENT AND THE
TERROR IN THE CÔTE-D'OR

Volfius was not the only priest imprisoned during year 2 in the Côte-
d'Or. The cases of three other priests offer further evidence about
the nature of the dechristianization effort in the department. Also
arrested during year 2 were Jean-Jacques Dubois, curé in the village
of Velard-sur-Oudre; Denis Chauchot, curé in the town of Is-sur-
Tille; and Jean-Baptist Grosdidier, episcopal vicar and formerly curé
in the town of Champagne. While these were not the only priests
arrested in the Côte-d'Or during the Terror, they share with Volfius
the distinction of having returned to the ministry as constitutional or
Gallican clergy when the churches reopened in 1795. The accounts
of their imprisonments indicate the way the committees of surveillance worked and the degree of support the constitutional clergy
enjoyed in their communities.

Early in November 1793, authorities in Dijon arrested Dubois after
the village of Velard-sur-Oudre's committee of surveillance denounced
him. Dubois's arrest occurred during the period when the representatives on mission Milhaud and Guyardin issued the order restricting
public displays of faith. Despite this denunciation, twenty other citizens of the village immediately objected to his arrest and wrote a
petition calling for his release.[65] The directory of the district of Dijon

soon acted in Dubois's favour, ruling that Velard-sur-Oudre's committee of surveillance, having only six members, was incomplete and
therefore illegal. On 5 November (15 *brumaire*), the commune elected
a new committee of surveillance. Ruling Dubois's arrest a calamity and
judging the priest to be a good patriot, the new committee petitioned
the district of Dijon to release him, "if not as Priest, at least as a good
Citizen." The departmental directory concurred and ordered Dubois
released on 8 November. Dubois was not only a priest in Velard-sur-
Oudre but also a municipal officer. Upon his release, the department
ordered that he execute the degree establishing a new revolutionary
calendar, another aspect of the effort to detach France from its traditional moorings in the Judeo-Christian tradition.[66] Establishing
the foundation of the French Republic on 22 September 1792 as the
beginning of the new era, France was already in year 2 when the convention decreed the new calendar in the fall of 1793.

Dubois's arrest was brief and relatively uncomplicated. The twenty
citizens who petitioned for his release quickly out-maneuvered the
original committee of surveillance. How long Dubois remained a
curé following his release is not recorded. Possibly he resigned sometime in the winter or spring of 1794.

Denis Chauchot, curé of Is-sur-Tille, was first denounced by
Citizen Charpy in a letter to the department. Charpy's letter is lost,
but something of its contents can be learned from the minutes of
the village's committee of surveillance. A member of the committee,
Charpy charged Chauchot with writing an objectionable hymn and
publicly displaying his faith. Is-sur-Tille's committee of surveillance
rejected this denunciation made in its name and disputed the accusations against Chauchot. Writing to the provisional national agent,
the committee requested that he set aside Charpy's denunciation.
As an added caution against any untoward behavior on the part of
Chauchot, the committee ordered the priest to refrain from singing
hymns.[67] The committee's action did not signal an end to Chauchot's
troubles. The following month, Bernard de Saintes issued an order
for his arrest for wearing ecclesiastical garb. Echoing the law of 18
August 1793, Bernard de Saintes explained that this prohibition
ensured that no religion was favoured over others in France.[68]

The arrest of Jean-Baptist Grosdidier, epsicopal vicar and former
curé of Champagne, is the best-documented of the three cases under
discussion. On 1 March 1794, Bernard de Saintes ordered Grosdidier
arrested by the tribunal of Is-sur-Tille. An unnamed accuser charged

Grosdidier with collecting the *casuel*, a fee paid to priests for officiating at baptisms, weddings, and funerals. The National Convention
had suppressed its collection in September 1792.[69] Authorities
arrested and imprisoned Grosdidier in Is-sur-Tille on 10 March.
The day of his arrest, Grosdidier resigned his ecclesiastical functions before at least one member of the directory of Is-sur-Tille.
He did not submit his letters of ordination at that time because, as
he explained in his statement, he was unable to find them.[70] From
prison, he wrote to the directory of Is-sur-Tille requesting a *certificat
de civisme*, a letter attesting to his patriotism.[71] The directory issued
a statement the same day, declaring that the curé "had constantly
manifested his attachment to the revolution." In addition to being
an episcopal vicar, Grosdidier was an elector, the president of the
Société des sans-culottes républicains of Champagne-sur-Vingeanne,
and the mayor of Champagne.[72]

At the time of his arrest, Grosdidier was forty-five. He had spent
his career as a priest. Before the revolution, he had served as the
curé of Champagne-sur-Vingeanne, and after it as an episcopal vicar.
With the revolution's ecclesiastical reforms, Grosdidier experienced
a significant decrease in his salary: previously 2,400 *livres*, it fell to
1,200 with the enactment of the Civil Constitution of the Clergy.[73]

Grosdidier's arrest was not the only trouble he faced in March
1794. Because of his imprisonment, some citizens objected to his
possessions remaining in the rectory. In an attempt to protect his
residence and property, Grosdidier submitted a petition to the
departmental directory in Dijon. The department ruled the question
outside of its competence and referred Grosdidier's petition to the
district directory in Is-sur-Tille.[74] Was Grosdidier forced to surrender
the rectory in Champagne? The answer is not to be found among the
papers preserved in the archives. That he may have lost his residence
demonstrates the escalating difficulties he faced once caught in the
judicial processes of the Terror.

In the course of his imprisonment, which lasted eleven months,
Grosdidier gathered various documents to demonstrate his faithfulness
to the revolution. Among these were several *certificats de civisme* from
the communes where he had lived, the earliest issued by Dijon months
before his arrest.[75] At the time of his arrest, Grosdidier requested and
received additional declarations of his republican credentials from the
Société des sans-culottes républicains of Champagne-sur-Vingeanne
and the directory of Is-sur-Tille. In June, the committee of surveillance

in Champagne-sur-Vingeanne issued a statement declaring that "the Citizen [G]rosdidier formerly minister of the catholic cult has always behaved as a good patriot, since the beginning of the revolution." Continuing, the committee wrote that Grosdidier had not preached moral fanaticism but had always urged the execution of the law, and a love of liberty and equality. Because of his outstanding character, they requested that he be freed.[76]

Despite the various attestations of his revolutionary credentials, Grosdidier's case did not go well for him. The tribunal of Is-sur-Tille ruled against him, convicting him of accepting the *casuel*. This conviction meant that he lost his salary. Grosdidier appealed the tribunal's judgment and requested that he be transferred to the prison at Gray in the department of the Haute-Saône to be closer to the court handling his appeal. Changing his place of incarceration, however, only complicated his case.[77] When he sent requests related to his case to the representative on mission in the Haute-Saône, he was told to address them to the department of the Côte-d'Or. The department of the Côte-d'Or, however, referred him back to the Haute-Saône due to his imprisonment there.[78] Grosdidier's conviction, despite his appeal, cost him some local support. In October, the general council of the commune of Champagne-sur-Vingeanne refused to issue him a certificate of civism because of the tribunal of Is-sur-Tille's judgment against him.[79]

Part of Grosdidier's difficulty was that, after the fall Robespierre, Bernard de Saintes returned to Paris, where he joined the Committee of Public Safety.[80] In September 1794, the National Convention sent a new representative on mission, Jean-Marie Calès, to the department of the Côte-d'Or. In November, Grosdidier requested that Calès hear his case. Explaining his situation, Grosdidier compared his arrest to the infamous *lettres de cachet* of the old regime and attributed it to the fanaticism of Bernard de Saintes.[81] Also in November, Grosdidier wrote to citizen Burard, a clerk (*sécétaire greffier*) in the tribunal of Dijon's office of conciliation. Grosdidier argued that Calès had jurisdiction over his appeal because the order for his arrest and his previous position were in the department of the Côte-d'Or. His residence in Gray was only a temporary expedient to help resolve matters after he lost his salary.[82] The priest's long ordeal came to an end in late January 1795, when the National Convention's Ccommittee of General Security and Surveillance issued him a certificate of release.[83] Following his release, the tribunal of Is-sur-Tille denied his request to recover his salary, citing the earlier judgment against him.[84]

In the background of both Chauchot's and Grosdidier's arrests was Bernard de Saintes. In the case of Chauchot, there is no documentation concerning the course of his imprisonment and date of his release. In the case of Grosdidier, it seems possible that Bernard de Saintes's interest in the case kept the curé imprisoned despite the multiple attestations of his revolutionary credentials. In his study of the Terror in Dijon, Larry Lee Baker argued that, while local experiences drove the terrorists of the city, executions occurred only when a representative on mission was in town and were especially likely during visits of Bernard de Saintes.[85] Michel Péronnet and Serge Lochot credited the representatives on mission, especially Bernard de Saintes, with a large role in the Terror and dechristianization movement in the Côte-d'Or.[86] From the testimony of Volfius, and the cases of Grosdidier and Chauchot, it appears that Bernard de Saintes was instrumental in the dechristianization of the department. Undoubtedly he found among the patriots of the Côte-d'Or those willing and able to carry out this agenda. Also present, however, were local revolutionaries who at times moderated the effort to *défanatiser* the region, as they did in the case of Dubois.

A final expression of dechristianization in the Côte-d'Or that again underscores the significance of Bernard de Saintes was clerical marriages. Eighty-eight constitutional clergy serving in the Côte-d'Or married during the revolution.[87] Xavier Maréchaux found that 135 clergy from the Côte-d'Or married; however, not all these individuals served as constitutional clergy in the department, and several had other relationships to the department (i.e., birth, residence after marriage, retirement, or membership in the regular clergy).[88] Some were constitutional priests, but in other departments. A few refractory clergy with a relationship to the department also married. Regarding the constitutional clergy serving under Volfius, Maréchaux's research reveals the success of the efforts to encourage priestly marriages in year 2. Forty constitutional clergy married between September 1793 and September 1794. The peak of clerical marriages came during the spring of 1794, coinciding with Bernard de Saintes's campaign to obtain clerical abdications. At least twenty-four constitutional priests married from February to April 1794, with twelve marrying in April alone. These three months mark the peak of constitutional clergy marriages in the department.

Eleven of the constitutional priests who married sought to return to their vocation after the Concordat of 1801, and ten successfully did so: six had divorced, three were widowers, and one's status at the time of his request is unknown.

AN ATMOSPHERE OF DECHRISTIANIZATION

Freeing the Côte-d'Or of religious "fanaticism" went beyond priestly resignations, arrests, and marriages. Bernard de Saintes and his local collaborators made several efforts to enlighten the department's citizenry. Speeches such as that presented at the Temple of Reason in Dijon in February continued to be delivered and published. In late March, Dijon's mayor, Pierre Sauvageot, spoke at the temple.[89] He attacked Christianity as a faith based on absurd dogmas, such as the virgin birth, miracles, the trinity, and a god who appears in a morsel of bread. The Enlightenment, Sauvageot declared, had freed the French people from this religion of priests and kings. Reason was the mother of liberty and shook the universe to its foundation. Hell, purgatory, heaven, and all the mysteries of Catholicism were the fables of priests. Even Protestants, he argued, rejected these ideas. Heaven, which priests place in the sky, Sauvageot declared, was on earth for good republicans.[90]

A second avenue of public education was the regular *instruction républicaine* column in *Le Nécessaire*. Like most of the paper's articles, the column was unattributed. It first appeared 5 March 1794 (15 *ventôse*), in the same issue that inaugurated the lists of priestly resignations. It was not until the end of March that the column addressed religion. In a report on the holy shroud of Christ held in the cathedral in Besançon, the author noted that for years pilgrims had come to worship the relic, which had been handled only by the archbishop. Raising the cloth, he would hold it toward the people, who strained to see a faint outline of a man on it. Never, the column noted, could the venerable canons have imagined that their cloth would be examined and exposed as just an old piece of fabric with faint colors. Reporting that the shroud was now on display at the *société populaire* in Bescançon, the column concluded, "the first miracle that this shroud has done is to bring back to reason those who seemed condemned to never hear her."[91]

Despite the successes of the dechristianization campaign, moving the people from "fanaticism" to "reason" was not an easy task. The

resilience of Christianity in the countryside was the subject of the following issue's *instruction républicaine*. Noting that signs of fanaticism
were disappearing everywhere, the writer regretted that still some
refused to abandon their toys and priests.[92] People continued to sing
the mass and pick up their mutilated statues. "Citizens," the writer
asked, "when will you become men, when will you know the grandeur of your being?"[93] They had overthrown a tyrant who had seen
them only as property, the author reminded his readers. Why cry over
their lost priests? Did they desire the priests to know their secrets,
be involved in their domestic affairs? Did they want to entrust them
with the honour of their wives and daughters? Concluding, the author
dismissed those who longed for their priests. "Flee, flee all of you who
ask for priests; go live in a place where dishonour, slavery, tyranny and
superstition reign, you do not have the dignity to be republicans."[94]

In the *instruction républicaine* published on 9 April (20 *germinal*),
Le Nécessaire printed a speech given by Villemin, a priest and
municipal officer of the village of Fontaine-Soyer, celebrating the
establishment of a temple of reason in the former church of Saint-
Apollinaire. The temple bestowed a new degree of glory on a place
formerly mired in superstition. Continuing, Villemin wrote that one
could see the light of a new free man, an individual without prejudice, who knew and asserted his rights.[95] Within the month, the
journal reported that Villemin had resigned his clerical functions.[96]

With the exception of Villemin's column, the *instructions répub-
licaines* were anonymous. It seems likely that the same author wrote
many of them. In mid-April, the paper published a long column that
was continued in the next three issues.[97] The author argued that, in
the ordinary course of events, the march of enlightenment is slow.
People resist change and cling to their prejudices, errors, and habits. But there are times of rapid change such as revolutions, during
which the people see the ridiculousness of received ideas. Warning
that fanaticism could regenerate itself from a fragment, the author
called on readers to abolish it entirely.[98] He also argued that fear, tyranny, and ignorance were the mother of superstition and that people
followed their curés because they fear damnation.[99]

In late April, the *instruction républicaine* argued in favour of a
belief in a Supreme Being, addressing the conspiracy to undermine
the scaffolding of the republic by accusing it of atheism. The description of the Supreme Being in the article is in line with the ideas of
eighteenth-century deism: one found him in nature, and the harmony

of the universe provided proof of his existence. To celebrate this Supreme Being, the author outlined a liturgy for each *décadis*, the tenth and last day of the week in the revolutionary calendar and the day designated for rest. Including hymns, incense, and a celebrant (a municipal officer), the liturgy contained elements of the Catholic mass. The municipal officer was to read a short address on morality. Only a garland of flowers was to decorate the temple. These simple ceremonies, the article argued, would lead villagers to abandon their longing for foolish spectacles.[100]

In May and June, the journal devoted one column each month to religion.[101] Each exhorted true republicans to engage in the re-education of the people, whom the priests had trained to be ignorant. Only the propagation of republican morals would overcome this ignorance. Journals, *sociétés populaires*, temples of reason, and national festivals should set themselves to this end. In June, the festival to the Supreme Being in Paris served as a model for these efforts. Religious topics continued to appear albeit infrequently in the *instruction républicaine* until October 1794, with the final articles devoted to a critique of the proofs of revelation.[102]

Dechristianization in the Côte-d'Or was an energetic and creative enterprise. Towns and villages across the department dedicated temples of reason, and, from their pulpits, revolutionary speakers exhorted their fellow citizens to abandon the superstition and fanaticism that held them captive. Bernard de Saintes's presence in the spring of 1794 was critical to inspiring local patriots to attack what they viewed as fanaticism. His promotion of some patriots at the expense of others also helped to shape the character of the Terror and the dechristianization movement in the department. In their propagation of a republican faith, the patriots of the Côte-d'Or emphasized reason and the liberty it brought. The monopoly of priests over the spiritual realm was at an end, or so it seemed, to those who celebrated the reign of reason in the spring of 1794.

Dechristianization in the Côte-d'Or also involved wanton destruction of church property and the suppression of liberty for the department's priests. As the experiences of Volfius, Dubois, Chauchot, and Grosdidier indicate, priests, regardless of prior support for the revolution, were suspect simply because they were clergy. They could be denounced by single individuals presenting themselves as the representative of a committee of surveillance. In the spring of 1794, as the Terror heated up in the department, local efforts to moderate the actions of the more zealous terrorists met with failure. Churches across the department closed, and a parade of priests resigned their positions and surrendered their letters of ordination.

The years 1792 to 1794 in the Côte-d'Or can be characterized as an extended dénouement of the Civil Constitution of the Clergy. Ironically, the revolution's most ambitious religious reform declined with more vigour than it lived. The official support enjoyed by Volfius in the heady days of 1791 faded quickly and left the bishop proclaiming an alliance between the church and the state that his fellow patriots in the departmental and district directories were ever less willing to endorse. For the refractory clergy, the antipathy of local patriots toward their rejection of the Civil Constitution was not long contained. A year before the violence of the Vendée, the departmental authorities, backed in short order by the Jacobins of Dijon and their supporters in the street, declared the refractory clergy to be tiresome troublemakers who were best kept close at hand. Despite the hostility of local revolutionaries toward these clergy, only a little over a third departed during the deportation efforts in 1792. The experiences of Catholic clergy, both refractory and constitutional, in the Côte-d'Or reveal the ambivalence of the revolutionaries toward the church of most French men and women. This institution, as old as any in the history of France, could neither be harnessed nor overcome, and after the Terror the revolutionaries would find it most convenient to part ways with Catholicism, offering, on occasion, equal opportunity harassment to both the constitutional clergy who supported the French Republic and the refractory clergy who rejected it.

The Campaign for Religious Liberty and Establishing the Gallican Church

Dijon's Jacobin Club learned of Robespierre's fall on 2 August 1794, six days after it occurred. With Robespierre's death, the Terror ended in Paris. Its conclusion in the provinces came more slowly. At the end of the month, the Mâcon Jacobins wrote to warn that moderation was threatening France's liberty. In response, Dijon's club sent a petition signed by four hundred individuals to the National Convention, urging it to continue the Terror. Four days later, the club received a second letter from Marseille. Inspired to announce their position, Dijon's Jacobins published their petition and sent it to other *sociétés populaires*, quickly gaining the support of forty provincial clubs and nine sections of Paris. This pamphlet brought the Dijonnais into the national spotlight.[1] In their single mention of clergy, Dijon's Jacobins urged the National Convention to remove all priests (and nobles) from public office. They also called for a limited freedom of the press. In his study of the Jacobin Clubs in France, Michael Kennedy concluded that the petition from the Dijon club was the best-known of the protests after 9 *thermidor*.[2]

The National Convention rejected the Dijonnais's demand for a return to the Terror and urged citizens to quit demanding blood and scaffolds. It also voted to send a new representative on mission to Dijon, Jean-Marie Calès, deputy from the department of the Haute-Garonne, dispatched the previous year to the Army of the Ardennes.[3] Calès was not a Jacobin, as he made clear in a speech at Sedan in which he referred to the club's members as "a lot of naughty children."[4] Given the changed political atmosphere, year 3 (22 September 1794–21 September 1795) in the Côte-d'Or was a period of realignment. Moderate republicans replaced radicals on local government councils, and the new officials allowed most who led the Terror to fade out of politics, singling out only a few individuals for retribution.

DECHRISTIANIZATION AND RELIGIOUS LIBERTY IN YEAR 3

Calès arrived in Dijon on 17 October 1794. His first concern was to free individuals unjustly imprisoned the previous year. Following the advice of Dijon's six sections, he freed three hundred people. On 9 November, he removed elected officials he deemed too radical, purging five members of Dijon's directory along with district personnel in Beaune and Semur-en-Auxois. In general, he removed officials put into office during year 2. He also prohibited *sociétés populaires* from meeting.[5] In Dijon, he removed the Jacobin mayor, Pierre Sauvageot, and replaced him with a moderate who had been an early supporter of the revolution, Jean Durande. A former royal councilman (échevin), Durande was an early member of the Société des amis de la constitution but had not held public office since 1790. His council included four other former royal councilmen. They sought a middle course, guarding against extremes on both the left and the right. Durande's principal goal was to recover municipal independence after the Terror, as the previously Jacobin-dominated council had relied heavily on the National Convention's representatives on mission and the laws of the Terror for its legitimacy.[6]

Although the Terror had ended in the Côte-d'Or, the battle against the church continued. For Calès there were four areas of concern: bells; liturgical vessels and sacramental garments; access to churches; and the surveillance of priests. In mid-December 1794, Calès issued an order outlining actions national agents should take related to the church and the clergy. He ordered them to break all remaining bells, allowing towns with populations of 3,000 or less to retain one bell. Larger towns were allowed one bell for each quarter. He instructed national agents to collect liturgical vessels and sacramental garments, and to imprison anyone who refused to surrender these items. They were to close churches with fewer than 3,000 parishioners and take control of the keys, thus regulating use of the buildings. Calès ordered districts to complete a census of all priests, providing their name, age, place of residence, former parish, current means of subsistence, and the dates they swore the various oaths required by the revolution. Agents were also to ensure that priests resided no closer than ten leagues to their former parishes and that priests not native to the department returned to their birth place within a *décadi* (i.e., ten days). Calès exempted married priests, those actively engaged in commerce or agriculture, and the elderly or infirm from these requirements. He also instructed national agents to report anyone celebrating mass, arresting those guilty of doing so and referring their case to him. They were also to break all crosses and to assess a fine of 150 *livres* on any municipal officer who permitted one to remain.[7]

Calès had hardly issued his order before he had to retract some portions of it. Seven days after the first order, he permitted any priest who was living with his family and had a record of good conduct, as well as those residing alone who had displayed patriotism above suspicion, to remain at his residence even if it was not ten leagues from his former parish. Priests originally from other areas could remain if they had an enterprise that supported them. Despite the relaxation of his order, Calès cautioned district authorities to be sceptical of attestations of patriotism coming from villages. He also allowed villages and towns that were above suspicion with respect to religious fanaticism to retain their bells, and left bells attached to clocks in place.[8]

Calès's order reveals the enduring anti-clericalism of the National Convention. It also betrays either an ignorance of local conditions or an actual intention for all churches in the Côte-d'Or to remain closed outside of Dijon, as only parishes in that city reached the threshold of 3,000 parishioners. The department as a whole was largely rural, with only small villages. With a population of 22,000, Dijon was twice as large as Beaune, the department's second-largest city.[9] Arnay-le-Duc's redistricting in 1791 offers insight into the size of parishes in the diocese. After closing and combining parishes, Arnay-le-Duc's administrators retained forty-five parishes ranging in size from 456 to 1,350 parishioners.[10]

In response to Calès's order, clergy submitted statements to their district directories. A handful of examples remain in the department's archives. François Chapuis, a former constitutional priest, described himself as a farmer. For over ten years, he wrote, he had cultivated a vineyard. Since resigning as the priest of Prâlon, he had lived entirely on the profits of his agriculture. Attesting that he rarely entered Prâlon, and that he was a sincere friend of the revolution, he asked to remain in his residence under the surveillance of the authorities. In 1794, Chapuis was fifty-four years old. Born in Dijon, he had served the parish of Prâlon for eighteen years. A supporter of the revolution, he had sworn all the oaths. The apparent end of his clerical career in the spring of 1794 left him dependent on the proceeds of his vineyard.[11] The municipal officers of Prâlon confirmed Chapuis's patriotism and reported his conduct above reproach.[12]

Jean-Jérôme Quillot, also a former constitutional priest in the district of Dijon, sent his statement to Calès on 31 December. Born in Dijon, Quillot was sixty-three. He began his clerical career as a vicar in the parish of Morebeau. In 1766, he became the priest at Saint-Julien. Residing in Dijon in the section *La hâlle*, Quillot wrote that he had taken all the revolutionary oaths without restrictions or delay. His only means of subsistence was a pension of 1000 *livres* from the republic, and with it he supported himself and an elderly sister. In conclusion, he wrote that he had seized every opportunity to be of service to the republic and that circumstances required him to remain in Dijon.[13] Marinet, captain of the *gendarmerie*, confirmed Quillot's statement, reporting that he had always loved the government and had never retracted his oaths. He added that Quillot had conducted mass only in parish churches, meaning that he had not conducted mass in private homes, an activity associated with the refractory clergy. This was a further indication of his allegiance to the revolution and not its clerical opponents.[14]

In their prompt response to Calès's order, Chapuis and Quillot demonstrated their adherence to the republic and its laws. Once it was possible to do so, both men returned to their work as constitutional clergy. In doing so, they joined the very small number of former constitutional clergy in the Côte-d'Or who became active in the Gallican church, the revived constitutional church whose story we will turn to shortly.

Some districts responded for their priests. Arnay-sur-Arroux reported that seven former priests resided in the municipality of Arnay and that all lived at least ten leagues from their former parish. The district asked if Arnay could retain its two bells, one attached to a clock and the second used to call people to the market, the observance of the *décadi*, and other assemblies, and as an alarm in case of fire. The department approved the district's request.

Calès's order reflected the national debate about religion and the threat it posed. In year 3, the National Convention passed two important laws that re-established the relationship between religion and the state. On 20 September 1794, it voted to suppress the budget for the constitutional church, declaring that "the Republic will no longer recognize nor salary any religion." With the law of 3 *ventôse* (21 February 1795), it proclaimed the religious neutrality of the state, declaring tolerance for all religions but prohibiting anyone from appearing in public in religious garb. The law of 3 *ventôse* subjected all religious ceremonies to police surveillance. Further, it decreed the end of endowments and taxes to support religion.[15] Taken together, these two laws ended the Civil Constitution of the Clergy and its ideal of integrating religion into the state.[16]

THE *ÉVÊQUES RÉUNIS* AND RE-ESTABLISHING RELIGIOUS LIBERTY

In mid-November 1794, a small group of constitutional bishops met in Paris to discuss the state of their church. Four, Jean-Baptiste Royer (bishop of the Ain), Jean-Pierre Saurine (bishop of the Landes), Eléonor-Marie Desbois de Rochefort (bishop of the Somme), and Augustin Clément (constitutional priest, and later bishop, of Seine-et-Oise), had suffered arrest during the Terror. They were joined by the physician Charles Saillant, an active layman. In December, Henri Grégoire, constitutional bishop of the Loire-et-Saône and member of the National Convention, also joined the group. Known as the *Évêques réunis* (United Bishops), this group worked to re-establish Christian worship in France and to revive the constitutional church. Studying the work of this group, historian Rodney J. Dean has underscored that, despite the leading role Henri Grégoire eventually played in the Gallican church, he did not initiate this effort nor carry it forward alone.[17] Like Grégoire, Royer and Saurine were members of the National Convention, but their support for the persecuted Girondin deputies had resulted in their arrests in October 1793.

The United Bishops first worked to reinstate public worship in France.[18] Among the opening salvos of this campaign was Grégoire's speech on religious liberty delivered to the National Convention on 1 *nivôse* (21 December 1794). A member of the Committee on Public Instruction, Grégoire timed his remarks to coincide with the National Convention's discussion of the *fêtes décadaires*. In his speech, he challenged the legislature to give the French the benefits of liberty.[19] What is not prohibited by the law is permitted, he reasoned, and thus the people should be left alone to hold their religious beliefs. He declared that the French enjoyed less religious liberty than the Turks, the Moroccans, or the Algerians, all subjects of despots. He challenged the idea that Catholicism was incompatible with the republic and argued that one found patriotic Catholics everywhere. He accused the National Convention of working to destroy the church. "If you were of good faith, you would admit that your intention, manifested in the evidence so far is to destroy Catholicism. You are embarrassed about the choice of means." Grégoire accused the deputies of failing to support religious freedom, which both natural right and the law protected. Further, he declared that liberty existed nowhere in France and that this was making the people hate democracy. It was necessary, he argued, to re-establish religious freedom.[20]

Grégoire's proposal recognized the reality of a changed religious and political landscape. He accepted that all religions should enjoy equal protection and that no one should be compelled to accept any faith. He also incorporated the recent legislation prohibiting external symbols, processions, and bells into his vision of a return to religious liberty. The revolutionary calendar need not be a barrier; people could exercise their religion using a different calendar from that governing the rest of their lives. He concluded his speech with the proposal that the National Convention guarantee all citizens religious freedom as long as they did not disturb public order and tranquility.[21]

Grégoire's speech received a hostile reception that December morning. Hecklers repeatedly interrupted the address and accused him of being premature in bringing up the subject of tolerance.[22] Despite this hostility, the speech struck a chord with the larger public and appeared in several editions and in reprints in various journals. The United Bishops reinforced Grégoire's argument by encouraging others to publish as well. Durand de Maillane, a member of the National Convention who, a few years earlier, had been on the committee that created the Civil Constitution of the Clergy, took up Grégoire's themes in his pamphlet *Opinions sur les fêtes décadaires*, as did P.C.L. Baudin, deputy from the Ardennes, in three pamphlets, including *Du fanaticism et la liberté des cultes*. Jean-Baptiste Royer wrote a pamphlet linking freedom of religion to the ideas of the enlightenment *philosophe* the Abbé de Mably, while Yves Audrien, member of the National Convention and later constitutional bishop of Finistère (1799), wrote a pamphlet defending Grégoire's speech.[23]

Various local efforts to reopen churches and resume religious practice echoed the United Bishops' campaign. On 2 January, women in Vaux in the department of the Yonne, inspired by reports that churches had opened in neighbouring villages, demanded the keys to the village church.[24] Grégoire's episcopal vicars reopened churches in the Loire-et-Cher. In Normandy, village schoolteachers (*instituteurs*) offered masses with the aid of former cantors while, in Alsace, parishioners lashed out at symbols of the revolution's radicalism, dismantling Jacobin mountains and breaking busts of Marat, Le Pelletier, and Voltaire.[25]

Significant for the effort to reopen churches were the actions of Jacques Guermeur and Mathieu Guezno, representatives on mission to the Army of the Coasts of Brest and Cherbourg.[26] By the fall of 1794, the National Convention's commanders had forced a truce on the counter-revolutionaries in the Vendée. In December, the National Convention sent Guermeur and Guezno to conclude a peace treaty with the rebels in the Vendée. Upon arriving, they released a number of suspects, and, on 24 *nivôse l'an* 3 (13 January 1795), they issued an order guaranteeing religious liberty in the departments of Morbihan, Ille-et-Vilaine, and Côtes-du-Nord. Guermeur and Guezno argued that no peace was possible without this provision. In part, the order read, "No individual nor group of citizens may be disturbed or harassed in the free and peaceful exercise of their religion."[27] Claude Le Coz, constitutional bishop of Ille-et-Vilaine, celebrated Guezno and Guermeur's action in a letter to Grégoire, reporting that an immense crowd came out for the reopening of the cathedral in Quimper in the department of Finistère.[28]

As the work of Augustin Gazier in the last decades of the nineteenth century and Rodney J. Dean much more recently demonstrate, the National Convention's passage of the law of 3 *ventôse* guaranteeing religious liberty followed a number of developments supporting the reopening of France's churches. In the end, it was Boissy d'Anglas, a Protestant, who presented the decree granting freedom of worship to all religions not prohibited by the state. The decree may have granted a measure of religious freedom, but at the same time Boissy d'Anglas's motion maligned the church, depicting Catholicism as "servile by nature, auxiliary to despotism by essence, [and] stupefying for the human species." In his study of the law of 3 *ventôse*, Albert Mathiez concluded that it "did not give Catholics true liberty. It threw them tolerance like alms."[29] Despite the negative portrayal of religious faith in the new law, the United Bishops celebrated this victory, reprinting the act's text in full in the second volume of their journal *Annales de la religion*.[30]

THE UNITED BISHOPS
AND THE GALLICAN CHURCH

After the passage of the law of 3 *ventôse*, the United Bishops worked
to reorganize the constitutional church as the Gallican church. In
the winter of 1795, the bishops identified themselves either by their
diocese òr by the city that served as their episcopal seat. The following year, however, they all named themselves by their episcopal
seat. This highlighted their break with the Civil Constitution of the
Clergy and asserted their legitimacy against the continuing claim of
the refractory clergy that they were usurpers (*intrus*).[31] In their effort
to revive the constitutional church, the United Bishops rented several
churches and other buildings in Paris. In addition, Desbois founded
a bi-weekly periodical, the *Annales de la religion*, which he edited
with Grégoire, and a publishing house, the *Librairie chrétienne*.[32]

On 15 March, the United Bishops issued an encyclical.[33] Addressing
themselves to the former constitutional bishops and the vacant
churches, they tackled the Terror and the church's recovery from it.
Attributing it to a small number of corrupt men, they asked the churches
to pardon those who had committed excesses and urged everyone to
turn their attention to God. They reasoned that, although God had
permitted the persecution because of the irreverence of the church,
not all were at fault. Referring to the experience of the prophet Ezra,
they explained that the impious had led the constitutional church to
sin.[34] Now, detached from the state, the Gallican Church was stronger
and more immune to corruption. Separated from politics, it enjoyed
a reciprocal, open relationship with the state. It functioned in a trans-
parent way, not in secret like the refractory clergy. In re-establishing
the Gallican church, the bishops emphasized a return to the primitive
discipline of the church's councils.[35]

Echoing the debate over the Civil Constitution of the Clergy, the
United Bishops tackled the issue of legitimate leadership. The church
was the faithful, led by legitimate pastors. Affirming their connection
with Rome, they noted that while Jesus Christ was the invisible head
of the church, the pope was its visible head. Christ consecrated bishops as successors to the apostles and gave them authority over the
church. Explicitly condemning presbyterianism, or a shared authority between the laity and the clergy, they endorsed the hierarchy of
the church, noting that bishops were superior to priests, who were
superior to deacons.[36]

The United Bishops were careful to emphasize both Christianity's submission to the state and its autonomy from it. Because the Gospels commanded respect for the state, they would submit to the laws of the republic, pray for it, and take an interest in its affairs. Despite this respect, they could not accept innovations that went against the church's moral teachings or its ancient discipline. With respect to recent developments, the bishops recognized civil marriage but not divorce. They also did not recognize the right of married priests to retain their spiritual functions.[37]

Concluding their encyclical, the bishops presented a provisional rule for the new Gallican church. Addressing the issue of how to deal with clergy who had fallen during the Terror, they were careful to distinguish between priests and bishops who had committed apostasy and those who, although resigning their positions and delivering their letters of ordination, never renounced their faith. Apostates and those who had profaned the objects and images held sacred by the church (the Eucharist, the scriptures, the holy oil, and so on) they judged unworthy to be priests. To return to the priesthood, a priest or bishop had to be repentant and not culpable of the most egregious acts of apostasy or persecution of the church. For those who could be reconciled to the church, the United Bishops recommended that priests consult St. Cyprian's treatise *De Lapsis* concerning how to treat fallen Christians. In a direct assault on the refractory clergy, who continued to judge the sacraments of the constitutional clergy as invalid, the United Bishops declared it a scandal to deny the efficacy of sacraments performed by one's opponents or to prohibit anyone from hearing their offices.[38]

With respect to the institutional organization of the Gallican church, the bishops proposed retaining the ecclesiastical jurisdictions established by the Civil Constitution of the Clergy. Provisionally, they suggested maintaining all existing parishes. And, despite the difficult times in which the church found itself, the bishops underscored the importance of canonical standards for ordination. No one under thirty was to be ordained. Individuals younger than thirty years of age were to be placed with a curé for formation. The first task of bishops and of presbyteries in vacant dioceses was to establish which priests had remained faithful during the Terror. Only these individuals should be authorized to administer the sacraments. The bishops also stressed that instruction was an integral part of the celebration of mass. A relaxation of piety had led some to believe that it was enough to hear mass without the homily or the celebration of the Eucharist. Again in a swipe at the refractories, the United Bishops underscored that only one mass and one Eucharist were to be administered in each church, and that it was the priest of that church who should celebrate those rites.[39]

As Dale Van Kley has argued, Abbé Grégoire's position on church and state changed between 1790 and 1795. In 1790, as a clergy deputy with Richerist leaning, Grégoire was willing to sacrifice the church's corporate voice. Five years later, as a bishop, he was not willing to do so, especially for a dechristianized republic. In the years following the Terror, he increasingly embraced Jansenist ideas, endorsing the idea of the separation of church and state and rediscovering the conciliar tradition.[40] In keeping with these ideas, the United Bishops proposed in their letter that the Gallican church hold a national council. Two years later, it held the first of two such councils.

REOPENING THE CHURCHES IN THE CÔTE-D'OR

In the Côte-d'Or, the reopening of the churches occurred over several months. Local circumstances played as large a role in this process, as did the United Bishops's encyclical. Volfius read the bishops' missive but, for a variety of reasons, did not return to his position as bishop until August 1795. The letter inspired other constitutional clergy in the diocese to return to their parishes, although, there, they faced opposition from both anti-clerical republicans and anti-republican refractories. The case of Denis Chauchot, constitutional priest of Is-sur-Tille who was briefly imprisoned during the Terror, illustrates some of the struggles they faced.

In late March, Chauchot wrote to the department's administrators requesting permission to resume his work as a priest. He also asked that the *maison nationale*, formerly the village's church, not be sold. Responding to Chauchot, departmental authorities noted that the law of 3 *ventôse* granted freedom of religion but prohibited the public exercise of any faith.[41]

At age sixty-four, Chauchot was hardly a novice to either ecclesiastical or revolutionary politics. A strong supporter of the revolution and its ecclesiastical reforms, he had been a vocal proponent of the Civil Constitution of the Clergy, even sending copies of his writings to Grégoire.[42] It seems unlikely that he would have been unaware of the National Convention's action granting religious freedom. More probable is that he was testing the waters, attempting to discern if the department would tolerate a resumption of religious services in Is-sur-Tille. The events that followed his celebration of mass in May suggest that, despite the actions of the National Convention, local opinion remained divided on the wisdom of allowing Catholic religious services in the community.

On 16 May, Chauchot conducted services in the *maison nationale* in Is-sur-Tille. It was an event of some note in the village. One citizen, Baron Couvreur, saw fit to remove the cross from the church's steeple, initiating the day's troubles.[43] Although some accused Chauchot of instigating the conflict, he defended himself by declaring that he feared an insurrection if he did not celebrate mass. As evidence of his hesitation, Chauchot related his reluctance to lead services in a church being used to store arms.[44] The village's officers and general council supported Chauchot's version of events, absolving him of any responsibility for what occurred.[45] The district of Is-sur-Tille, however, denounced Chauchot for violating the law of 3 *ventôse* and disturbing public order, and they sought to bring him before the criminal tribunal. The department endorsed the version of events advanced by the municipality and reprimanded only citizen Couvreur, ordering him to return the cross to the church's steeple. As a precaution against future incidents, the department ordered that the keys to the *maison nationale* be held by the secretary of the district and that only those in compliance with the law of 3 *ventôse* be permitted to use the building.[46]

The citizens of Is-sur-Tille were not the only ones in the department to seek the return of Catholic worship in their village. At the end of June, the department received a petition from the inhabitants of Agencourt, requesting a priest and the reopening of their church. They also sought a teacher for the children of the commune. The directory granted the petitioners the use of the church building but stipulated that they must choose a priest who was in compliance with the recently passed law of 11 *prairial*, which required all clergy to swear an oath of loyalty to the republic.[47] This law was a response to the revival of refractory clergy that had followed the law of 3 *ventôse*. Some priests returned from exile, but many others just came out of hiding, including four old regime bishops. The law of 11 *prairial* created yet another split among the clergy. Some refractories, following the lead of the abbé Jacques-André Emery, former superior of the Sulpicians, took the oath and became known as *soumissionnaires*.[48]

VOLFIUS'S RETURN AND THE
GALLICAN CHURCH IN THE CÔTE-D'OR

In mid-July, two former constitutional priests reported to Abbé Grégoire on the strength of the refractory clergy in the Côte-d'Or. The United Bishops' letter had inspired Louis Bitouzel, a priest in Beaune, and Jean-Baptiste Grosdidier, only recently released from prison, to return to their parishes.[49] Separately, they wrote to Grégoire to report on conditions in the department. Both noted that refractory priests were engaged in an aggressive campaign to obtain public retractions from the constitutional clergy. Bitouzel named four centres of this activity – Autun, Châlons-sur-Saône, Dijon, and Besançon. According to Bitouzel, the constitutional priests retracted their various oaths of allegiance to the state, and then several witnesses signed their statements. Alarmed by these activities, Grosdidier wrote that the refractories had "redoubled their audacity." Most worrisome to Grosdidier were the widening divisions and multiplying hatreds that he feared were preludes to civil war. He reported that the refractories had established a tribunal in Dijon to take the retractions of constitutional clergy and to determine their penance. Both Bitouzel and Grosdidier expressed concern about the prospect of the National Convention allowing the deported priests to return.

In their letters to Grégoire, Bitouzel and Grosdidier commented on the failure of Volfius to resume his functions. Bitouzel believed that it was unlikely that Volfius would return as bishop, given his recent letter to the Dijon paper, *L'Original, ou Journal du Départment de la Côte-d'Or*.[50] Grosdidier accused Volfius of sacrificing his priests during the Terror. He also judged him for failing to return to leadership. His absence, Grosdidier wrote, left the diocese's priests uncertain about whom they should follow, leading some to join the refractories.[51]

In his letter to *L'Original*, Volfius discussed his resignation during year 2 and argued that he had not committed apostasy but had merely responded to what was then necessary.[52] Although he argued his case forcefully, privately he struggled to reconcile his resignation in the spring of 1794 with the idea that now, under different circumstances, he could resume his functions as bishop. Grégoire was well aware of Volfius's dilemma from his correspondence with the bishop. Grosdidier and Bitouzel, apparently not confidents of Volfius, appear to have had no knowledge of the bishop's personal crisis.

Volfius's correspondence with Grégoire began in March 1795 following the passage of the law of 3 *ventôse* establishing religious tolerance. Although aware of the law, Volfius remained discouraged about the prospects for the church in the Côte-d'Or. Writing that no one in Dijon was interested in tolerance and that for many people the idea was odious and contemptible, Volfius gave the impression of being in a deep depression. "I live," he wrote, "in the most profound retreat and am resolved to remain there."[53] Over the next five months, he continued to write to Grégoire, slowly modifying his judgment of himself and of the prospects for the Gallican church in the Côte-d'Or.

Grégoire initiated the correspondence with Volfius in early spring as the United Bishops began to organize the Gallican church. In his response, Volfius praised Grégoire's speeches before the National Convention and his steadfastness during the months of dechristianization. About himself, Volfius reported on the events of the previous year that had led him to resign. Although he had acted under considerable pressure, Volfius could not absolve himself of what he judged to be weakness.[54] Three weeks after his first letter to Grégoire, he sent a second, enclosing a copy of the statement he had submitted to the *Affiches de Dijon* at the time of his resignation.[55] In this letter, the question of whether or not he could in good conscience return to his position as bishop consumed Volfius's attention. Giving a fuller account of the events that led to his resignation, he asked the bishop of Blois to judge: could he return to his functions, as had other constitutional priests in the diocese? In this second letter, Volfius's mood, while still far from hopeful, appeared more elevated. He closed the letter with a discussion of an article on a "religion of man" (*un culte aux hommes*) that he was considering publishing. It would unite all priests for the good of religion and the nation, and end the schism that divided the church.

In early July 1795, Volfius announced his return as bishop in a letter published in *L'Original*.[56] Curiously, the letter was dated three months earlier, 10 *germinal l'an* 3 (30 March 1795). This letter demonstrated none of the doubts expressed earlier by Volfius to Grégoire. Instead, Volfius argued forcefully that, in resigning his functions, he had not resigned his faith. Further, he noted that he had made it clear to Bernard de Saintes that he would declare nothing that violated his conscience. It was the temper of the time, the "rage of the faction ... that spoke for the nation," that had pressed the clergy to resign and hand over their letters of ordination. Fearing that scenes of the Vendée would be repeated in the department, Volfius had resigned.[57] Despite the troubles of that time, Volfius wrote that he had never doubted that religion would re-establish itself, because "a great nation cannot long exist without religion."[58] The schism within the Catholic Church, however, remained a problem, and it was to this issue that Volfius devoted the second half of his letter. A bishop recognized by only one part of his flock could not survive. What was necessary now was for all Catholics, especially the clergy, to unite and provide a great example to the nation, as it was through their divisions that their mutual enemies sought to destroy the church. This united front was necessary because the people, "tired of so many battles and commotions, needed to be recalled to morality, to concord, to the sweet affections of the heart."[59]

The need to end the schism between the constitutional and refractory clergy was a central concern for Volfius. He returned to the theme in August in a letter he signed with fourteen other constitutional clergy in Dijon that appeared in the *Annales de la religion*.[60] In it the constitutional clergy appealed to the refractory clergy of the diocese to unite with them for the good of religion. They argued that there were no dogmatic barriers between them, only differences on some points of discipline. With the demise of the Civil Constitution of the Clergy, Volfius and his colleagues believed that these differences could be easily overcome. They proposed a meeting at the cathedral on 14 August, urging the refractories to come with the issues most important to them to join with them in rebuilding the church in the department. They argued that those supporting the division had little concern for the faith.[61] They appealed to the refractory clergy to practise their faith openly now that it was legal for them to do so, warning that secrecy lent itself to fanaticism, abuse, and immorality. Establishing confessionals in private homes was an open door to sin. Finally, they argued that Christians lived under the law of the land in which they found themselves. Thus if the refractories refused to practise their faith openly, they would be declaring themselves enemies of the republican government.[62] This open letter was the only piece Volfius published in the *Annales de la religion*, although later issues did carry news of him and events in the Côte-d'Or. Volfius was not naive about the likely reception this appeal would receive in the refractory camp. Yet, as he wrote to Grégoire, he hoped that it would at least demonstrate to the public his own disposition toward his ecclesiastical opposition.[63]

That same month, Volfius reported to Grégoire that he had resumed his functions as bishop.[64] He had returned to his ministry because he was convinced that he was needed. Left without a leader, the priests of the diocese were turning to the refractory camp. On 8 *thermidor* (26 July 1795), he presided over the reopening of the cathedral. A great crowd attended, with "a lot of curious individuals and aristocrats." Some "young people" who seemed to have had "a plan to make trouble" also came, but in the end they were "satisfied with the very august ceremony." Volfius reported that "we prostrated ourselves" to make an "honourable amend" for the "sacrileges committed in the temple, the faults of the people and the weakness of the priests." In doing this, "tears ran on all parts," and a lot of people "showed great devotion." The following Sunday, the cathedral was no less crowded, he reported, and since the churches reopened parents brought at least two hundred children for catechism. Nonetheless, the activities of the refractory clergy remained a concern. According to Volfius, they insulted the constitutional clergy, calling them wolves, and did not hesitate to remarry, rebaptize, and re-confess parishioners who had received any of these sacraments from a constitutional cleric. They also conducted much of their activity in secret, although they operated openly in the countryside. "Vagabond monks" and "so-called apostolic vicars ... deputies of the bishop of Lausanne" supported them in their work to gain the retractions of constitutional clergy.

Despite his decision to return to his ministry, Volfius remained concerned about his record during the Terror. In concluding his letter, he returned to the subject of the *Lettre encyclique* of March.[65] He wrote that he did not know if he should sign it and have his name listed among its adherents because he was not sure if the letter condemned the type of actions he took during the Terror. Apparently, Grégoire and the other United Bishops were not as troubled as Volfius over his past, because his name did appear in a published list of adherents to the letter before the end of year 3 (22 September 1795).[66]

Volfuis gave some indication of his relationship with departmental authorities in a letter to Grégoire in mid-August.[67] He requested the abbé's aid in establishing a temporary commission of the arts in the department to replace the one originally created by Calès. The department had put a professor from the *école centrale* in charge of that commission. Volfius argued that the work of the commission was outside of that man's expertise. Volfius's appeal, over the heads of the departmental authorities to a deputy of the National Convention, suggests that the bishop's influence in the department was minimal.

Reports of devotion and camaraderie at the time of his return as bishop were soon replaced by news of difficulties. In mid-September, Volfius wrote to Grégoire that he had only four or five old and infirm priests still with him.[68] The others had left. Most were waiting the outcome of events before resuming their careers. In all, he estimated that he might have twenty "lazy priests," many of them his former vicars, whom he was unable to convince to serve two or three parishes. He had especially harsh words for the priest of Fontaine, who had served in the Constituent Assembly. Volfius urged Grégoire to "treat him as he merits," and complained that he came poorly dressed to services despite having been asked to adopt ecclesiastical garb. He also said mass reluctantly and failed to resume other clerical duties.

Across 1795, the churches reopened in France. The law of 3 *ventôse* appeared to allow refractory priests an equal footing with the former constitutional priests. The National Convention, however, soon felt the need to restrict the religious expression of the republic's most virulent clerical critics. On 11 *prairial* (30 May), it instituted an oath of loyalty for all clergy wanting to conduct religious services. In the Côte-d'Or, year 3 saw a moderation of the radical Jacobinism that had held sway during the Terror. Initially, Jean-Marie Calès placed the department's clergy under strict surveillance. The tolerance decreed by the law of 3 *ventôse* had to be worked out in the face of opposition from both anti-clerical republicans and anti-constitutional refractories. From the reports given by Bitouzel, Grosdidier, and Volfius, it would be generous to refer even to a rump constitutional church in the Côte-d'Or in year 3. A handful of constitutional clergy returned to their parishes and openly allied with Volfius once he returned as bishop. All three reported the better organization of the refractory priests and their success in gaining the retractions of former constitutional clergy. The religious liberty of year 3 provided a decisive opening for the activities of the revolution's clerical critics in the Côte-d'Or. For the former constitutional priests, the state's actions presented a new challenge: organizing a pro-revolutionary church without the support of the revolutionary state. Despite the changed context, Volfius and the some former constitutional clergy returned to the task of creating a church for the new political order.

8

Religious Pluralism and
the Early Directory, 1795–1797

The summer of 1795 saw a royalist revival in France due in part to the death of Louis XVI's only surviving son, who died in prison in June. The child's death made his uncle, Louis-Stanislas the count of Provence, the Bourbon pretender. Living in exile, the count of Provence issued the Declaration of Verona, establishing his intention to restore France to its pre-revolutionary state. These developments coincided with Britain's effort to ignite a civil war led by French émigrés. The British secretary of war, William Windham, believed that, sufficiently supported, the émigrés might turn the tide in England's ongoing war with France. On 27 June, eighty-seven transport ships carrying 3,000 men sailed into Quiberon Bay off the southern coast of Brittany. The ships carried armaments, munitions, and uniforms for a force of 17,000; as well as provisions to sustain an army of 6,000 for three months. Protected by a British fleet, the soldiers disembarked on the beaches surrounding the village of Carnac.[1] Once landed, the émigré force awaited the arrival of a second army of 2,000 men, equipped and supplied by the Dutch, that was making its way through Spithead toward Quiberon.[2]

General Lazare Hoche, commander of the Armies of Cherbourg and Brest, was at his headquarters in Rennes when he learned of the landing. Mobilizing 22,000 men, he marched on the émigrés who had joined with the Chouans, irregular forces composed of a cross-section of revolutionary France's opponents.[3] Hoche's military career traced the recent turmoil of the revolution. Although distinguishing himself in September 1793 in the war with Austria, he found himself imprisoned the following summer, denounced by Saint-Just, the youngest member of the Committee of Public Safety.

After Robespierre's fall in which Saint-Just shared, Paul Barras, deputy in the National Convention and a rising star, intervened, delivering not only Hoche's freedom, but also command of the Army of Cherbourg. In November 1794, the National Convention placed him over the Army of Brest as well.[4]

In Hoche's first months in the Vendée, representatives from the National Convention led by Albert Ruelle negotiated a tentative peace with the chiefs of the Vendée and the Chouans led by François-Anthanase Charette de La Contrie, at the chateau of La Jaunay outside Nantes. In coming to terms with Charette, Ruelle granted a critical concession, religious liberty. Hoche followed these negotiations with talks in Rennes, reaching a similar agreement with insurgent leaders in Brittany in early April.[5] Like the actions of Guermeur and Guezno in the departments of Morbihan, Ile-et-Vilaine, and Côtes-du-Nord, discussed in the preceding chapter, these developments were in the background of the National Convention's decree of 3 *ventôse l'an 3* (21 February 1795) granting freedom of worship.

The British-sponsored invasion in June 1795 overturned this fragile peace. Fanning the flames of civil war, the count of Provence named Charette as commander-in-chief of the region's royalist forces. Charette met the British-equipped émigrés with several thousand poorly armed, undisciplined, ragged, and underfed troops. The count of Puisaye and the count of Hérvilly received him and his irregular forces coolly. Many of the Chouans drifted away as the émigré commanders debated whether to wait for the second army to arrive or to advance toward the Vendée and Paris. In the end, the British effort to stoke civil war in western France failed miserably. Assisted by intelligence from deserters of the revolutionary armies whom the British had returned to France with the émigrés, Hoche pushed the royalist forces onto the narrow Quiberon peninsula, inflicting a punishing defeat and harsh reprisals. Capturing 9,000 men, including 1,000 émigrés, Hoche enforced the revolution's laws. A military commission condemned 752 to death. They were executed at the end of July.[6]

Charette's leadership had important consequences for the Vendée's refractory clergy. Among those landing with the expedition were forty to fifty refractory clergy, including the abbé Jean Brumauld de Beauregard, vicar-general of the bishop of Luçon, Marie-Charles-Isidore de Mercy. From exile in Switzerland, Mercy had written to Beauregard, also in exile but in England, and authorized him to organize a synod of the clergy faithful to Rome should he return to the diocese. Working with Charette, Beauregard held this synod on 4 August 1795 at Poiré-sur-Vie. Attended by fifty-seven clergymen, the synod outlined a plan to identify refractory clergy and nuns still in the diocese as well as to inventory the resources available to them. A particular concern was rehabilitating baptisms and marriages performed by constitutional clergy. The synod at Poiré-sur-Vie was an unusual gathering for refractory clergy in revolutionary France made possible by the presence of the Chouans and emigré forces.[7]

The renewed royalist challenge raised again the question of the clergy's loyalty to the state. In an effort to secure clerical submission, the National Convention enacted two important laws in its last weeks. First, on 7 *vendémiaire* (29 September 1795), it instituted a new oath that required all clergy to affirm that sovereignty resided in France's citizenry, not in any dynastic claimant, and to promise to submit to the republic's laws. Priests conducting services without taking the oath faced imprisonment.[8] Volfius took the oath about a month after its passage.[9] The second law, passed on 3 *brumaire* (24 October 1795) at the convention's second-to-last session, took aim at clergy who had been deported or whose failure to comply with the various oaths demanded since 1791 made them deportable. This law followed the convention's action the previous month that banished non-juring clergy for life and renewed all the penalties enacted against priests in 1792 and 1793. These included the denial of amnesty and the warning that any non-juring priest found in France had fifteen days to leave before he faced the firing squad.[10] Despite the draconian tenor of the law of 3 *brumaire*, the early Directory (1795–6) was a period of religious pluralism that allowed both the refractory and the constitutional clergy to be active. Surveying these years, Bernard Plongeron and Astérious Argyriou concluded that they constituted a "false and fugitive lull" in a larger storm against religion, a reflection that rings true for the religious history of the Côte-d'Or.[11]

RELIGIOUS CONTROVERSY IN THE CÔTE-D'OR

In the Côte-d'Or, the revolutionary newspaper *Le Nécessaire* reported three incidents of religious trouble as 1795 drew to a close.[12] The first, which involved the uprooting of a liberty tree, occurred in Saint-Romain, a village southwest of Dijon close to the department's border. Local authorities declared their outrage at this trampling of the laws protecting private property, and the department followed up by ordering municipal officials in Meurfaut, a neighbouring village, to replant the tree. The second incident involved a refractory priest in Perrigny-sur-l'Oignon, a village about fifty kilometres to the east of Dijon, who urged his listeners to forget the duties of citizenship. When the local bailiff tried to arrest the man, the crowd attacked the bailiff. The justice of the peace and the National Guard of Pontailler, a village on the Saône River's opposite bank, defended the bailiff, but a furious crowd repulsed them and blood flowed. Ultimately General Carteaux, commander of the division of Dijon, sent an armed force that arrested and imprisoned the priest. In reporting the incident, *Le Necessaire* noted that cries of royalism were heard in the melee.[13] The final incident occurred in Flavigny, where a young girl supported by a priest attracted followers. Claiming to be the envoy of the divine, the girl preached and taught the catechism. In response to these activities, the public prosecutor in Flavigny denounced the girl. The newspaper's point in offering these stories of religious disorder was to illustrate what it called a great fermentation of religious activity in the department that required official action. Flavigny, located in the northwestern quadrant of the Côte-d'Or, rounded out the *tour-de-département* created by these three incidents, underscoring the pervasiveness of these developments. In the editor's judgment, religion was only a pretext for these actors; the real concern was the challenge to public order they presented.[14]

At the same time, the department's Gallican clergy expressed concern about the new openness permitted the refractory clergy. In January 1796, François Sivry, Gallican curé of Combertaut, a village southeast of Beaune, wrote to departmental authorities to denounce Jacques Cloutier and the brothers Simon and Louis Bigot, for their roles in sponsoring visits by the non-juring priest, Father Gerard.[15] A former Capucin, Gerard appeared in Combertaut in July and November, saying mass and leading vespers in private homes. On each visit, Cloutier and the Bigots rang the village's bell to announce the priest's arrival and offices. In Sivry's judgment, Gerard's visits had widened the divisions in the village. Some citizens, Sivry believed, had too little courage to resist the opinions of Louis Bigot, the village agent, who he described as a "counter-revolutionary man, a royalist and a most outraged fanatic." Cloutier and Simon Bigot were also prominent citizens, the former having served as mayor and the latter preceding his brother as town agent. The Bigots and Cloutier welcomed Gerard even though they knew he was a non-juring priest who had retracted his earlier oath. Following the priest's second visit, Louis Bigot took him to Autun, where, as an apostolic vicar, Gerard re-consecrated an altar. For Sivry, all of these actions amounted to a violation of the nation's laws and the principles of the rights of man because the Bigot brothers and Cloutier were actively working to make their religion dominant. The village's religious troubles, Sivry concluded, were the responsibility of a small faction of five or six individuals.

Sivry's letter rests in the departmental archives with other papers concerning the priest, but it is not apparent what effect it had on departmental authorities. From reports in *Le Nécessaire*, it is clear that policing religion remained an important concern for public administrators. In mid-March, the journal printed two notices concerning religion. The first ordered all municipal administrations and their agents to enforce laws on the exercise of religion and to police the exterior of all temples.[16] The following week, the journal printed a second order that explained explicitly what the department expected of the municipal authorities.[17] They were to destroy all exterior signs of religion, make sure that no bells announced religious ceremonies, and place the key to all bell towers with the municipal agent. Bells were to announce communal assemblies and three points of the day, morning, noon, and evening. Agents were to replace any liberty tree destroyed. Failure to enforce these regulations would result in suspension.

Bells were the subject of some concern in year 4 (September 1795–September 1796), and not just because of their use by refractory clergy. In late January 1796, several citizens of the commune of Champagne wrote to the department to complain about the ceremonies of the village's constitutional curé, Jean-Baptiste Grosdidier.[18] They asked that Grosdidier be required to move his services from the common temple because the ringing of the bells was so loud that it made the ceremony unavoidable. The department responded to the petition by asking the administrators of the canton of Beaumont to verify that the bells were so loud as to be inescapable. If they found this to be the case, they were authorized to take steps to stop the annoyance. As related earlier, Grosdidier had a long and contested history as a priest in Champagne-sur-Vingeanne. These renewed complaints suggest that neither he nor his opponents had tired.

In early May, *Le Nécessaire* again reported on the laws prohibiting bell ringing and the requirement that local officials enforce them. This time, the journal referred its readers to the reminder, recently issued from Paris, concerning the law of 3 *ventôse l'an* 3.[19] In addition to establishing official tolerance for religion, the law limited practices that brought religion into the public sphere. It prohibited the ringing of bells to call citizens to a religious assembly, subjecting offenders to imprisonment for their first offence and deportation for their second.[20] In Paris, the United Bishops responded to the state's prohibition of bells by arguing in the *Annales de la religion* that this rule singled out Catholics, as only they used bells. Further, they rejected the notion that Catholic assemblies were a threat to public order.[21]

Most of the evidence concerning the refractory clergy's activities comes from their opponents – republican officials and constitutional clergy. However, one refractory priest in the Côte-d'Or wrote a confession of his activities to the department. The priest, Jean-Baptiste Arnoux, was the son of the large landowner (*grand cultivateur*), Louis Arnoux from the village of Charey in the district of Beaune, which was an area especially hospitable to refractory clergy. Beaune's *société populaire* complained of local officials' failure to enforce religious laws and of the open activity of refractory clergy in the city. In May 1796, the department received an unsigned letter purporting to be from Father Arnoux.[22] In the letter, the author declared his intention to denounce himself, as no one else dared to denounce him because his father was a dangerous despot in the village of Charey.

There is some evidence to demonstrate the activity of Arnoux's father to counter efforts to deport his son. In April 1795, an order for Arnoux's deportation was issued, but it is unclear what body ordered it. In July 1795, the district of Beaune repealed the order after Louis Arnoux presented a certificate from the municipality of Charey declaring that his son had submitted to all the laws of the republic as demanded by the law of 11 *prairial* (30 May 1795). The elder Arnoux also presented evidence that his son had taken, albeit belatedly, the oath required by the law of 14 August 1792.[23] Nonetheless, Father Arnoux was deported at some point, because, in year 8 (September 1799–September 1800), the department issued an order recognizing the district of Beaune's repeal of the deportation order and permitted the priest to return to France.[24]

The letter from Jean-Baptiste Arnoux could be a fake, an elaborate forgery created by opponents who sought to bolster the case against the priest. It could also be genuine. Arnoux's father worked to reverse the order deporting his son, and there is no indication that the priest was present. The letter's description of Arnoux's life as a non-juring priest is interesting because it corroborates the reports given by constitutional clergy concerning the activities of the refractory clergy. Arnoux wrote that he was a courier of the aristocrats and spent two to three nights each week in a house on the rue Fraternité in Beaune, where he conducted religious services "under the eyes of the municipality." He was aided by his sister, who made the preparations for marriages and baptisms that he conducted in the evening. Nuns visited him in the house, deriding the "peaceful and patriotic priests." They even supported his work in the hospital of Beaune. Two juring priests, Girard and Durand, saw the large number of people from the countryside who came to him for instruction. He remarried couples and rebaptized infants, rejecting sacraments first performed by constitutional clergy. He also received constitutional priests who had retracted their oaths, taking them to his father, who gave them provisions. In the letter, Arnoux declared that he had not sworn the oaths required of clergy and explained the certificate presented on his behalf was due to the influence of his father. The mayor of Charey, he wrote, did not dare to refuse the elder Arnoux. Why reveal all this information? At the end of his letter, the author explained:

> I enter here into detail that which would make one suspect me of being a fool or an imbecile, not at all; it is a motive of curiosity. [Done] in order to learn if all of your laws are illusory, as I have not too much place to doubt. I give you a faithful and sincere picture of that which is taking place at Beaune, because if I find myself making the voyage to Guyana as I desire, I would not be angry to see for companions those who have worked with me and the retractors who are multiplying.[25]

Although Arnoux's letter is not fully verifiable, other reports confirm the assertiveness of the refractory clergy and their allies. In late June, *Le Nécessaire* reported that émigrés and deported priests remained in contact with friends in France by using Swiss peddlers as their mail carriers.[26] These peddlers carried letters to small villages under the pretext of selling wares. Visiting specific houses, they delivered letters and received payment for doing so. Villagers had recognized one of these postmen, eliminating, as far as

Le Nécessaire's editor was concerned, any doubt about the danger
of enemy emissaries circulating in France. The following week, the
journal reported that the ministry of police had issued orders prohibiting Swiss peddlers from carrying émigré correspondence and
urging vigilance on the part of municipal administrations.[27]

The seeming vitality of the refractory clergy stands in stark contrast
to the struggles of the constitutional or Gallican clergy. In mid-July,
Volfius responded to a request from the Abbé Grégoire for information on the various districts of the department.[28] For the northern
districts, Volfius reported, he had no information, despite having written to several former constitutional priests. Most of the clergy in those
districts had retracted their oath or left the church. Some had married. Only a few clergy remained in small communes. Elsewhere in the
department, Volfius had established the *archiprêtres* envisioned by the
United Bishops, and communication was easier. As for his standing in
the community, Volfius reported some small progress, writing that he
was no longer embarrassed when he spoke publicly and that people
were asking him to elaborate on his ideas. In national developments,
a major matter of concern for Volfius was the finance minister's proposal that church organs be sold because "the Catholic religion took
too much preponderance over other religions by the majesty of its
ceremonies." Volfius feared this could lead to Catholics being denied
the use of churches because their liturgy was deemed too grand. He
reported that he had lost the use of Saint-Benigne, Dijon's cathedral
church, the previous winter, when General Cartaux took it over to
establish an artillery park. Volfius also commented on a national plan
to sell the organs in various churches, judging it an act of vandalism
and appealing to Grégoire to oppose it. Commenting specifically on
Dijon's three organs, he noted that those in Saint-Michel and Notre-
Dame were masterpieces, while Saint-Benigne's was perhaps superior
to others of its kind in France.

THE *SECONDE LETTRE ENCYCLIQUE*

Volfius's relationship with Grégoire evolved significantly from
the spring of 1795 to the summer of 1796. Initially expressing
a sense of desolation and despair in his letters, Volfius gradually
regained his self-confidence and intellectual assertiveness, offering,
by the end of the year, a critique of the United Bishop's *Seconde
lettre encyclique*.[29] The second encyclical proposed provisional

regulations for the Gallican church until a national council could be held to decide matters more formally. Most of the letter addressed issues of church discipline and hierarchy. Publicly Volfius endorsed the new letter, but privately he expressed disagreement with its historical understanding of the French Catholic Church.[30]

The United Bishops traced the history of the Gallican church from its founder, Pothin de Lyon, in the second century to the martyrs of the Terror.[31] Their choice of some clerics and omission of others troubled Volfius. For instance, with respect to recent leaders, Volfius wondered at the inclusion of Gouttes, the constitutional bishop of Autun, who had been guillotined during the Terror, and the omission of Lamourette, the constitutional bishop of Lyon. Because Gouttes was denounced by one of his vicars for holding anti-republican ideas, Volfius judged his execution as the result of a hatred of religion, not his faith. Lamourette, on the other hand, left memoirs written in prison that indicated his devotion to religion. Turning his attention to earlier figures, Volfius questioned the inclusion of Bénigne of Dijon, a simple priest in his judgment, and Martin Letellier of Reims, "the most brutal man in the kingdom." Further, he asserted that one could not place among the fathers of the church James of Soissons and Colbert of Montpellier because they did not write several of the works attributed to them.[32] Volfius disagreed with the placement of the "two Lamis," whom he described as Germans, on this list.[33] Where, he asked, were Bossuet and Fénélon? Why include Richelieu, a supporter of despotism, and Fleury, ruthlessly ambitious, among the gifts of the French church to the government? In his comments on the letter's treatment of Jansenists and Jesuits, Volfius's argued that the United Bishops portrayed the Jansenists as the penitent persecuted saints of the Gallican church and made only the feeblest of efforts to highlight Jesuit contributions, praising the work of Xavier, a Spaniard, and Kirker, a German. Volfius's offence at the virtual absence of the Jesuits from the encyclical may have arisen from his early studies to become a Jesuit priest. Volfius also offered pointed criticism of the United Bishops's praise for France's recent literary and philosophical luminaries. Rousseau's paraphrase of the psalms was not religious because that philosopher understood them to be a celebration of the nation. Samuel Clarke and Isaac Newton, Volfius wrote, were not Christians but Socinians, and although Descartes proved the existence of God, this did not equal belief in God.[34] Mably believed in natural religion, not Catholicism, and Voltaire, in contrast to the claims of the encyclical, did not respect religion but actually derided it. In conclusion, Volfius noted that the *Seconde lettre encyclique* made several slights toward Rome, hardly the path to reconciliation.

Volfius's critique of the second encyclical highlights the diversity of opinion within the constitutional clergy. As they sought to restructure the Gallican church, Grégoire and the United Bishops embraced much of the Jansenist critique of the church.[35] Revealing no inclination toward Jansenism, Volfius struggled with the issue of reconciling constitutional and refractory clergy and, by extension, Paris and Rome throughout his career as bishop.

After his report to Grégoire in July 1796, Volfius did not write the bishop again until March 1797, when he sought clarification concerning allowable dispensations for marriage.[36] Specifically, Volfius sought direction concerning couples related by marriage (brothers-in-law and sisters-in-law), lay brothers who married without seeking a dispensation, and priests who had renounced their vows. In addition, he expressed concern about the tone of comments in the *Annales* concerning the Prince Bishop of Basle, a cleric firmly allied with Rome. Volfius found the *Annales*'s treatment of the prelate too violent and sarcastic and not in keeping with the journal's professional standards.

For the period from the summer of 1796 until the fall of 1797, there is little evidence concerning the activities of Volfius and his constitutional colleagues in the Côte-d'Or. Volfius published no pastoral letters or other communications. Likewise there were few administrative actions related to religion during these months. One exception is a letter from the public prosecutor of Is-sur-Tille concerning the town's constitutional priest, Denis Chauchot, who has left a fairly rich paper trail in the archives.[37] In the winter of 1797, Chauchot found himself (again) on the wrong side of the authorities, who accused him of violating the law of 7 *vendémiaire* (29 September 1795) and imprisoned the cleric for one month. How he violated this law was not recorded. From past incidents, it is apparent that Is-sur-Tille had at least a few republicans who watched their constitutional curé with great interest.

CARION'S *JOURNAL DE LA CÔTE-D'OR* AND RELIGION

One source of information on the activities of clergy, constitutional and refractory, during the fall and winter of 1798 is the *Journal de la Côte-d'Or, par Carion,* successor to *Le Nécessaire*.

The sympathies of the *Journal* were with the constitutional clergy, whom it portrayed as harassed and ill-treated patriots. This is not surprising, given that Vivant Carion, its publisher, was briefly a constitutional priest, ordained in 1791.[38] Evidence of this patriotism included the *Te deum* that the constitutional clergy chanted in Dijon to celebrate Napoleon's victories in Italy. "Priests are very useful and respectable," the *Journal* declared, "when they stick to their place, observe the laws, and teach patriotism."[39] The *Journal* reported on the climate of hostility that Volfius faced: "Religious intolerance sharpens it daggers, designating already its victims; it is through the patriotic bishop who lives here peaceable and retired, that it wants to begin its delicious Bartholomew. Each day brings to the soul of this honest man new bitterness, and to his life new dangers."[40] In opposition to the parable of the Good Samaritan, the journal offered the tale of a pious girl who refused to aid a constitutional cleric. Initially seeing a citizen in need, she turned away from him when she saw that he was a priest who had "submitted to the law," and as she departed, she said, "Go look for another." Finally, the paper reported that the citizen Girard, formerly a constitutional cleric, was the victim of arson, and noted that he lived beside a number of refractory priests.

In July, the *Journal* published a long letter to the editor criticizing Camille Jordan, an exile only recently returned to France.[41] A native of Lyon, Jordan had fled France during the National Convention's bloody attack on the city in 1793, going first to Switzerland and then England, where he developed an admiration for the English constitution. At the end of 1796, he returned to France and ran for the Council of 500, the lower house of the legislature, the following May. Elected deputy of the department of Rhône-et-Loire, Jordan presented a report in mid-June that questioned the need for the state to regulate religion or the bells of France.[42] In the Côte-d'Or, Jordan's proposal received support from the short-lived publication *La Glaneuse*. It was an article in *La Glaneuse* on Jordan's initiative that provoked the letter writer to the *Journal*. Accusing *La Glaneuse* of presenting philosophy as seeking to destroy the "sublime and comforting idea of God," the letter writer warned that such efforts only turned the people toward fanaticism and civil war. Further, priests who took the oaths required by the state did not urge citizens to act against other priests, nor did they divide wives from their husbands or daughters from their parents.

The misdeeds of the refractory clergy continued to interest Carion and appear in the pages of the *Journal*. In mid-February, the paper reported on a "mutiny" in Autun.[43] Although the exact cause of the trouble was unknown, one report indicated that it had orginated with individuals recently catechized by a refractory priest. The mutineers insulted and threw stones at the National Guardsmen, forcing them to retreat. After several days of trouble, General Pille arrived with some gendarmes and artillery men to put down the mutiny.[44] Pille, a division general in the Midi in 1797, began his revolutionary career as an organizer of the volunteer militias in the Côte-d'Or. In Autun, he was joined by General Augereau, and the two restored calm with no loss of life.

The *Journal* also carried the gruesome account of an ex-nun's murder by her husband, a former priest.[45] Before murdering his wife by attacking her with a pitchfork in her "sexual parts," the man had declared publicly that his marriage was a sacrilege. The murder also resulted in the loss of a fetus of six months. This account came to the paper from a correspondent in the department of Puy-de-Dôme. In his introduction to the letter, the editor of the *Journal* wrote that he printed it out of a desire to alert authorities to the religious fanaticism that was growing ever stronger in the nation.

In the winter and spring of 1797, the valorous and reprehensible deeds of the clergy and former clergy were not the big stories for the *Journal de la Côte-d'Or*. They were the filler pieces. The lead stories were Napoleon's campaign in Italy and the preparations for the Directory's first elections in March and April. These national stories, especially the spring elections, form an important part of the context for the next major developments in the Directory's policies toward religion.

9

Targeting Fanaticism
and Cultivating Citizens

After eighteen months of governing, the Directory held its first elections in the spring of 1797. Almost all departments swung to the right, giving conservatives the upper hand in both houses of the legislature. France's refractory clergy and émigrés were among the beneficiaries of this shift in government. The increased support for the refractory clergy concerned leading Gallican clergy in the Côte-d'Or. In May 1797, Volfius wrote to Grégoire, urging him to remain vigilant against the refractories.[1] Volfius expressed concern about François Robert, recently re-elected deputy for the Côte-d'Or to the Council of 500. According to Volfius, Robert was a religious turncoat. Formerly a friend of the constitutional church, he now supported the refractory priests. Volfius hoped that a direct appeal from Grégoire might persuade Robert to reconsider his position.[2] He also sounded a note of caution, that the softer attitude in Paris had emboldened local refractories, and their numbers were large and growing. The bishop estimated that three-quarters of the population followed the refractories, especially in the countryside. A further issue was the material situation of the constitutional clergy. Complaining that the refractory clergy lived in comfort while the constitutional clergy struggled, Volfius reported that communes failed to pay even the meagre salaries promised by the state. In closing, Volfius declared the government's persecution of constitutional priests shortsighted because they had demonstrated their patriotism while the refractory clergy organized the people against the government.

Guy Bouillotte, curé of Arney-sur-Arroux and former deputy to the Estates-General and the National Assembly wrote to Grégoire in May 1797.[3] Boulliotte's assessment of the situation echoed Volfius's.

Praising Grégoire as a principal supporter of the French church, Bouillotte wrote that discord rocked religion in particular and asked that the legislature take action against the non-juring clergy by enforcing existing laws. In the Côte-d'Or, Bouillotte reported that refractory clergy were active both publicly and privately. Tolerance of their activities widened the schism in the church and hurt the republic. Several clergy around him refused to celebrate mass in the churches. This created trouble that threatened to turn into civil war. Further, apostolic missionaries had invaded the countryside. Like Volfius, Bouillotte appealed to Grégoire to use his position to seek a more favourable treatment for the Gallican clergy.

The conservative tide in favour of the refractory clergy crested in mid-summer with concerted efforts to revise the revolution's religious legislation. Camille Jordan's report questioning the need for any state regulation of religion was the first volley. Throughout the summer, the bicameral national legislature debated abolishing the various oaths required of the clergy. In mid-July, the pro-refractory camp won a big victory in the Council of 500, with a vote to overturn all the oaths demanded of the clergy. This victory for the refractories was short-lived. The Council of Elders (*anciens*), the legislature's upper house, approved the measure only on 24 August and, by that point, the Council of 500 partially reversed itself by passing a bill requiring clergy to declare their adherence to the constitution and the laws of the republic. A joint committee presented the final text of this new oath on 27 August (10 *fructidor* in the revolutionary calendar), just one week before the coup d'état of 18 *fructidor* (5 September 1797).

The coup d'état was similar to the legislative purge of the Girondin in 1793; this time, however, the leadership came from a divided executive, not a faction within the legislature. Further, the three directors who spearheaded the coup appealed not to the people of Paris to support them, but to the army. General Hoche, commander of the Army of Sambre and Meuse, marched his troops to Paris under the pretext of heading to Brest, while Napoleon sent Lieutenant Augereau. On the night of 17–18 *fructidor* (4–5 September), troops surrounded the legislature and took control of Paris, arresting two directors, Lazare Carnot and François Barthélémy, as well as fifty-three deputies and several other prominent conservatives in the capital. The next day, a rump Directory announced the discovery and elimination of a royalist plot. It shuttered thirty newspapers and annulled the spring elections in forty-nine departments, including those of the Côte-d'Or, unseating 177 deputies. In the end, the Directory deported fifty-three individuals and two directors to Guiana.[4]

THE OATH OF 19 *FRUCTIDOR*

The relative religious tolerance of the Directory's first years ended on 19 *fructidor l'an* 5 (6 September 1797). That day, the legislature reinstated the penalties against the deported clergy and those eligible to be deported. Refractory clergy had fifteen days to leave France or face death or deportation to Guiana. Even those clergy who had sworn the oath of 7 *vendémiaire l'an* 4 acknowledging the republic now had to swear an oath declaring their hatred of royalty and their fidelity to the constitution of 1793.[5] Refractory priests who were over seventy or infirm did not face such penalties and were subject only to surveillance.

In the Côte-d'Or, compliance with the law of 19 *fructidor* produced a long list of priests resident in the department.[6] This list, compiled by departmental authorities, does not distinguish constitutional priests who swore all the oaths required by the authorities from *soumissionaires* (or refractory priests who swore the oath of 7 *vendémiaire*). In all, 173 priests from the department took the oath of 19 *fructidor*. Volfius did so on 17 December 1797. The largest number of oath takers came from the canton of Châtillon-sur-Seine, where fifteen priests took the oath, although four of these actually worked in different cantons. Twenty-four priests who participated in the diocesan synod of the Côte-d'Or's Gallican church held in 1800 took the oath, but they were likely not the only constitutional clergy who did so.[7]

Taking the oath of 19 *fructidor* was not a simple matter. It required a priest to demonstrate that he had sworn the oath of 7 *vendémiaire* and had not retracted it. Municipal authorities verified a priest's compliance with the earlier oath; then the department issued a statement permitting the priest to take the current one. The priest's canton recorded the swearing of the oath. The entire process created at least three official letters and in some cases more, as priests collected attestations of their compliance with the earlier law.[8] The administrative effort related to the oath of 19 *fructidor* parallels that of the first oath required of clergy in 1791. Significantly, however, the oath of 19 *fructidor* did not demand an endorsement of any religious reform. It required only submission to the republic and its laws.

From 1794 to 1797, the constitutional church in the Côte-d'Or had experienced a modest and troubled redevelopment as the Gallican church. Embracing the vision of Grégoire and the United Bishops in Paris, Volfius and a handful of clergy had worked to re-establish a pro-revolutionary Catholic Church in the department. The initial enthusiasm that greeted the reopening of the cathedral in Dijon dissipated quickly, and, as the years passed, the department's constitutional clergy found themselves working at the margins of a lively and growing refractory Catholic Church that was more readily embraced by the populace. Under these circumstances, the Gallican clergy welcomed the state's renewed interest in policing religion. However, the refractory clergy remained active and were troubled only infrequently by the authorities.

Bells continued to interest the state because of their ability to call citizens together. In mid-December, Jean-Marie Sotin, minister of police for the republic, sent a letter to the departments warning of various factions active in France. The hidden fanaticism of some Catholics was of special concern. He asked administrators to be especially vigilant and pay attention to small details such as the ringing of bells. Bells, Sotin warned, reminded people of the hours of prayer. Those arguing that bells were rung to keep track of the day were disingenuous, he wrote, because agricultural labourers do not work to the rhythm of a clock like miners, blacksmiths, or manufacturers. The solution to this subterfuge was to enforce the law that permitted bells to be rung only in cases of public danger, fire, flood, or the approach of an enemy.[9] In the Côte-d'Or, administrators quickly acted on Sotin's directive, forbidding the ringing of bells except in emergencies. To ensure compliance, the department ordered that the keys and pulls for the bells be deposited with the national agent of each commune.[10] This was not the department's first effort to regulate the peeling of bells: it had issued similar regulations two years earlier.

The activities of the refractory clergy and their supporters continued to be a cause of concern for the Gallican clergy. In the early winter of 1799, Jean-Baptiste Grosdidier, the maligned Gallican cleric in Champagne-sur-Vingeanne, wrote to the department's central administration requesting aid in reversing a local order evicting him from the presbytery.[11] Enemies of the republic, as he saw it, had succeeded in obtaining an order forcing him to leave the two rooms he occupied. The village's teacher was to take the space. Grosdidier labelled this development the work of royalists and fanatics, and he charged two former nuns of the Robelet family with leading the campaign against him. Each day, he wrote, they worked to make him appear an "object of horror." As evidence of their fanaticism, he pointed to their possession of a book written by Jouffrey, a "known fanatic."[12] Besides the Robelet family, Grosdidier reported that several bourgeois in the community admired Jouffrey's book. Grosdidier's troubles are interesting because they provide evidence of the use of primary-level teachers (*instituteurs*) in the Côte-d'Or by the refractory camp. The revolutionaries paid little attention to primary education; it was only during the Terror that the *sans-culottes* supported it, arguing that educating the masses would further the aims of the revolution. Later, national educational reforms focused on developing a few elite schools.[13] This neglect left an opening for teachers sponsored by the refractories to set up schools in the countryside. These clerical schools taught basic Latin and the catechism.[14]

Grosdidier was not the only individual concerned about the activity of the refractory clergy. In March, the department's central administration wrote to François de Neufchateau, the minister of interior, seeking his advice about citizens in Dijon who were harbouring refractory clergy.[15] Neufchateau advised the Dijonnais to take action against non-juring priests who spread superstition and troubled public peace. Noting that the law provided them with sufficient authority to act, he advised them to coordinate their actions with the justices of the peace and informed them that he had sent a copy of their letter to Sotin, the minister of police.

The matter was not easily resolved. In late summer, the new minister of police, Joseph Fouché, responded to department's administrators' further reports of trouble.[16] In their correspondence, the commissioners in Dijon noted the difficulty of enforcing laws regarding refractory clergy. The people welcomed these clergy and subverted efforts to investigate their activities. Many of the department's justices of the peace refused to visit homes suspected of harbouring refractory clergy, or, if they did visit, the inhabitants were warned in advance of their coming. Fouché's response was unyielding: it was their duty to denounce individual administrators in the communes who were not carrying out their functions. Individuals harbouring refractory clergy were to be investigated and brought before the tribunals. He advised using secret agents to carry out this work. Noting that they had also contacted the minister of justice concerning the recalcitrant magistrates, Fouché asked them to consider if they were using all the means at their disposal to address the problems. He urged them to reject public functionaries who did not carry out the law, and requested that they inform him about the results of their efforts to address these problems.

Problems policing the refractory clergy continued unabated. In January 1800, Fouché responded to a letter from the superintendent of police in the Côte-d'Or concerning the failure of the department's commissioners to enforce the laws regarding non-juring clergy.[17] Fouché urged the superintendent to maintain his vigilance, noting that all laws not repealed should be executed. Only the priests who took the oath of 19 *fructidor* were eligible to exercise their functions. Non-juring clergy could not seek refuge in the department's jail (*maison de detention*), nor could they return from exile and resume their ministries.

REPUBLICAN FESTIVALS AND THEOPHILANTHROPY

The refractory clergy were not the Gallican clergy's only competitors. The state challenged the Gallican clergy's position as it established civil alternatives to Catholicism. In December 1794, the National Convention instructed the Committee of Public Instruction to organize a cycle of republican festivals.[18] In mid-February, the committee proposed a series of festivals celebrating nature, law, reproduction, genius, and force. The National Convention endorsed the idea in early May, passing a decree calling for the establishment of *les fêtes décadaire*. The decree of 7 *vendémiaire* that required clergy to swear an oath acknowledging the sovereignty of the people also made the *décadi* a day of rest.[19] The newly elected bicameral legislature of the Directory finalized seven national festivals on 25 October 1795. These celebrated the foundation of the republic, youth, marriage, gratitude, agriculture, liberty, and old age.[20] The Directory later added three festivals commemorating important dates in the revolution (the anniversary of the death of Louis XVI, 14 *juillet*, and 10 *août*).[21] Pierre Daunou, the spokesperson for the Committee of Public Instruction, expressed the hope that these festivals would make patriotism the common religion of the French.[22]

Initially this effort to establish a civil religion struggled, due to poor funding and ridicule by the press and priests. With only a few exceptions, public administrators executed their roles in these events without enthusiasm.[23] Albert Mathiez, writing at the beginning of the twentieth century, attributed the failure of the *fêtes décadaires* to a conflict between rationalists and deists. The rationalists sought to destroy Catholicism and any belief in the supernatural, whereas the deists acknowledged metaphysical questions and sought to establish *fêtes décadaires* in the spirit of year 2's Cult of the Supreme Being.[24]

The only new religion to develop a following was theophilanthropy, founded by Jean-Baptiste Chemin-Dupontès, a Parisian bookseller and adherent of the Cult of the Supreme Being. In September 1796, Chemin-Dupontès published a manual for the new religion, which professed belief in the immortality of the soul and the existence of God. Theophilanthropy was a family cult with daily rituals led by the father and was intended to be an open freemasonry. In early 1797, Chemin-Dupontès reissued his manual with the support of four other individuals, and the cult celebrated its first public service in the chapel of the Hôtel-Dieu de Sainte-Catherine in Paris. Theophilanthropy quickly gained adherents in Paris, and, by April, Chemin-Dupontès and his collaborators were holding two services a week, one on Sunday and one on the *décadi*. They established a committee of fifty-two that included eight deputies from the Council of 500 and eight members of the Council of Elders to govern the new faith.[25] The coup of 18 *fructidor* enhanced theophilanthropy's standing in Paris by allowing it to gain control of several parish churches. Theophilanthropy was much less popular in the departments. In the Côte-d'Or, the religion found the largest group of followers in the city of Beaune. The high point for theophilanthropy was 1797, although it continued to hold public celebrations until the coup d'état of 18 *brumaire* 1799. After 18 *brumaire*, Chemin-Dupontès taught theophilanthropy in a school on the Rue Saint-Étienne in Paris.[26] Adherents presented the faith as a natural religion, meeting each *décadi* in a simple temple. Their practice included the rites of baptism, in which they presented an infant toward the Father sky; first communion, which followed four months of study; marriage; and last rites.[27]

Both the Gallican and refractory clergy rejected theophilanthropy. Grégoire believed it to be the real enemy of Catholicism because it offered a moral code expunged of dogma and clerical hierarchy.

He was less hostile toward the *cultes décadaires*, but still saw them as a poor successors to the cults of reason and the Supreme Being advocated by some during the tumult of year 2 (September 1793–September 1794).[28]

LE CULTE DÉCADAIRE

In August 1798, the Directory made a concerted attempt to establish the *culte décadaire*. A driving force behind this effort was Merlin de Douai, member of the Directory's five-man Executive Council. In the spring of 1798, the directors again feared unfavourable election results. Having overturned the results of the previous year's election to unseat royalist deputies, the directors worried that Jacobins, the radical left, would become the new threat. Indeed, as anticipated, deputies with Jacobin pasts did well in the April elections. Douai, aided by two other directors, Jean-François Reubell and Louis Marie La Révellière-Lépeaux, manoeuvred to overturn the results. The law of 22 *floréal* (11 May 1798) empowered the agents of the central government in each department to work against newly elected deputies deemed too independent of established authority.[29] Despite opposition from some, including Minister of Police Sotin, Douai and his supporters successfully quelled the Jacobin challenge. Reviving the *culte décadaire* in August, Douai hoped it would serve as a sort of school for citizenship.[30] On 20 August (13 *fructidor*), the legislature passed a law requiring municipal administrations to hold each *décadi* special meetings for all citizens. Presided over by a local official, the gatherings included readings of official proclamations, the celebration of marriages, and the announcement of births, deaths, adoptions, and divorces. To ensure an audience, the law required schoolteachers to bring their students, and, to attract the general public, it instructed city councils to organize gymnastic exercises and games for the day.[31] The *culte décadaire* of 1798–9 had a short, ambitious life. François de Neufchateau, minister of the interior, was in charge of the new religion as part of his oversight of public education. He established a liturgy for the weekly ceremonies and special programs for the national festivals. He also initiated a project to create a five-volume *Manuel républicain* that could be used in the schools. It was to include a catechism on the Constitution, a new history of France by the abbé Mably, a treatise on pratical medicine, and a two-volume universal morality. Along with the *Manuel*, he hoped to produce a *Recueil des belles actions* chronicling events and prominent individuals since the revolution.[32] In the end, the Directory did not complete either project. Nevertheless, both indicate the aspirations of the proponents of the *culte décadaire*.

In the Côte-d'Or, the civil authorities did work to establish the *culte décadaire* in 1799 by publishing posters announcing the new faith and explaining its practice.[33] The cult's protocol was a mix of military parade and Catholic mass. The National Guard played a central role, opening the doors of the national house (*maison nationale*), supervising the entrance, accompanying the official procession, and maintaining order. The services included patriotic hymns, the reading of a *décadaire* bulletin, remarks from the administration, and the announcement of marriages. Each celebration concluded with the hymn, *Amour sacré de la patrie*. The posters advised citizens to conduct themselves with due solemnity. In the Côte-d'Or, the towns of Dijon, Beaune, Châtillon-sur-Seine, Is-sur-Tille, and Semur-en-Auxois established temples for the *culte décadaire* in 1799.[34]

There is evidence that the department's constitutional clergy resisted the new symbols and cults of the revolution. In the spring of 1799, municipal authorities reprimanded Denis Chauchot, constitutional curé of Is-sur-Tille, for using a tapestry to cover the statue of Liberty in the *hôtel de la patrie*. The authorities ordered Chauchot to uncover the statue or face denunciation before the central administration. It seems that Chauchot complied with the order, as there is no record of further proceedings against him.[35] Three years later, Balanche, previously constitutional curé of Arnay-sur-Arroux, wrote to Grégoire, by then a member of the *sénat conservateur*, to ask his assistance in getting a statue of Liberty removed from the alter of the village's only church, as the statue, recently placed in the church, was offensive to some parishioners. Balanche asked Grégoire to request that the commune remove the statue and work to restore Catholicism to the nation's churches.[36]

WAITING FOR POPE PIUS VI

The biggest development for Volfius in 1799 was the expected arrival of Pope Pius VI in France. In February 1798, General Berthier entered Rome and declared it a republic, forcing the pope to flee to Tuscany, where he established a papal government in exile. When

Austria organized a second coalition against France, the French
arrested the pope. In March 1799, the pope began a slow progres-
sion from Tuscany toward Paris.

In the Côte-d'Or, news of the pope's journey preceded him. At
the beginning of June, Volfius wrote to Éléonore-Marie Desbois de
Rochefort, the bishop of Amiens and one of the United Bishops, concerning newspaper reports that the pope and General Karl Mack,
the former German commander of the Neapolitan forces, were to
travel through Dijon.[37] General Mack had arrived, Volfius noted,
but the pope had not. Volfius wrote that the expected papal visit
greatly pleased the refractory, royalist clergy in Dijon. In Briançon,
near France's southeastern border, bishops in the pope's retinue met
with Gallican priests and were surprised to learn that the revolutionary church had held a national council in Paris and had sent several
letters to the pontiff. Putting himself at the service of Desbois, and
implicitly the larger Gallican church, Volfius awaited the pope.

By the end of July, Pius had yet to arrive. Having suffered a seizure
that left him largely unable to use his legs, he had, by mid-July, made
it only as far as Valence in southeastern France.[38] Volfius learned
through his brother, Alexandre-Eugène, the central commissioner,
that the pontiff was nonetheless expected soon.[39] The central commissioner received a letter instructing him on the protocol for the
pope's passage through the city. He was a hostage, not a prisoner,
and all consideration was to be given to his age and infirmities. No
suspect person, including Gallican clergy, were to speak with him.
Volfius reported to Desbois that local Jacobins were preparing to
meet and had already written several ardent motions about the
pope's anticipated visit; he feared trouble from that quarter. Despite
the prohibition on Gallican clergy meeting with the pope, Volfius,
with the aid of his brother, was seeking permission to do so.

In mid-August, Volfius again wrote to Desbois seeking advice
about whom he should include in the delegation that would meet
with the pontiff.[40] He suggested the metropolitan bishop of Jura
and one of the bishops in Paris. Commenting on a recent attack on
the pope in the *Annales de la religion*, Volfius wrote that it might
encourage some French Catholics to be cautious about the pope,
but it was unlikely to be read by Pius VI or his court. He also noted
that he had compiled a number of decrees and other works to share
with the pope, but many attacked the court of Rome and were not
likely to help reconcile the Gallican and Roman churches. Volfius

asked Desbois to send any material he wanted presented to the pope as well as instruction concerning how he should proceed should the pope, who was in very poor health, die in Dijon. In closing, Volfius noted that he had less access to departmental and municipal administrators because his brother was no longer central commissioner. In the end, Volfius's preparations were not needed. The pope died in Valence on 28 August, a week after Volfius's final correspondence with Desbois.

Volfius's enthusiastic anticipation of Pope Pius VI's visit to Dijon was in keeping with his desire to see the refractory and Gallican clergy reconciled. Despite his position as a Gallican bishop, Volfius did not rule out the possibility that he might meet with the pope. His views on the division with Rome were quite moderate. For Volfius, reconciling with Rome did not mean surrendering the Gallican church's vision or its role in revolutionary France. Rather, it meant working from the broad ground of agreement in doctrine and practice that existed between the two camps to find a solution to the schism. In 1799, Volfius did not repent the commitments he had made in 1791, when he swore an oath of allegiance to the Civil Constitution of the Clergy, but his years of political and ecclesiastical experience convinced him that the Catholic Church in France would be better served by being united than by remaining divided.

Reviving Conciliarism in the Gallican Church: National Councils and the Synod of the Côte-d'Or

The constitutional church had its origins in legislative initiatives, first the Civil Constitution of the Clergy and then the ecclesiastical oath of 1791. The Gallican church, by contrast, had its beginnings in the efforts of the United Bishops. As each church came into being, there were calls for a national church council. In May 1790, as the Constituent Assembly opened its debate on the Civil Constitution of the Clergy, Jean de Dieu-Raymond de Boisgelin, the archbishop of Aix, called for a national church council to discuss the proposed reforms. Dismissed as a tactic to stall or derail the legislation, the assembly refused Boisgelin's proposal. Following the Terror, the United Bishops returned to the idea of a national church council and received support for the endeavour from bishops and clergy who rallied to the Gallican church. The urgency for a national council was greater than in the past: with the Gallican church no longer attached to the state and still rejected by Rome, the national council provided the Gallican bishops with a link to the conciliar tradition that, through much of Christian history, rivalled the papacy in its claim to authority. Despite the interest in a national council, the United Bishops did not organize one until 1797. Still, the Gallican church held two national church councils in its short six-year lifespan, the first such councils since the Middle Ages.

The national councils of the Gallican church had important eighteenth-century precedents.[1] The provincial council of Utrecht held in 1763 and the Synod of Pistoia held in 1786 were two recent models for the United Bishops. A common link among these initiatives was a Jansenist theology that supported conciliarism. The Gallican church's two national councils made several proposals that aligned the church with the republican revolutionary trajectory of France. These included election of clergy by parishioners, a purge of baroque forms of piety, and a recognition of national liturgical styles, including the use of the vernacular in worship. In addition, the two councils and the United Bishops's second episcopal letter envisioned a series of consultative assemblies from the diocesan synod to the national council.

On 15 August 1797, the first national council of the Gallican church held its opening ceremony in the cathedral of Notre-Dame in Paris. The abbé François de Torcy, attending on behalf of the bishop of Reims, reported that, although sufficiently majestic and solemn, the service avoided ostentatious display and attracted a modestly dressed and serious crowd of men and women. For de Torcy, this solemn gathering signalled the church's return to Christianity's first era.[2] Meeting from August to November, 107 participants (31 bishops, 70 priests, and 6 theologians) deliberated in the Hôtel de Pons in the faubourg Saint-Germain. Volfius did not attend the national council, but sent a representative, the *procureur* E.-C. Desvignes. The abbé J.-B.-L. Mignard of the diocese of the Côte-d'Or also attended as a clergy delegate.[3] Each day, the council published it debates and proceedings in the *Journal du concile nationale de France*. For its part, the Directory was largely indifferent to the proceedings; however, the council had a wider audience among European Catholics. Italian, German, and English correspondents attended its meetings. In the end, the council issued several decisions concerning dogma and discipline, some of which conflicted with revolutionary legislation. For example, the council ruled marriage a sacred and indissoluble union between two Catholics and rejected the state's legal acceptance of divorce. The council also conflicted with the state when it declared that a priest should wear a cassock to celebrate mass, despite laws prohibiting clerical attire in public. The council stressed civic duties such as paying taxes and established an episcopal hierarchy for the French colonies. It also approved a decree of pacification establishing conditions for reunion with the refractory clergy, although the refractory clergy and Rome rejected this vision for reuniting the French church. At the council's conclusion, a number of issues remained unresolved, so the delegates proposed a second council to follow diocesan synods. Among the issues deferred were the church's positions on civil divorce and clerical marriages, as well as the suppression of confession and other practices some viewed as incompatible with the republic.[4]

THE DIOCESAN SYNOD OF THE CÔTE-D'OR

In their second episcopal letter (1795), the United Bishops called upon the church to renew the tradition of diocesan synods, a practice that had fallen out of favour, they wrote, due to the despotism of the seventeenth and eighteenth centuries.[5] This call resulted in twenty-five dioceses convening assemblies before the meeting of the first national church council. Following that council, an even greater number of dioceses, forty-five, held synods. In addition, six metropolitan councils met, including Besançon, the metropole of the east.[6] The diocese of Dijon held its diocesan synod in 1800 as part of the Gallican church's preparations for the second national council.[7] In his introduction to the *Actes du synode diocésain,* Volfius noted the diocese's delay in holding a synod and attributed it to several factors, including anarchy and disorganization. Once convened, the diocese benefited, Volfius wrote, from the models provided by the other dioceses as well as the example of the national council.[8] At the synod's end, the diocese published its resolutions. Among the concerns addressed were abuses in discipline, disorganization in the diocese, and the Gallican clergy's position with respect to the state and the refractory clergy.[9]

In its *Actes,* the synod of the Côte-d'Or insisted on the orthodoxy of the Gallican church and its clergy.[10] The heretics were the refractory clergy who re-administered the sacraments and taught that the faith and virtue of the priest determined their validity. The synod also acknowledged its adherence to the church's historical practice of submitting to state authority as long as doing so did not contradict the faith or discipline of the church, natural morals, or reason. Finally, the synod condemned all revolts that claimed religion as their principal justification. Despite nearly ten years of existence, the Gallican/constitutional church of the Côte-d'Or remained concerned about challenges to its legitimacy and its relationship to the state. Besides these overarching concerns, the synod addressed matters of liturgical practice and clerical discipline.

Among the concerns of the Côte-d'Or's Gallican clergy were procedures for administering the sacraments and clerical discipline.[11] The sacrament of marriage received the most attention. The delegates stressed the importance of submitting to the state's authority and recognizing the validity of civil marriages. Procedurally, the church's blessing followed the civil contract. A second concern was baptism.

The synod urged parish priests to take an active role in encouraging parents to present their children for baptism. The discussion of clerical discipline focused on proper decorum.[12] Even though the state prohibited priests from wearing ecclesiastical garb daily, they were to cut their hair round and without a tail, and to dress in a modest and serious style. The synod forbade priests from frequenting cabarets and places of public amusement, especially in their parish, or attending balls and spectacles. It also prohibited them from hunting. The acts placed the greatest emphasis on the authority of the Gallican bishop, declaring as outlaws all priests working in the diocese without Volfius's official sanction.

In its discussion of the liturgy, the synod ruled that there should be only one mass in each parish on Sundays, with the exception of Christmas.[13] This standard, if successfully applied, would force the refractory and constitutional clergy to work together, because it did not allow for separate services. The synod also declared indirectly that the diocese's parishes should follow the church calendar and not the republican one. It did this by outlining movable and immovable festivals. Most festivals were ruled immovable, meaning they had to occur on the date traditionally assigned by the Christian calendar. The movable festivals were dependent on the date of Easter. Regardless of their designation, the synod rejected placing either the movable or the immovable festivals arbitrarily on a *décadi*. Gallican bishops and diocesan synods across France faced the issue of whether mass could be said on the *décadi* instead of Sunday. The *décadi* hosted the services of the official *culte décadaire*. A few Gallican bishops responded to state pressure to participate in the official cult by combining the mass with the services of the *culte décadaire*. More took positions similar to that of the Côte-d'Or Gallican clergy, maintaining a distinction between Catholic services and the new state cult. In the *Annales de la religion,* Jean-Pierre Saurine, Gallican bishop of the department of Landes and a member of the United Bishops, published a protest of the state's effort to force Catholics to move their services to the *décadi*.[14]

The first national council of the Gallican church called on diocesan synods to re-establish *archiprêtrés*. The Civil Constitution of the Clergy had suppressed *archiprêtrés* in its effort to streamline the church offices. The first national council concluded that the large dioceses without subdivisions created by the Civil Constitution of the Clergy presented a hardship for rural populations. By

re-establishing *archiprêtres*, the council hoped to increase the influence of bishops in their dioceses and to provide local leadership
for clergy.[15] The diocesan synod in the Côte-d'Or noted that, in
this action, they were responding to the directive of the national
council.[16] The diocesan synod divided the Côte-d'Or into twenty-
eight districts and placed an *archiprêtre* over each. Each of the
twenty-eight *archiprêtres* was to conduct annual announced visits
to the churches in his area. In addition, he was to regularly sur-
vey the morals, discipline, and ministry of each priest under his
jurisdiction and to hold rural synods and monthly ecclesiastical
conferences. The monthly meetings were to focus on morals and
discipline and any difficulties experienced. The neatly organized
archiprêtres were more symbolic than practical in the Côte-d'Or
in 1800. The diocesan synod had only twenty-eight clergy in attendance, and the opening paragraphs of the *Actes du synod diocésain*
described them as "all the clergy of the Diocese of Dijon."[17]

The Gallican clergy in the Côte-d'Or attending the 1800 synod
shared Volfius's commitment to reunion with the refractory camp.[18]
Declaring the schism to be the biggest challenge facing the French
church, the Côte-d'Or's Gallican clergy asserted that no issues of
faith or discipline were at stake in this division. Counselling each side
to submit to the other, they directed women, artisans, and labourers
to be silent about religious matters. These groups, the priests of the
synod declared, had never had a voice in religious matters. Final
judgment on the schism could come only from the church leadership.

In the final section of its report, the synod discussed the duties
of citizens to provide for their pastor's subsistence and outlined a
system to elect lay administrators in each parish.[19] It then concluded
with a list of acclamations for the unity of the church, including for
Pope Pius VII (only recently ascended to the Holy See), their dissident brothers, the persecutors of religion, the martyred, the synod,
the national council, the Gallican Church, and the citizens of the
diocese.[20] The state is absent in these acclamations, but prayers for
it were offered in Latin in a two-page attachment following the list
of synod participants.[21]

Volfius sent a copy of the *Actes du synod diocésain* to the departmental administration. In his letter introducing the document, he
stressed that the department's Gallican clergy remained faithful and
committed republicans. "I have the honour," he wrote, "of sending
a copy of the acts of our synod. I hope that you will recognize here

that which has always been in the heart of the constitutional priests of the department of the Côte-d'Or – love of the republic, submission to the government and to the law, and a spirit of conciliation and of peace."[22]

THE SECOND NATIONAL COUNCIL OF THE GALLICAN CHURCH AND THE CONCORDAT OF 1801

At the conclusion of the first national council in 1797, the assembly set up a permanent committee composed of three bishops and a secretary to lead the church until the next national council. Henri Grégoire and other United Bishops that remained in Paris led this group. In 1800, the permanent committee proposed a second national council to open on the Feast of the Ascension in 1801.[23] As it happened, the council did not convene until a few weeks later, holding its opening session on 29 June. The diocesan synod in the Côte-d'Or occurred a full year before the second national council of the Gallican church. Volfius did not attend the second national council but sent his former vicar, Jean-Baptiste Grosdidier, to represent the diocese.[24]

Napoleon's negotiations with Rome entirely overshadowed the second national council. Following the election of Pius VII in March 1800, Napoleon decided that the time was right to seek an end to the schism in the French Catholic Church, and, by late November, he succeeded in opening negotiations. For Napoleon, the national council of the Gallican Church provided not so much an alternative path for resolving the schism as a strategy in the ongoing negotiations. The second national council met with the consent of the state. Aware of regime's negotiations with the papacy, the leadership of the council sought to present the Gallican church as the more acceptable partner, issuing as their first decree a statement on submission to spiritual and civil authorities. However, talks between the state and the papacy were already at an advanced stage. Two weeks after the national council's opening session, the papal and French negotiators reached an agreement, on 15 July, and the Gallican bishops and clergy meeting at Notre-Dame were faced with defeat. When called upon by Napoleon to close their assembly in mid-August, they had yet to resolve the essential question of how the Gallican bishops might resign, and they had given little thought to the position of the former constitutional clergy in the reunited church.[25]

In the Concordat of 1801, the French government recognized Roman Catholicism as the religion of the majority of the French. It guaranteed freedom of public worship for Catholics as long as they conformed to the laws of the republic. The agreement acknowledged that the state would established new diocesan and parish boundaries and anticipated the establishment of a new episcopacy named by Napoleon and sanctioned by the pope. Ultimately, through the Organic Articles, Napoleon established 60 dioceses (including ten archdioceses), down from 83 under the Civil Constitution of the Clergy and the 135 under the old regime. Each diocese would have a cathedral chapter and a seminary. The state returned to the French Catholic Church all properties not sold, and it guaranteed the income of pastors and bishops, allowing Catholics to establish endowments, but only with government bonds.[26] To establish the episcopacy of the reunited church, Napoleon pressed the pope to require all bishops to resign. This the pontiff did on 15 August with the brief *Tam multa*.

Pius VII did not consider the Gallican bishops legitimate, so he did not consider that *Tam multa* would apply to them. With respect to those bishops, the papal secretary of state and lead negotiator with France, Cardinal Consalvi, sought instructions about the manner of their reconciliation with Rome when he returned to the Vatican. He suspected that Napoleon might name some of these individuals to the new concordataire episcopacy. With regulations fashioned by his cardinal, Pius VII sent the brief *Post multos labores* to Mgr. Giuseppe Maria Spina in Paris. Spina, archbishop of Corinth, was a lead papal negotiator. Although Spina received *Post multos labores* at the end of July, he did not informed either Napoleon or the second national council of the brief, which required the former constitutional clergy to submit a statement of obedience and submission to the Holy See.[27] It also included instructions to Spina to obtain from the Gallican/constitutional bishops an affirmation of Pius VI's rejection of the Civil Constitution of the Clergy and other ecclesiastical legislation as well as a formal retraction of their oath to uphold that constitution. In essence, the brief required the Gallican bishops to reject unequivocally their revolutionary careers.[28] The work of reconciling the constitutional bishops and clergy with Rome ultimately fell to Cardinal Caprara, who arrived as papal legate in October.

As the Gallican bishops closed their second national council in mid-August, they considered the problem of their position in light of the new Concordat. Not knowing the full details of the agreement, three questions animated their final debates: Must sitting Gallican bishops resign? What should be the manner of this resignation? Into whose hands should they submit their resignations? The bishops determined that a mass resignation would be justified only if the papacy and the French government were to suppress all the dioceses of France in concert and establish a new Gallican church. This church would not have previously existed, and so a bishop could legitimately resign from a diocese of the suppressed church. As to the manner of the resignation, the bishops concluded that it must be spontaneous, and not ordered by either the papacy or the government. Finally, because the metropolitan bishops had installed them, they concluded that they should submit their resignations to them. Pressed by the government to close their national council on 16 August, the bishops debated whether to resign immediately or to continue in their dioceses. In the end, with much unknown about the agreement and varied opinions on the floor, they settled the question by taking no action.[29]

At the end of September, Napoleon's minister of religion, Jean-Étienne Portalis, learned of *Post multos labores* and the requirements it place on the former constitutional bishops to declare their submission and obedience to Rome.[30] The Gallican bishops did not learn of the brief until mid-October, after many had resigned their positions. For the former constitutional bishops as well as Napoleon's administration, the requirements of *Post multos labores* went beyond the letter and the spirit of the Concordat. Portalis attempted to find a middle ground between the pope's demands and the former constitutional bishops' refusal to repent their revolutionary oaths by publishing a model letter of submission in *Le Moniteur*. However, this template pleased no one. France's former constitutional bishops were loath to go beyond an affirmation of their adherence to the Concordat, a position supported by Napoleon.[31] At the end of October, the United Bishops wrote to Napoleon and declared that the former constitutional bishops presented their "resignation pure and simple, but voluntarily, freely and spontaneously, of their episcopal seats." The former bishops then published this letter in the *Annales de la religion*.[32] In the end, all fifty-nine of the bishops of the Gallican church resigned, but only fifty-eight of the ninety-four surviving refractory bishops did so.[33] Some of the refractory bishops who refused to recognize the new Concordat established a schismatic French Catholic Church known as the *Petite Église*.

Napoleon did not promulgate the Concordat until April 1802, and, when he did so, he unilaterally appended to it the Organic Articles. These articles established the state's authority over the French church and defined the limits of Rome's prerogatives. The first article prohibited the publication of any papal bull, brief, or instruction in France without the government's permission. The second forbade any papal nuncio, legate, or apostolic vicar from exercising authority in the French church without the government's approval. The Organic Articles made clear that the French church, though reunited with Rome, would remain clearly subordinate to the French state. This subordination included domestic initiatives. Article 4 required state approval for any national council, metropolitan synod, or diocesan synod – in fact, for any deliberative assembly within the church. As Dale Van Kley has noted, the Concordat and Organic Articles dealt the coup de grâce to the conciliar reform efforts within eighteenth-century Catholicism.[34] Many of the document's seventy-seven articles regulated the appointment, functioning, and compensation of bishops and priests. They also required faculty at diocesan seminaries to affirm their adherence to the Gallican Liberties of 1682, and established one catechism and one liturgy for France. Although the articles were drafted in October by Portalis and the abbé Bernier, one of Napoleon's negotiators of the Concordat, the papal legate Cardinal Caprara reacted with surprise at their attachment to the Concordat.[35]

The promulgation of the Concordat reopened the issue of the former constitutional clergy's role in the new church. On 9 and 11 April, Napoleon named ten former constitutional or Gallican bishops to the new church's episcopacy. Later he added two more. The revolutionary credentials of these former bishops were strong. Five had served in revolutionary assemblies –, Bécherel, Charrier de La Roche, Saurine in the Constituent, and Le Coz and Lacombe in the Legislative. Seven had been imprisoned during the Terror. Although Grégoire's name appeared on an early list, Napoleon, in the end, judged him as too symbolic of the constitutional church. Napoleon's choices did favour those who had worked with Grégoire to re-establish the revolutionary church after the Terror. Six of the nominated attended the national council of 1797 and seven that of 1801.[36] For Caprara, the nomination of the former constitutional/ Gallican bishops renewed the campaign for their submission to Rome in line with the instructions attached to the bull *Post multos labores*. Beginning in mid-March, when Napoleon announced the first names of the former constitutionals he intended to nominate, Caprara worked to secure their retractions. In the face of significant intransigence on the part of several of the former bishops with respect to revoking their revolutionary oaths and pledging submission to Rome, the abbé Bernier proposed a solution: the papal legate might provisionally install these bishops until the pope rendered a definitive judgment. Caprara rejected this innovation in canon law. After two months of negotiations, Napoleon supported the former revolutionary clergy by decreeing that, by accepting the Concordat, they rejected their earlier commitments. This left the twelve former constitutional bishops in an irregular position, holding their appointment as bishop but not their canonical institution because Rome retained the bulls of institution. It was only in 1804, when Napoleon sought Pius VII's participation in his coronation, that the former constitutional bishops's incomplete installation was resolved. Pius refused to admit any unreconciled bishop to the cathedral for the coronation. After much negotiation and with the addition of amendments to the propose formula, all of the former constitutionals were reconciled to the satisfaction of Rome.[37]

The issue of the retractions also haunted the former constitutional clergy. In May and June 1802, as new concordataire bishops assumed their posts, some demanded retractions from the former constitutional priests in their dioceses. The papal legate, Cardinal Caprara, attempted to standardize these statements, supporting the use of Bernier's formula: "I abandon the benefice that I have occupied without canonical institution. I submit entirely to the judgments of the Holy See on the ecclesiastical affairs of France and I profess a true and sincere obedience to the Sovereign Pontiff and to my legitimate bishop."[38]

But the former constitutional clergy refused the demand that they deny their revolutionary careers. Jean-Antoine Maudru, formerly constitutional bishop of the Vosges, organized a party of 200 former constitutionals in the Meurthe and the Vosges, and wrote an open letter rejecting the proposed declaration. Napoleon declined to support any requirement of the constitutional priests beyond their acceptance of the Concordat of 1801 and their statement of communion with their new bishop.[39] The papacy's unfulfilled demand for retractions was a sleeping dog not left to lie, resurfacing not only in 1804 with Pius VII's journey to Paris for Napoleon's coronation but also in 1815 after the Bourbon restoration.[40]

Napoleon did not select Volfius to be a bishop in the newly reorganized French Catholic Church. In a letter to Pius VII in October, Volfius pledged his support for the Côte-d'Or's new bishop, Henri Reymond, formerly constitutional bishop of Isère.[41] Reymond named Volfius canon of Dijon and allowed him to retire to engage in literary pursuits.

As the Gallican bishops and clergy gathered for their second national council, they did not expect the sudden end of their church, despite their genuine interest in reconciling with Rome. Although Napoleon allowed the Gallican clergy to convene, he used the second national council to strengthen his negotiators engaged with the pope's envoys.[42] As he well knew, he had nothing to fear from, and everything to gain by, presenting the French people with a united Catholic Church endorsed by Rome. Further, Napoleon's concern was not just France, but also Catholic territories in Belgium, along the Rhine, and in Italy that were now subject to or allied with the French.[43] It was practical politics to endorse a faith already embraced by so many subjects of the growing French Empire. Despite the sudden reversal of their fortunes, the Gallican clergy cooperated with the Concordat of 1801. Few parishioners had embraced their vision of a national French Catholic Church supportive of the republic and co-equal with Rome. Further, no longer did clergy and public officials declare an enthusiasm for a purified, primitive Christianity that would support the revolution. Revolutionary France had changed. With a territory expanded by war, France did not need a new vision of Catholicism, but rather a unified church carefully subordinated to the state. Despite this, Napoleon refused to abandon completely the former constitutional clergy. Although enjoying a minority presence in the new Concordataire church, they remained within it as both bishops and priests.

Conclusion

Throughout his revolutionary career, first as chaplain to the National Guard units of the Côte-d'Or and later as constitutional bishop, Jean-Baptiste Volfius was a committed and thoughtful patriot as well as a priest who took his religious vocation seriously. Without the revolution, Volfius, son of a *procureur* at the *parlement* of Dijon, could scarcely have dreamed of becoming a bishop. Non-noble bishops, long a minority in the French episcopacy, became even more uncommon in the eighteenth century with nine such individuals elevated to a see from 1700 to 1749, and only an additional two from 1749 to 1790, the eve of the ecclesiastical oath.[1] Yet, Volfius's decision to build the constitutional church in the Côte-d'Or with meagre resources and in the face of ongoing opposition belies the assessment of opportunism. As constitutional and then Gallican bishop of the Côte-d'Or, Volfius was a principled advocate of the revolution and of a church that would support it.

Other constitutional clergy in the Côte-d'Or shared Volfius's commitment to the revolution and the constitutional church. Their position as priests and patriots eventually placed them at odds with a revolution that cut its ties to Catholicism, becoming ever less tolerant of even the constitutional church. Navigating the revolution as a priest, even one allied with the new order, demanded careful attention to the debates in Paris and in local centres of political power such as Dijon, Is-sur-Tille, Beaune, and Arnay-le-Duc. The effort of the revolutionaries to reform and regulate religion was both national and local. It involved the public administration of oaths and enforcement of laws relating to varied aspects of religious life. In very short order, to be a constitutional priest was to be a patriot under siege by other patriots. Whatever initial advantages juring priests enjoyed or anticipated, the state's ambivalent commitment to the Civil Constitution of the Clergy quickly undermined their position in the communities they served.

The presence and activity of refractory priests in the rural communities in the Côte-d'Or created yet another challenge for the constitutional clergy. Openly endorsed by Rome, these non-juring clergy also enjoyed the support of rural authorities. Their activities and those of the apostolic vicars sent by bishops living in exile troubled the constitutional clergy of the Côte-d'Or throughout the ten-year existence of the constitutional church.

The history of the constitutional clergy and church in the Côte-d'Or demonstrates a failure of will among the successors of the Constituent Assembly. The promise of a rationalized Catholicism that provided the people – the new sovereigns of the nation – a greater role in choosing church leadership was not realized. It was not just a question of electing one's bishop or priest. Initially, the revolution held out the promise of demystifying the faith. The *société populaire* in Besançon displaying the shroud of the cathedral challenged the former Catholic hierarchy and the monarchical state that had aligned with it. In Dijon, the city provided a similar opportunity to examine relics when it took over the abbey of Saint-Bénigne.[2]

After the Terror, as representatives of the Gallican church, France's constitutional clergy were significantly diminished in numbers and struggled to build a national Catholic Church independent of the state and of Rome. The United Bishops' turned to the church's conciliar heritage as they attempted to revive the vision of the Civil Constitution of the Clergy in a new political reality. It was only by achieving agreement with Rome that Napoleon ended the schism in the French Catholic Church. Despite the rejection of the Civil Constitution, the Concordat of 1801 left other religious legislation in place. It accepted the state's authority to seize and sell church properties, thus recognizing a decade of state-organized plunder of the French Catholic Church. In addition, with the Organic Articles, Napoleon reasserted his right, held by the French monarchy since the sixteenth century, to name the bishops of France.

To be a priest and a patriot in the first decade of revolutionary France presented both opportunities and challenges. Within two years, the constitutional clergy moved from the vanguard of the revolution to its storehouse of failed ideas. It is tempting to write off the constitutional clergy and their church as a lost cause. However, history belies this judgment. The church of the Concordat and Organic Articles retained many of the reforms instituted by the Civil Constitution of the Clergy. Diocesan boundaries continued to adhere to departments, even if some departments were combined to form single dioceses. Further, the church's episcopacy and clergy remained subordinate to the state. The state set and paid ecclesiastical salaries and enforced long-desired reforms such as the requirement of residence within one's diocese. Yet some revolutionary reforms were lost as the constitutional/Gallican church experiment came to a close. The election of bishops and parish priests, modelled on the civil elections of deputies to the revolutionary assemblies, did not survive the reunion with Rome. Likewise, the bishop's council did not retain its role in diocesan governance, nor did the progressive levels of consultative governance remain.

The history of the constitutional clergy in the Côte-d'Or demonstrates the resourcefulness and persistence of these provincial revolutionaries. Throughout the existence of the constitutional church, its clergy lived in open struggle with their ecclesiastical opponents. This history reveals that the dynamic between revolution and counter-revolution was active for ten years across France. For Volfius and the constitutional clergy of the Côte-d'Or, the differences between those who were with them and those who opposed them never seemed insurmountable. Underlying their project was an optimism about the rightness of the revolution's reform of the church. Liberty and equality were for all, and, viewed from the revolutionary commitments of Volfius and his constitutional colleagues, the fact that the church would change in this new age appeared not only desirable but inevitable. With the luxury of hindsight, some might find it easy to accept the judgments of opportunism or moral frailty offered by opponents in their lifetime and the century that followed. Walking with them through their story, however, it is less easy to dismiss their revolutionary convictions about the possibilities for the church in the new order of liberty, equality, and fraternity.

Epilogue

In February 1816, after fifteen years of retirement, Volfius published a curious declaration of faith in the *Journal de la Côte-d'Or*.[1] He explained that his statement came following conversations with an enlightened ecclesiastic who judged his 1801 pledge to adhere to the Concordat insufficient and recommended a further retraction of his revolutionary career. Before his fellow canons of the cathedral, the priests of Dijon, and other clergy of the diocese, Volfius declared, "I remain inviolably attached to the four articles of the assembly of the clergy of 19 March 1682, and to the consequences which resulted from them. Alexander VIII condemned them in a bull, but the bishops, the clergy and the nation preserved them as being the rampart of the liberties of the Gallican church."[2] With this declaration, the former constitutional bishop and champion of the revolution, gave no ground. Despite its militant tone, the fact that Volfius made a public statement in 1816 was celebrated by the conservative journal *L'ami de la religion et du roi*, which interpreted Volfius's declaration as an admission of error.[3]

Jean Collin, the vicar general of the diocese of Dijon, was the enlightened ecclesiastic who prevailed upon the retired eighty-one-year-old to right himself with Rome.[4] In a letter following the declaration, Collin reported his confidence in Volfius's sincerity.[5] Not all of the former bishop's critics shared the vicar's enthusiasm. An unsigned letter published in the *L'ami de la religion et du roi* in late April 1816 judged the retraction "a little vague, incomplete and insufficient." Although a good *littérateur,* the writer concluded, Volfius was a poor theologian. He admitted his error in accepting a seat that was not vacant and in swearing the various oaths of the revolution, yet he had taken no action to correct either failing. For the letter writer, Volfius had apologized for his actions, but had not repented. To complete his public retraction, he needed to make reparations to the Holy See.[6]

Apparently, the pressure on Volfius was considerable because he made a second retraction. Two versions of this retraction exist. The first, dated 25 April, is of questionable authenticity because it is not written in Volfius's hand or accompanied by his signature, although it is signed with his name. It could be a copy of an authentic document but was not marked as such (other copied documents from the era were identified as a copy and signed and dated by the scribe who created them). The author of this letter, allegedly Volfius, wrote to Pius VII that he wished "to throw himself at the feet of your Holiness." He confessed as error his entire career as constitutional bishop and his actions during the Terror. His greatest expressions of regret related to the surrender of his letters of ordination.[7] This retraction is most likely the statement celebrated by L'ami de la religion in July 1816, when it reported that, prevailed upon by the grands vicaires of Dijon, Volfius made a second humble retraction read in the cathedral of Dijon on 25 April 1816.[8]

A second letter, dated 25 May, presents a statement more in keeping with Volfius's earlier published sentiments. It is also in Volfius's handwriting and contains his usual signature, witnessed by several individuals.[9] In this letter, he expressed his submission to the Holy See and recognized as errors his acceptance of the position of constitutional bishop and his actions that promoted the schism in the church. This letter lacks the desolate tone of the 25 April statement, which contained declarations such as "O douleur inconsolable! O eternal reproche de ma conscience!"[10] Pius VII accepted Volfius's retraction. In a letter dated May 1816, Michael Cardinal de Perro, the grand penitentiary in Rome, wrote, "M.J.B. Volfius, Priest, earlier Constitutional Bishop of the Côte-d'Or, is reconciled with the Church ... [and] is in communion with Our Holy Father the Pope."[11] A cathedral service dedicated to the "reintegration of Sr. Volfius, former constitutional bishop," announced the public retraction and its acceptance by Rome. The celebrated sinner declined to attend, begging off due to his age and infirmity. Doubtless, he would have sat uneasily through an address that characterized his revolutionary convictions and career as a "sudden abandonment of the fundamental principals of social order and of his religion."[12]

Collin's energetic pursuit of Volfius's public retraction was possible in 1816 because the bishop of Dijon, Henri Reymond, was in Paris, retained there by Louis XVIII.[13] Reymond was no fan of the returned Bourbons and refused to say a *Te Deum* in 1814 when Louis XVIII took power. He further revealed his political allegiance with his celebration of Napoleon Bonaparte's return to power during the spring of 1815. In a pastoral letter, he judged the emperor's return an act of providence. On 1 June, he participated in the ceremony on the *champ de Mai* and signed an act in support of Napoleon. When Louis XVIII returned to power after Napoleon's second defeat, he ordered Reymond to Paris and detained him for a year. It was during Reymond's absence that Collin and the other vicars of Dijon pursued their campaign to gain a sufficiently repentant public retraction from Volfius. In 1817, Reymond returned to his diocese and remained there until his death on 20 February 1820.

Jean-Baptiste Dubois, a doctor of the Sorbonne who refused to take the ecclesiastical oath in 1791 and spent a decade in exile, succeeded Reymond. In 1801, Dubois returned to France, serving as vicar general of Arras and then of Metz. In 1817, Louis XVIII named him bishop of Aire, but when the Concordat of 1817 failed to be ratified, Dubois did not take his seat. In March 1820, the king transferred him to the reunited dioceses of Dijon and Langres. His bishopric was short-lived: he died in Paris on 6 January 1822.

A campaign to obtain retractions from the former constitutional clergy marked Dubois's short episcopate.[14] Most clergy retracted in 1821, a few made their amends later (two in 1824, and one each in 1830, 1833, 1834, and 1840). Thirty to forty priests signed one undated statement. Two retracting priests, Parîn and Lunette, attached the list of questions they were asked. The questions focused on a disavowal of revolutionary oaths and careers as well as reconciliation with the Rome, made possible by sincere contrition and an acceptance of censure.

The desire to acquire, fifteen and then twenty years after the Concordat of 1801, the retractions of Volfius and other constitutional clergy in the Côte-d'Or demonstrates the lingering bitterness of the revolution's legacy for the reunited church. There remained among some in the new church's hierarchy a desire for a more public and humbling rejection of the constitutional church. With Napoleon's fall, the former constitutional clergy lost their last protector, even if only of their dignity in defeat.

Volfius died 8 February 1822. Sadly, it appears that, in his last years, a woman in his employ along with her sister and male friend took advantage of him. In a lawsuit filed in 1824, Volfius's niece and nephew challenged a will signed by the former bishop in November 1820.[15] In this will, Volfius left his possessions to Marie Guedeney, Rose-Edmée Guedeney, and Esprit Sylvestre, who lived with him at the end of his life. His niece, Mme Lesage, and nephew, M. Mielle, alleged that he intended to make several pious gifts to St. Bénigne upon his death, and to give the rest of his fortune to them, his relations. In his last years, their suit alleged, he suffered from failing mental and physical capacities and was isolated from his family by Sylvestre and the Guedeney sisters. Prior to their residence in Volfius's home, his niece and nephew charged, the former bishop had enjoyed close relations with his family. Following the arrival of Sylvestre and the Guedeneys, he had not received letters sent to him or calling cards left for him.[16] The lone published court brief, prepared on behalf of his niece and nephew, does not reveal how this case was adjudicated. Yet, the argument of Lesage and Mielle that Volfius would have wanted some portion of his estate to go to St. Bénigne is in keeping with the commitment to the church he displayed during his career.

The conservative journal *L'ami de la religion* was not particularly kind to Volfius in its obituary. It attributed his election as bishop to the position of his brother Alexandre-Eugène as a deputy to the National Assembly. It judged his revolutionary convictions and commitments as motivated first by ambition and then by fear. Finally, calling into question his intellectual capacities, it noted that he had not studied a lot of theology, although it judged him a "cultivated, gentle and sociable individual."[17] A more positive assessment of the former bishop was made at mid-century, when a biographer in Hoefer's *Nouvelle biographie générale* judged him a "man of pure morals, gifted with a great oratorical talent, and having mastered in depth ancient and modern literature."[18]

Careers of Eleven Constitutional Clergy Elected in the District of Arnay-le-Duc in March 1791

In April 1791, the district of Arnay-le-Duc, southwest of Dijon, sent a letter to the Côte-d'Or department, reporting that it had filled seventeen vacant parishes. These vacancies were the result of either priests' death or their refusal to take the ecclesiastical oath. Arnay-le-Duc's revolutionary administrators were efficient, beginning to fill the empty parishes in late March. The department did not send the table detailing its actions along with the letter that spring, but provided it the following year in further communication.[1] Of these seventeen constitutional curés, it is possible to follow the careers of eleven through the biographical notes compiled by Eugène Reinert, a vicar and parish priest in the diocese of Dijon from 1900 until his retirement in 1951.[2] Reinert devoted his career to studying the clergy of northern Burgundy in the revolutionary era, amassing extensive notes and even drafting portions of a manuscript. His efforts now provide an important collection for researchers. The data are housed in Dijon's bibliothèque municipal, which, fittingly enough for this study, is located in the former building of the Collège des Godrans.

What happened to these eleven men who were elected as parish priests in the spring of 1791? It is interesting that three left the parish to which they were elected before a year had passed. Thus, when the *procureur* of Arnay-le-Duc submitted the table to the department, it was already out of date. Yet, even with these parish changes, the careers of these men reflect in miniature the history of clergy in the diocese of Dijon prior to the revolution and of constitutional clergy in the Côte-d'Or during it. Seven of the eleven men were under the age of forty when they were elected to a parish in 1791. Six were between the ages of twenty-nine and thirty-five, with most ordained in the mid-1780s. As Eric Wenzel has demonstrated in his study of the clergy of the diocese of Dijon, most clergy began their careers as a vicar, *desservant*, or *mépartist*.[3] On average, clergy in the Côte-d'Or spent ten years in such positions. So, the younger men who were elected in 1791 actually advanced more quickly than they might have expected to, receiving a parish less than a decade after their ordination. The older men also came from positions as vicars, with the exception of Antoine Brun, who was a Capuchin.

One individual, Antoine Henri Lardillon, did not jure the oath to the Civil Constitution of the Clergy and refused the parish of Thury to which he was elected. He built a revolutionary career as a refractory priest, leaving the district of Arnay-le-Duc in 1792 but returning to the region in 1796 to be a missionary to the region of Chagny in the neighbouring department of Sâone-et-Loire. After the Concordat, he became a priest in the parish of Givry, also in Sâone-et-Loire.

The revolutionary careers of the other ten men documented by Reinert reflect the findings of this study on the constitutional clergy of the Côte-d'Or. All of these men, except for Louis Jean Nouveau, who died in October 1791, resigned the priesthood in 1792. One, Théodore Nyault, was detained for seven months, arrested at the order of the representative on mission, Bernard de Saintes, and released by his successor, Jean-Marie Calès. Only two, Pierre Claude Rasse and François Roussin, returned to their vocation in the period 1795–1801. Neither is described by Reinert as retracting their revolutionary oaths. Two priests did retract their revolutionary oaths in this period, Étienne Cornesse (1796) and Théodore Nyault (1800?). Three priests married after resigning their positions and submitting their letters of ordination during the Terror, Jacques Chapuis (who was forty-four in 1791), Joseph Houdaille (age not noted, probably in his early thirties), and Jean Vaudrey (thirty-two). As the preceding chapters have demonstrated, the dechristianization efforts in the department decimated the constitutional clergy. Very few returned to work in the Gallican Church. The two retractions, and Reinert's attention to them, underscore the efforts made by refractories and apostolic missionaries to return the constitutional clergy to Rome's fold in the years before the Concordat. After the Concordat, four of these priests – Nyault, Cornesse, Rasse, and Roussin – served parishes in the Côte-d'Or, and they appear to be evenly split between former constitutional and refractory clergy. Lardillon also served a parish after 1801, but in the department of Sâone-et-Loire.

All of these men, with the exception of Lardillon, remained in the Côte-d'Or throughout their careers, either in Arnay-le-Duc or a neighbouring district. Two of the three men who married became manual labourers or farmers after leaving their vocation. Jacques Chapuis took a position as a teacher in the district and then served as a municipal agent in Viévy.

Table A.1 | Names of outgoing and replacement priests,
Arnay-le-Duc, 1791

Cure	Curé démissionaire	Curé remplacant
Labussière	Lefranc	Payse (religieux)
St. Martin de la Mer	Renard	Houdaille*
Voudenay	Moreau	Rasse*
Allerey	Moreau	Cornefre [Cornesse]*
Créancey	Duchesne	Brun (Capucin)*
Grosbrois [Grosbois]	Caveau	Chapuis*
Thury	Battaul	Larvillion [Lardillon]*
Bellenot	Boüyes	Roussin*
Chatellenot	Detairsche	Maréchol [Maréchel]*
Ste Sabine	Clavin	Pagneau
Esfey	Pagniev	Ronyer (Capucin)
Thoisy les efers (sp?)	Sirux	Vaudrey (Benedictin)*
Sombernon	Gaudet	Nyault*
Bussy la Selle	Gerard	Nouveau*
Nenilly	Rameau (décée)	Boucheren
Savigny sous Malain	Troingros (sp?)	Saunois (Capucin)
Sussey	Travayon	Soirot (curé d'Oguy succurselle de Sufrey)

Source: This information is from a table enclosed with a letter from the Procureur
Sindic [*sic*], District of Arnay le Duc, to Procureur Gen Sindic [*sic*], Department of
the Côte-d'Or, 28 March 1792, ADCO, L1144.

Note: Names with asterisks are individuals who appear in Reinert's four-volume
manuscript, *Dictionnaire d'écclésiatiques*, Fonds Reinert, MS 3238 (1–4), BM Dijon.

Abbé Reinert's Research on the Ecclesiastical Oath of 1791 in the Côte-d'Or

Part of Eugène Reinert's research, discussed in appendix A, focused on oath taking in the Côte-d'Or department in the spring of 1791. And, while this research should not be taken as complete, it does provide important information about the nature of this process in the department (see the summary in table B.1). With respect to its limitations, it is, first, necessary to address Reinert's sources. Unfortunately, he did not indicate his sources with respect to oath taking. It is clear throughout his papers, however, that he was an exhaustive researcher, utilizing departmental and district archival records, records in the National Archives, and even, at times, parish records. He also read widely and cited various articles and books about the clergy in northern Burgundy. While the Côte-d'Or was a special focus, his research quickly carried him beyond the department's borders as he followed clerical careers. His papers include compilations (like the one from which I created the summary table [table B.1]), copied archival material, a small amount of original archival material, his notes, and an incomplete manuscript he was writing. Reinert's extensive collection of material provides credibility for the varied efforts he made to compile material to answer particular questions. He used various descriptors as he tallied the oaths taken in the Côte-d'Or, and he was not consistent in these descriptors or in the information he gave about the entries. On some dates, he named the juring individuals; on others he did not. At times, he named only curés and simply provided a tally of other clergy. Sometimes, he provided notes with contextual information. For example, on 15 March, he provided a note criticizing the district of Beaune for suspecting the oaths of two individuals that were later confirmed on 8 April. However, he wrote no entry for 8 April.

In addition to the daily tally he was constructing, Reinert also addressed in his manuscript the difficulty of clarifying the matter of oaths statistically, using the district of Beaune by way of an example.[1] He noted that the official list of March 1791 for the district stated that it had 39 parish priest (curés) and 28 (*dessertes* [sic] *desservants*). Of these 67 clergy, 57 took the oath without restrictions (46 of these were *titulaires* – i.e., in a parish position), and 11 took the oath "à pourvoir" (presumably, with restrictions). In addition, the district indicated it had 46 juring and 43 non-juring clergy. These numbers do not add up. Reporting 67 priests, the district counted 68 oaths. It then went on to decide it had 46 juring clergy, when it stated that 57 took unrestricted oaths. Despite the seeming completeness of this report, Reinert concluded that the district had 75 curés and *desservants*, a number decreased to 57 with the reduction of parishes. Correcting for what he judged to be errors, Reinert calculated that, when vicars were added, the district had 89 clergy, accounting for the total juring and non-juring clergy reported. Yet, a second list of juring and non-juring clergy also existed, and it indicated 61 juring clergy and 41 non-juring. To deal with this discrepancy, Reinert peeled away the excess jurors as former religious (12 oratorians and 1 confessor), leaving 48 jurors and 41 non-jurors. In the end, Reinert judged that there were 38 authentic jurors (i.e., curés or vicars) and 5 former religious who had jured. Reinert was thorough in his cross-examination of evidence, and from his records it is clear that oath taking and reporting was a messy, fluid affair in the spring of 1791. Municipalities and districts administered the oath and then conveyed the results to the department, where the oaths might be refused, forcing a second attempt at the local level to secure an acceptable oath.

Given the lack of precision in the historical data, what information can this summary of Reinert's research provide? First, it indicates that there were three peak dates for the taking or recording of acceptable oaths, 18 and 28 February and 20 March. The earliest date came at the end of the week following Volfius's election as bishop on Sunday, 13 February, and 20 March was the date of his return to Dijon after having been installed as bishop in Paris. Reinert's notes do not indicate whether these larger ecclesiastical events in the department influenced oath taking, but it seems probable that they did. Large numbers of clergy gathered in Dijon on these dates, and on both the new ecclesiastical organization was a focus. Looking at the figures for the oaths judged unacceptable, there is a clear peak on 3 and 4 March. If the three categories of accepted oaths, accepted oaths with restrictions, and unacceptable oaths are considered, it is apparent that, from early February until the end of March, clergy and administrators in the Côte-d'Or were grappling with the Civil Constitution of the Clergy and the requirement that clergy swear the ecclesiastical oath. Reinert's research also indicates that, in this early period, very few clergy decisively refused to jure. The column labelled "non-juring" in table B.1, which encompasses all those indicated by Reinert as refusing, has entries for six days, and these represent only seventeen individuals. Overall, Reinert's research provides information for 358 individuals, not all of whom were parish priests or vicars. Included in this number are former religious as well as *desservants* and *mépartists*. The size of Reinert's data set adds weight to the conclusions it suggests. A substantial number of clergy (208) (columns 1 and 2), in the department took the ecclesiastical oath in a manner that the department judged to be acceptable. A smaller number (127) took the oath in an unacceptable manner or refused to take it (i.e., were non-juring).

Table B.1 | Summary of Reinert's research on oath taking in spring 1791, by date

Date	Accepted oaths, no restrictions	Accepted restricted oaths	Unacceptable oaths	Extensions	Non-juring	Vacant parishes	To provide a replacement
			REINERT'S DESCRIPTORS				
	Serments acceptés/ prête pur et simple	*Avec restrictions*	*Serments non-admis, serments inacceptables, déclarés nuls, inadmissibles*	*Sursis*	*Rejet le serment, serments rejeté, refus, refus de serment, insermentés*	*Cures vacant, pourvu remplace-ment*	*Pourvu remplace-ment*
Wed., 9 Feb.	10	3		3			
Thurs., 10 Feb.	1	3					
Sun., 13 Feb.	4		1				
Mon., 14 Feb.						5	
Wed., 16 Feb.						4	
Fri., 18 Feb.	48		4				
Sat., 19 Feb.	1						
Mon., 21 Feb.	3		10				
Tues., 22 Feb.	10		7		3		
Mon., 28 Feb.	46						
Tues., 4 1 Mar.		2			1		4
Wed., 7 2 Mar.					2		7
Thurs., 3 Mar.	14		32				
Fri., 4 Mar.	1		28		3		
Sat., 5 Mar.	3	5			7 (all from Dijon)		

Table B.1 | *continued*

Date	Accepted oaths, no restrictions	Accepted restricted oaths	Unacceptable oaths	Extensions	Non-juring	Vacant parishes	To provide a replacement
Tues., 8 Mar.	2 (district of Irnay) 6 (district of Semur)		20 (district of Irnay) 2 (district of Semur)				
Wed., 9 Mar.	1						
Sat., 12 Mar.	3						
Wed., 16 Mar.	2						
Fri., 18 Mar.	6						
Sat., 19 Mar.	6 (district of Semur)		1		1		
Sun., 20 Mar.	18		5				
Wed., 23 Mar.			1				
Thurs., 24 Mar.	9		1				
Fri., 25 Mar.	1						
Sat., 16 Apr.			3				
Totals	195	13	110	3	17	9	11

Source: Fonds Reinert, "Serments par ordre de dates," MS 3846, BM Dijon. This table is my summary of Reinert's data.

Notes

1 Charles Chauvin provides the text of this first oath demanded of the clergy, known as the ecclesiastical oath. His study offers as well the wording of the several other oaths the revolutionary assemblies in Paris would eventually demand of clergy. See *Le clergé à l'épreuve de la Révolution*, 59–60.

2 Many studies of the revolution's religious history include a chapter on the Civil Constitution of the Clergy and the subsequent ecclesiastical oath. See, for example, Nigel Aston, *Religion and Revolution in France*. The most expansive study of these developments is Rodney J. Dean's *L'Assemblée constituante et la réforme ecclésiastique*.

3 Timothy Tackett explored the various levels of oath taking across France in *Religion, Revolution, and Regional Culture in Eighteenth-Century France*. This important study details the varied factors that influenced a priest's decision to take or to refuse the oath, including the efforts of some to jure with reservations.

4 Of the seven juring bishops, only four were titular bishops, meaning they governed a diocese or archdiocese: Maurice Talleyrand de Périgord, bishop of Autun; Loménie de Brienne, archbishop of Sens; Louis Jarente de Sénac d'Orgeval, bishop of Orléans; and Lafont de Savine, bishop of Viviers. Also taking the oath were three coadjutors, or bishops *in partibus*: Jean Baptiste Gobel, Bishop of Lydda, coadjutor of Bâle; Martial de Brienne, coadjutor with his uncle at Sens; and Dubourg-Miraudot, bishop of Babylon. See Pierre de la Gorce, *Histoire religieuse de la Révolution française*, 1:387.

5 Tackett, *Religion, Revolution, and Regional Culture*, 40–3.

6 Dale Van Kley builds an intriguing case for a succession of breaks between the French bishops and the state as well as the French bishops and the lower clergy that dated back to the summer of 1788. These, he argues, culminated in the schism of 1791. See "The *Ancien Régime*."

7 Évêques, deputés à l'Assemblée nationale, *Exposition des principes sur la Constitution du Clergé.*

8 France's higher clergy and the clergy deputies within the National Constituent Assembly endorsed the bishop deputies' position. By November, 119 bishop and archbishops as well as 98 ecclesiastical deputies had signed their pamphlet (*Liste des évêques, députés à l'Assemblée nationale qui ont signé l'Exposition des principes sur la Constitution du Clergé*). The bishop deputies were inspired to take up the pamphlet published by Jean-René Asseline, the most recently appointed bishop in France's episcopate, having been ordained to the see of Boulogne only in January 1790. With about forty colleagues, Asseline published a pamphlet critical of the new legislation on 24 October 1790, *Instruction pastorale de M. l'évêque de Boulogne sur l'autorité spirituelle.* See Aston, *Religion and Revolution in France*, 152.

9 Several historians have studied the positions of Louis XVI, the French bishops, and Pope Pius VI during this conflict. At the turn of the twentieth century, Albert Mathiez emphasized the willingness of the French bishops serving in the Constituent Assembly to create an acceptable process for reforming the French church. He concluded that the papacy's silence left the French episcopacy little choice but to reject the civil constitution of the clergy, refuse the ecclesiastical oath, and create the schism in the French church. See Mathiez, *Rome et le clergé français*, 101–2, 148–9. In a more recent study, *Rome et la Révolution française*, 144–1, Gérard Pelletier concluded that the separation between the assembly and the French bishop deputies began much earlier, dating from February 1790, when François de Bonal, bishop of Clermont, left the assembly's Ecclesiastical Committee. Dale Van Kley trods a middle path in his assessment, noting the efforts of the French bishops to find an acceptable means of reforming the church, either through a national church council or papal endorsement of the Civil Constitution of the Clergy. Van Kley points out that Pius VI's long silence allowed the pontiff to issue papal bulls against the Civil Constitution after the French bishops had decisively taken this stand as well. Van Kley, "The *Ancien Régime*," 139–40.

10 Volfius to Messieurs du directoire du de parlemens a Dijon [*sic*], Dijon, 28 April 1792, folder L1091, Archives départementales de la Côtes-d'Or (hereafter ADCO).

11 Paul Pisani's *Répertoire biographique de l'épiscopat constitutionnel*
    provides a more even-handed account of each constitutional bishop's
    career than earlier works. An ecclesiastic, Pisani remained critical of the
    constitutional episcopacy, but not virulently so. A good example of the
    nineteenth-century bias against the constitutional clergy is Ludovic Sciout,
    Histoire de la Constitution civile du clergé. Working at the same time as
    Pisani, but in the secular, republican tradition, Albert Mathiez wrote three
    studies on religion and the revolution. His focus in these volumes was pol-
    itical. In addition to his study of the civil constitution of the clergy dis-
    cussed above, Mathiez wrote *Les consequences religieuses de la journée de
    10 août 1792* and *La théophilanthropie et la culte décadaire*.

12 John McManners brief study *The French Revolution and the Church*
    remains an important introduction in English to this subject. Paul
    Chopelin provides a succinct overview of recent work in his introduction
    to *Gouverner une église en revolution*, 7–14. Bernard Plongeron was
    among the first to study the theology of the constitutional church. His
    works on the religious history of the revolution, including the constitu-
    tional church and clergy, are extensive. The reader can find them listed in
    the bibliography as well as various notes throughout this work. Michel
    Vovelle began with an interest in the decline of religious practice in the
    eighteenth century, leading him eventually to study the alternatives to
    Christianity proposed during the revolution. See *Piété baroque et
    dechristianisation en Provence*; *Religion et Révolution*; and *The
    Revolution against the Church*. See Tackett, *Religion and Regional
    Culture*. Dale Van Kley has worked to link the revolution's religious hist-
    ory to that of the centuries preceding it, see *The Religious Origins of the
    French Revolution*; "Catholic Conciliar Reform in an Age of Anti-Catholic
    Revolution"; and "The *Ancien Régime*."

13 A good overview of works in the two decades since the bicentennial is
    Philippe Bourdin and Philippe Boutry, "L'Église catholique en Révolution."
    Two works synthesizing the revolution's religious history and asking new
    questions of it have appeared as well: Cousin, Cubells, and Moulinas, *La
    pique et la croix*, and Aston, *Religion and Revolution in France*.

14 Robert, Bourloton, and Cougny, eds., *Dictionnaire des parlementaires
    français*.

15 Among the works on Grégoire since the bicentennial are Plongeron,
    L'abbé Grégoire; Hermon-Belot, *L'abbé Grégoire*; Popkin and Popkin,
    eds., *The Abbé Grégoire and His World*; Dubray, *La pensée de l'Abbé
    Grégoire*; Goldstein Sepinwall, *The Abbé Grégoire and the French
    Revolution*; Guittienne-Mürger and Lesaulnier, eds., *L'abbé Grégoire et*

Port-Royal; and Chopelin-Blanc and Chopelin, *L'obscurantisme et les Lumières*.

16 Chopelin-Blanc, *De l'apologétique à l'église constitutionnelle*.

17 See Dean, *L'abbé Grégoire*.

18 Joseph F. Byrnes takes a broader approach to the constitutional clergy and bishops in his work *Priests of the French Revolution*. His study examines the history of the constitutional church through a chronological framework featuring varied priests and bishops. The united bishops are not absent from his study, but he also includes significant discussion of Claude Fauchet, constitutional bishop of Calvados; Jean-Baptiste Gobel, metropolitan bishop of Paris; Claude Le Coz, constitutional bishop of Ille-et-Vilaine (and later archbishop of Besançon); as well as of clergy, including radicals such as François Chabet and Jacques Roux. Claude Muller's short article examines the careers of three lesser-known constitutional bishops, François Antoine Brendel, Arbogast Martin, and Marc Antoine Berdolet. See "La Croix et la cocarde."

19 Sottocasa, *Mémoires affrontée*; Chopelin, *Ville patriote et ville martyre*.

20 See Flament, *Deux milles prêtres normands face à la révolution*; Perrouas and d'Hollander, *La Révolution française*; and Varry and Muller, *Hommes de Dieu et Révolution*.

21 Tackett, *Religion, Revolution, and Regional Culture*, 41, 320.

22 Rémond, *Religion and Society in Modern Europe*.

23 Michel Vovelle is foundational for this perspective, beginning with his study of wills and the decline of pious bequests in-eighteenth century Provence. See *Piété baroque et dechristianisation en Provence*. In *Religion et Révolution*, he turns to a consideration of declining religious expression, specifically in the revolutionary period.

24 Typical of this perspective are the works of Nigel Aston, *Religion and Revolution in France* and the older volume by John McManners, *The French Revolution and the Church*.

CHAPTER ONE

1 At the end of the Roman period, there were 114 dioceses in France. Only about twenty were created after this point. See "France," in Aubert, ed., *Dictionnaire d'histoire et de géographie ecclésiastiques*.

2 Bergin, *The Making of the French Episcopate*, 31–6. The monarchy's gain in the Concordat of Bologna came more at the expense of the canon chapters than the papacy. The 1519 accord overturned the Pragmatic Sanction of Bourges, which provided that colleges of canons and monks could elect

their own leaders. In 1519, the king gained the right to appoint these positions.

3　McManners, *Church and Society in Eighteenth Century France*, 183–5.

4　Palliot, *Le parlement de Bourgogne*, 22–7.

5　Farr, "Consumers, Commerce, and the Craftsmen of Dijon," 141–7.

6　Historians have differed about the number of attempts to establish a diocese at Dijon before 1731. Courtépée and Béguillet's five is the highest number; see *Description générale et particulière du duché de Bourgogne*, which was first published in 1774–85. In the nineteenth century, Philibert-Bernard Sautereau in *L'Évêché de Dijon et ses Évêques*, pointed only to efforts during the reign of Henri IV in 1592 and 1597, omitting any notice of efforts under Henri III or Louis XIII. Gabriel Dumay, in *Les Évêques de Dijon*, noted attempts in 1575, 1578, 1597, and 1630, thus retaining most of Courtépée and Béguillet's scheme. In each of these accounts, the sixteenth-century initiative for the diocese came from the Estates of Burgundy. At the turn of the twentieth century, Louis Prunel, in *Sébastien Zamet, Évêque de Langres*, provided the most extensive discussion of these early efforts. He noted three – one in 1578, another during the reign of Henri IV, and finally the effort led by Zamet in 1630, discussed below. Among more recent historians, Daniel Ligou, "De Louis XIV à la Révolution," 157–8, notes attempts in 1575, 1597, and during the reign of Zamet. Éric Wenzel in *Curés des lumières*, 12, also dates the first efforts (1572–3, 1575) to the reign of Henri III, and attributes their failure to the activities of the king's opponents, the Catholic League. Joseph Bergin used Dijon to illustrate larger points about the early modern French Catholic Church. He gave little credit to the sixteenth-century efforts, noting an attempt in 1590 by individuals in the Catholic League in *Church, Society and Religious Change in France*, 20, and an attempt under Henri IV in *The Making of the French Episcopate*, 31–3.

7　"Arrêt autorisant l'érection d'un évêché à Dijon," 2, 3, and 5 July 1597, Archives nationales de France (hereafter ANP), microfilm E1b.

8　Prunel, *Sébastien Zamet*, 33–6, 44–6.

9　Vignier, "Tentative d'érection d'un siège épiscopal a la Sainte-Chapelle." Unless otherwise noted, the details of this account of Zamet's effort follow Vignier's study.

10　Prunel, Sébastien Zamet, 528, provides a copy of the Consentement et advis du Conseil issued in favour of this project. The advice of Louis XIII's council was longer than the brief order issued in 1597. In this advice, the king's council pointed to the "abuse and disorder of the clergy of Dijon" as a justification for establishing the second seat in the city. The autonomy of Dijon's clergy, who held a general assembly from the late sixteenth century to negotiate their interests with municipal authorities, had provoked the bishops of Langres to refer to them as "autocephalous." See Gras, *Le diocèse de Dijon*, 17.

11   Prunell, *Sébastien Zamet*, 311.

12   Courtépée and Béguillet, *Description générale et particulière du duché de Bourgogne*, 340.

13   In the nineteenth century, Dumay, *Les Évêques de Dijon*, and Sautereau, *L'Évêché de Dijon*, followed Courtépée and Béguillet in their assessments, as did Ligou, "De Louis XIV à la Révolution," in the twentieth.

14   Gras, *Le diocèse de Dijon*," 17. Des Marches, *Histoire du Parlement de Bourgogne*, 20. Des Marches notes that Bouhier was even called bishop in a letter dated 12 April 1728 from the president of the *chamber de comptes* to Abbé Leblanc, who was only twenty-one at the time and was later to build a career in Paris as an author and member of the republic of letters. Leblanc was a favorite of Mme de Pompadour. He had close connections with the Bouhier family.

15   "De la Secretairerye Consistoriale," manuscript, n.d. G1, Archives départementales de la Côte-d'Or (hereafter ADCO).

16   "Extrait du reg. ^res du con.^el d'Etat," 9 August 1724, G1, Évéché de Dijon, Erection de l'Évéché, ADCO.

17   Gabriel Dumay in *Les Évêques de Dijon*, 3, wrote that Charles-François de Châteauneuf de Rochebonne was active in these negotiations for the first six years until his death, after which the bishop of Autun, Antoine-François de Bliterswyck de Montcley, took over. It is hard to credit this information because Rochebonne did not become archbishop of Lyon until 1732, and he died in 1739. While Bliterswyck de Montcley was bishop of Autun from 1724, he moved from that position to become archbishop of Besançon in 1731.

18   "Mémoire du chapitre de Langres contenant les raisons qui semblent devoir engager le roi de ne pas permettre l'érection d'un évéché à Dijon," fol. 131–8, MS 988-71, Collection de manuscrits de Pierre-Louis Baudot, Bibliothèque municipal de Dijon.

19   "De la Secretairerye [sic] Consistoriale," n.d., manuscript, G1, ADCO.

20   "Bulle de N.S.P. Le Pape Clement XII. Et Lettres Patentes de Louis XV. Roy de France et de Navarre. Portant Erection d'un Évéché à Dijon. Registrées en Parlement à Dijon le 8 août 1731," G1, ADCO.

21   A *mense* was revenue granted to a clergyman – in this case, the revenues of the abbey.

22 Roserot, *Dictionnaire topographique du département de la Côte-d'Or,* lxiii–lxiv.

23 McManners, *Church and Society in Eighteenth Century France,* 185.

24 Wenzel, *Curés des lumières.*

25 Ibid., 18–19.

26 Wenzel's description of the diocese of Dijon mirrors national trends as discussed by Timothy Tackett and Claude Langlois in "Ecclesiastical Structures and Clerical Geography on the Eve of the French Revolution," 358, 361. Tackett and Langlois note that only about a third of clergy nationally were involved in pastoral work as either a parish priest or vicar, and about 40 per cent of all clergy were concentrated in urban areas. Although Dijon was the only significant urban centre in the diocese, it exerted its dominance over the pastoral clergy, as noted by Wenzel, *Curés des lumières.*

27 Wenzel, *Curés des lumières,* 33–4, 41–2, 45.

28 Ibid., 14.

29 Ibid., 33, 45–50.

30 The first bishop of Dijon (described above) was Jean-Jacques Bouhier de Lantenay (1731–43); in 1743, he resigned in favour of his nephew, Claude Bouhier (1731–55), vicar general of the diocese. Claude-Marc-Antoine d'Apchon (1755–76) was the next bishop. Born in Montbrison to the west of Lyon, d'Apchon began his career in the military, variously reported as a dragoon captain or a naval officer. He left the military for an ecclesiastical career. In 1776, he resigned from the diocese of Dijon when Louis XVI named him archbishop of Auch. Jacques-Joseph-François de Vogüé (1776–87) of Aubenas in the Vivarais followed d'Apchon. Upon his death, René Des Monstiers de Mérinville (1787–1801), confessor to Marie-Antoinette, became bishop. There are several accounts of the bishops of Dijon; the most entertaining is from Antoine Colas, vicar to Bishop d'Apchon, and a fan of neither de Vogüé nor Des Monstiers de Mérinville. Phillip Voillery published Colas's reflections in 1883, adding a final section on Des Monstiers de Mérinville and Volfius. See, Colas and Voillery, "Les premiers évêques de Dijon" and "Les premiers évêques de Dijon (Suite)." Two other nineteenth-century works are A.S. Des Marches, *Histoire du parlement de Bourgogne,* 21–5, and Gabriel Dumay, *Les Évêques de Dijon.*

31 Wenzel, *Curés des lumières,* 145–51.

32 Dinet, *Religion et société,* 187.

33 As Dale Van Kley demonstrates, France's Jansenists laid the groundwork for a century for the campaign against the Jesuits. By the mid-eighteenth

century, Jansenism, originally a pious reform movement in seventeenth-century French Catholicism, found friends among the magistrates of the king's courts. Utilizing the cases of French creditors attempting to regain losses against a Jesuit mission in Martinique, the Jansenist magistrates of the Parlement de Paris launched one of the century's great religious and political reversals. Van Kley, *The Jansenists and the Expulsion of the Jesuits*; on the *parlement* of Dijon's actions against the Jesuits, see ibid., 165, 192, 200–2. The suppression of the Jesuits was a global phenomenon of significant impact. Jeffrey D. Burson and Jonathan Wright explore the varied connections and campaigns involved in these developments in *The Jesuit Suppression in Global Context*.

34 Dinet, *Religion et société*, 179–80. Volfius's decision to enter the secular clergy as the *parlements* acted against the French Jesuits was typical. Most former French Jesuits or Jesuit novices entered the diocesan clergy, as D. Gillian Thompson discusses in "French Jesuits, 1756–1814," 194–5.

35 Courtépée and Béguillet, *Description générale et particulière du duché de Bourgogne*, i–iii.

36 Ibid., 340.

CHAPTER TWO

1 Philippe Grateau notes the cultural significance of writing these *cahiers* for the French. In the countryside, he found peasants and villagers expressing support for the ideals of equality and liberty, at times using the rhetoric of the Enlightenment and at times not. In the diocese of Dijon, the pre-revolutionary pamphlets of the lower clergy (discussed later) also demonstrate support for these ideals and for the peasantry. See *Les cahiers de doléances*.

2 Baker, "Politics, Privilege, and Political Culture."

3 Dijon (Diocèse), Curés, *Vœu de quelques curés de campagne*, 15, French Revolution Collection, Newberry Library (hereafter NB).

4 Dijon (Bailliage), Clergé *Vœu des pasteurs du second ordre*, 16 (NB).

5 Dijon (Diocèse), Curés, *Vœu de quelques curés de campagne*, 14.

6 Dijon (Bailliage), Clergé, *Vœu des pasteurs du second ordre*, 4–5.

7 Ibid., 6–8.

8 Grateau, *Les cahiers de doléances*, 130–1.

9 Ibid., 10–11.

10 Dijon (bailliage), [clergé], *Chambre du clergé du bailliage de Dijon*.

11 Ibid., 3–5. Significantly, the curés argued that personal letters should be made inviolable. They accepted limitations on freedom of speech only in instances of national security.

12 Ibid., 6–11, 16–20.

13 These proposals are recorded in the pamphlet *Discours pronouncé par l'un de MM. les secretaries de la noblesse*, 1–2, 4, 15.

14 Ibid., 4–6.

15 Ibid., 9.

16 Ibid.,10.

17 Madival and Laurent, et Al., eds., *Archives parlementaires*, 3: 127–30; Péronnet and Lochot, *La Révolution dans le département de la Côte-d'Or*, 83.

18 Madival and Laurent, *Archives parlementaires*, 3: 130–7 ; Péronnet and Lochot, *La Révolution dans le département de la Côte-d'Or*, 83–4; and Baker, "Politics, Privilege, and Political Culture," 85–7, 90–4.

19 Madival and Laurent, *Archives parlementaires*, 3: 116; Baker, "Politics, Privilege, and Political Culture," 107–8.

20 Young, *Arthur Young's Travels in France*, 219. Amelot de Chaillou was appointed intendant for the province of Burgundy in 1784. His office was one of the first to cooperate with the new departmental administrations established in 1790. In May 1790, then in Paris, Amelot turned over his office and its personnel to the new departmental administrators. See Richard, ed., *Histoire de la Bourgogne*, 272–4, 312.

21 For Volfius's addresses on history, see *Discours pour l'ouverature du cours d'histoire*. Françoise Giraud discusses Volfius's speeches in 1779 and 1787 at Dijon's academy in "Volfius, évêque constitutional de la Côte-d'Or," 10–12. For Volfius's rhetorical manual, see *Rhétorique françoise à l'usage des collèges*.

22 Giraud, "Volfius, évêque constitutional de la Côte-d'Or," 9.

23 Ibid. Giraud concludes that the expulsion of the Jesuits from France is the more likely reason for the end of Volfius's theological studies. Some historians have attributed the premature end of Volfius's education to ineptitude. This judgment reflects the nineteenth-century hostility to the former constitutional bishop. See Abbé Chomton in his *Histoire de l'Église Saint-Bénigne*, 305.

24 Van Kley, *Jansenists and the Expulsion of the Jesuits*, 192, 200–2. As Van Kley notes and as is discussed in Chapter 1, the Parlement of Burgundy had little enthusiasm for the actions against the Jesuits

25 Delattre, ed., *Les établissements de Jésuites en France*, 4: 157, 301.

26 Giraud, "Volfius, évêque constitutional de la Côte-d'Or," 10–11.

27 Volfius, *Discours pour l'ouverature du cours d'histoire*, 10. Volfius declared, "L'autorité du monarque sera établie sur des fondemens inébranlables; plus d'intermédiaire entre le père & les enfans; il ne sera qu'un avec son peuple; il n'y aura plus dans une seule Nation des Nations divisées & rivals."

28 Ibid., 6.

29 Volfius, *Discours prononcé à la bénédiction des drapeaux patriotiques*, 6–8.

30 Ibid., 2. In a brief disclaimer, Volfius described how he came to give this speech and how it came to be published.

31 Ibid., 5, 8.

32 Pisani, *Répertoire biographique*, 246.

33 For a discussion of Alexandre-Eugène Volfius's role in the Parti patriote, see Baker, "Politics, Privilege, and Political Culture," 86–7, 109.

34 Giraud, "Volfius, évêque constitutional de la Côte-d'Or," 9, 13–14.

35 On the night of 4 August 1789, the Constituent Assembly voted to end the tithe and *casuel* (fees collected by clergy for marriages, baptisms, and funerals). In a frenzied session, nobles and clergy offered up a variety of privileges associated with their estate, renouncing them as remnants of feudalism. Carefully planned, this session was a response to a wave of unrest in France's countryside. The assembly nationalized church properties on 2 November after a month of debate.

36 Volfius, *Discours prononcé à la bénédiction des drapeaux de messieurs les volontaires-artilleurs de la garde nationale*, 4.

37 Ibid., 8–9.

38 Ibid., 10–11.

39 Ibid., 3–4, 12–14.

40 Péronnet and Lochot give the figure 342,986 for the department's initial population; see *La Révolution dans le département de la Côte-d'Or*, 90. Gérard Moyse credits André-Rémy Arnoult, an attorney at the Parlement of Dijon and deputy to the Constituent Assembly, with formulating the name "Côte-d'Or." Initially, the deputies had thought to name the new department after its chief city, Dijon. See Moyse, *Joyaux d'archives*, 127.

41 Péronnet and Lochot, *La Révolution dans le département de la Côte-d'Or*, 90–1. For a detailed discussion of the Parti patriote's takeover of Dijon's city council in July 1789 and the subsequent reversal of this development in the spring of 1790, see Baker, "Politics, Privilege, and Political Culture," 116–20, 156–7, 160–3.

42 In Dijon, 2,715 individuals were eligible to serve in political office given the tax requirement established by the National Assembly. The electorate was an even more restricted group, consisting of some 956 individuals. See Baker, "Politics, Privilege, and Political Culture," 153.

43 Péronnet and Lochot, *La Révolution dans le département de la Côte-d'Or*, 91.

44 Ibid.

45 Baker, "Politics, Privilege, and Political Culture," 164.

46 Ibid., 165–6.

47 Péronnet and Lochot, *La Révolution dans le département de la Côte-d'Or*, 95.

48 Ibid., 95, For Guyton de Morveau's role in the *club patriotique*, see 92.

49 Furet and Ozouf, eds., *A Critical Dictionary of the French Revolution*, 68–9.

50 These were the departments of the Côte-d'Or, the Ain, the Yonne, and the Saône-et-Loire, Péronnet and Lochot, *La Révolution dans le département de la Côte-d'Or*, 88.

51 Ibid., 93. All translations are mine unless otherwise noted. The text reads: "de maintenir de tout leur pouvoir la constitution du royaume, d'être fidèles à la loi et au roi et de faire exécuter les décrets de l'Assemblée nationale sanctionnés ou acceptés par le roi." This event was memorialized in a painting: see Péronnet and Lochot, *La Révolution dans le département de la Côte-d'Or*, 86. De Buffon's first name is noted in an article on his father, "Buffon, (Georges-Louis Leclerc)" in *Dictionnaire de biographie française*, 7: 630. The younger de Buffon was executed during the terror in 1794.

52 Volfius, *Discours prononcé le 18 mai 1790*, 1, 3–4.

53 Ibid., 3–5. For a discussion of the evolution of the meaning of this word see, "La patrie," in *Dictionnaire historique de la langue française*, 2:1452.

54 Volfius, *Discours prononcé le 18 mai 1790*, 5–8.

55 Ibid., 9–10: "Cette base n'est point autre que la déclaration de nos droits ... Les droits qu'elle énonce sont antérieurs à toute convention; c'est la chartre éternelle que nous tenons de Dieu."

56 Ibid., 23–4.

57 Volfius, *Discours de M. l'Abbé Volfius, Président de l'Assemblée électorale*, 4.

58 Ibid., 1–2.

59 Ibid., 2–3.

60 Ibid., 3–4.

61 Baker, "Politics, Privilege, and Political Culture," 134–5.

CHAPTER THREE

1 The figures for retractors in the Côte-d'Or are from Tackett, *Religion, Revolution, and Regional Culture,* 320. Pius VI issued two briefs prior to *Caritas quae.* One on 10 March addressed to the thirty signatories of the *Exposition des principes* sought the bishops' guidance to find a compromise solution. In a second brief on 13 April, the pope instructed clergy not to take the ecclesiastical oath or to retract it.

2 Ribas, "Les prêtres fonctionnaires publics," 82–3. Ribas writes that none of Dijon's clergy, with the exception of the ten professors at the Collège des Godrans, took the oath. Chidjou, "Le clergé constitutionnel de Dijon," 43–6 provides a table listing juring clergy in the canton of Dijon. He includes in this list M. Simon and M. Gellet, curés of Nôtre Dame and Saint-Jean, respectively, who swore the oath. Both Simon and Gellet were elected priests of these parishes after the former clergy refused to jure. Prior to being elected parish priests in Dijon, Simon was a vicar at Saint Oportune in Paris, and Gellet was a vicar in Orléans. See "Résultat du procès verbal de nomination aux cures," Archives départementales de la Côte-d'Or (hereafter ADCO), L 1795.

3 Volfius, *Lettre pastorale de M. l'évêque,* 3. All translations are mine.

4 Ibid., 13–14.

5 Ibid., 17.

6 Doyle discusses the Civil Constitution and its enforcement as a stimulus for the formation of patriotic clubs. The patriots, he notes, saw support of the Civil Constitution as a test of support for the revolution, just like the use of assignats. See Doyle, *Oxford History of the French Revolution,* 142.

7 [Assemblée constituante], *Décret sur la constitution civile du clergé,* 11.

8 Société des amis de la constitution, Beaune, to Messieurs, Dijon, 20 April 1791, folder L1180, ADCO.

9 Directoire du Département de la Côte-d'Or, *Extrait des procès verbaux,* 23 April 1791, folder L1180, ADCO.

10 Gouttes, *Lettre de M. Gouttes, curé d'Argilliers.* At the end of the pamphlet is an announcement of the weekly meetings of the Société des amis de la Constitution. In the departmental archives in Dijon, Gouttes's pamphlet is accompanied by a letter from the Société des amis de la Constitution in Beaune recommending the pamphlet to the department and its bishop (Volfius). In addition to circulating it to the departmental authorities, the writers note, they have also distributed it in their district. See Société des

amis de la Constitution, Beaune, to MM du directoire du département de la Côte-d'Or, Dijon, 1 April 1791, folder L1142, ADCO.

11 For example, Mirabeau, president of the assembly in February 1791, sent *Adresse des électeurs du département de la Seine Inférieure*, 1-2, folder L1142, ADCO. In this piece, the Seine-Inférieure electors applauded the Constituent Assembly for restoring the people's power to choose their pastors.

12 "Gouttes, (Abbé Jean-Louis)," in Michaud, Michaud, and Desplaces, eds., *Biographie universelle.* Gouttes's tenure as a constitutional bishop was brief. He was guillotined in Paris on 26 March 1794, during the height of the dechristianization campaign associated with the Terror when he refused to cease his ecclesiastical functions.

13 Gouttes, *Lettre de M. Gouttes*, 5–6.

14 Ibid., 6n.

15 Ibid., 7.

16 Ibid., 8–9, 11.

17 Jean-Louis Gazzaniga, "Pragmatic Sanction of Bourges," in Vacher, Dobson, and Lapidge, eds., *Encyclopedia of the Middle Ages*, 1177. See also, Dean, *L'Abbé Grégoire*, 319. The bourgeoisie did gain some influence over the appointment of parish clergy in the fourteenth and fifteenth centuries. Erwin Iserloh discusses bourgeois influence in free German cities during this period in "From the Middle Ages to the Reformation," in Jedin and Dolan, eds., *The Handbook of Church History*, 569–70. On elections in the medieval Catholic Church, see Basdevant-Gaudemet, "Election," in Vacher et al., eds. *Encyclopedia of the Middle Ages,* 475. For a discussion of the monarchy's continuing influence in the case of the upper clergy, see Bergin, *The Making of the French Episcopate*, 48–50.

18 René, Paris, to Directoire du district de Dijon, Dijon, 15 November 1790, folder L1791, ADCO.

19 Jannon et al., *Déclaration unanime.*

20 Ibid., 2–3.

21 Ibid., 3–5.

22 Ibid., 7.

23 Louis-Antoine Alotte, Morey, to Messieurs, Dijon, 19 December 1790, folder L1154/6, ADCO. See also an earlier letter, Louis-Antoine Alotte, Morey, to Monsieur, Dijon, 8 December 1790, folder L1154/6, ADCO.

24 Norel, "Extrait des minutes du secretariat de la municipalité de la commune de Dijon," 23 January 1791, folder L1808/21, ADCO.

25 Girardot, Dijon, to Messieurs, Dijon, 21 February 1791, folder L1808/21, ADCO.

26 Girardot, Dijon, to Messieurs, Dijon, n.d. (between 14 February and
   12 March 1791), folder L1808/21, ADCO.
27 Reinert's analysis of oath taking in the department and his conclusions
   about it are in an incomplete manuscript in the Fonds Reinert, MS3846, in
   the Bibliothèque municipale de Dijon (hereafter BM Dijon).
28 Ibid. Construction on the Burgundy canal began in 1784 and continued until
   interrupted by the Terror of 1793. It was under Napoleon in 1808 that the
   canal first opened for navigation. In the eighteenth century, only the passage
   from Saint-Jean-de-Losne to Dijon was built. By the 1880s, the canal, though
   incomplete, had reached its full length, 242 kilometres, extending northward
   to Laroche and connecting the Sâone and the Yonne rivers. Interest in constructing a canal in Burgundy dated from the early sixteenth century, but it
   was only in the eighteenth century that the Estates of Burgundy engaged
   engineers to submit plans. Support for the project grew slowly across the century. See Desaunais, "Le canal de Bourgogne et son trafic," 115–21.
29 Les administrateurs composant le Directoire du District de Saint Jean de
   Losne, to MM. Les administrateurs composant le Directoire du
   Département de la Côte-d'Or, Dijon, 12 January 1791, folder L1165/26,
   ADCO.
30 Nicolas, Maire, et al., Saint-Seine-en-Bache, to [Directory of the
   Department of the Côte-d'Or], Dijon, n.d., folder L1165/26, ADCO.
31 See Procès verbal, municipal officers of Combertaut, folder L1441/42,
   ADCO; Declaration of Pallegoix, maire, n.d., folder L1441/42, ADCO.
32 Tackett, *Religion, Revolution and Regional Culture*, 320. Tackett provides
   an account of the overall number of juring and non-juring clergy in the
   department. By the fall of 1792, the number of juring clergy in the department had decreased to 395. Counting oath taking in the Côte-d'Or is not an
   easy matter. In the departmental archives, the ecclesiastical oath of 1791 and
   the oath of 19 *fructidor* (6 September 1797) are the best documented, but
   even for these no unified department-wide accounting is available. Reinert
   worked to compile a list of oaths by date for the ecclesiastical oath of 1791.
   I have included my summary of Reinert's research in Appendix B. Reinert's
   work is also not exhaustive, but is interesting for the patterns it reveals.
33 There is not a list of constitutional clergy in the Côte-d'Or after the Terror
   of 1793–4. Such lists as do exist in the departmental archives of clergy
   active in the department do not distinguish between constitutional clergy
   and refractory clergy, who were, by that time, permitted to be active as
   well. François and Sivry are among the twenty-eight signers of the *Actes
   du synode diocésain*, held in Dijon on 8 July 1800 (19 *messidor, l'an 8*).

The report comments on the disorganized and embattled state of the constitutional clergy in the department at that time.

34 Bertrand, Dijon, to Directoire du département, Dijon, 21 January 1791; Perron, Dijon, to Directoire du département, Dijon, 21 January 1791; Lautrey, Dijon, to Directoire du département, Dijon, 21 January 1791; Champoulet and Robert, Dijon, to Directoire du département, Dijon, 22 January 1791; and Champoulet, to Directoire du département, Dijon, 23 January 1791, all folder L1080/5, ADCO.

35 Champoulet and Robert, 22 January 1791, ibid.

36 "Copie collationnée de l'arrête pris par le directoire du département de la Côte-d'or," 21 January 1791, folder 1080/5, ADCO; Norel, "Extrait du register des deliberations du conseil general de la commune de Dijon," 22 January 1791, folder 1080/5, ADCO.

37 Ribas, "Les prêtres fonctionnaires publics," 82–3. Ribas writes that, in taking the oath, these ten clergy were exceptional among the parish clergy in Dijon because the rest refused to do so in an act of solidarity with their bishop (Des Monstiers). Ribas's research differs from that of Abdoul Karime Chidjou, who lists several oath-taking clergy in the parishes of Dijon. See "Le clergé constitutionnel de Dijon," 43–6.

38 The *procureur-syndic* of the districts and the *procureur-général-syndic* of the department were legal agents for their respective directories.

39 Form letter, see rolder L210/2, ADCO.

40 René, Ev. de Dijon, *Lettre de M. l'évêque de Dijon a MM. Les électeurs du département de la Côte d'Or* (Paris, 1791), 8, folder L210/2, ADCO.

41 Ibid., 1–7.

42 Fonds Reinert, "Election de Volfius," MS 3882, BM Dijon. This information is in Reinert's manuscript. As is typical in his manuscript, which was not complete, Reinert did not indicate all his sources. Most of his work on Volfius was still in note and draft form. Reinert clearly saw Desmonstiers de Mérinville as the legitimate bishop and Volfius as an intruder. One of his notes is a quotation from Amanton's *Notice sur J.B. Volfius, prêtre du diocese de Dijon*. Amanton wrote "On voudrait jeter le voile du silence sur une époque de sa vie de M. Volfius, celle où il a eu le malheur de ne laisser sacrer comme évêque constitutionnel sous le titre d'évêque de la Côte-d'Or et de somber [*sic*] par nuit de cette première faute dans une multitude d'autres." Reinert's position on Volfius is also indicated in his discussion of his election, one of the few narrative sections on Volfius in his manuscript. Reinert focused on Mérinville's letter and those who supported the aggrieved bishop. Claude-Nicolas Amanton was a *conseiller de prefecture*

and a member of the academy of Dijon. He was also the owner of the *Journal de Dijon et de la Côte d'Or* from 1813. See Quérard, *La France Littéraire*, 44–6.

43 Cl. B. Navier, président de l'assemblée électorale, Dijon, to M. le président de l'Assemblée nationale, Paris, 17 February 1791, folder L210/2, ADCO. Navier wrote as well that, although the electors continued to respect de Mérinville, they hoped the National Assembly would be "justly severe" to him in response to his letter to them.

44 J. Le Clerc, S. Germain le Rocheuse, to M. le président, Dijon, 10 February 1791, folder L210/2, ADCO.

45 For excuses given by electors, see, Lacordaire, Recey, to M. le président, Dijon, 11 February 1791; L.B. Rochel, (Is-sur-Tille), to M. le president, Dijon; Pétot, Villey, to M. le président, Dijon, 11 February 1791; Vieffy, Creanecy, to Monsieur, Dijon, 11 February 1791; all located in folder L210/2, ADCO.

46 In her discussion of Volfius's election, Françoise Giraud points to the season as one explanation for the absence of some electors. She judges the absences to be reasonable and not excessive in a way that would indicate widespread disaffection with the project of electing a new bishop. See "Volfius," 25.

47 Bertrand, maire, Ausonne, to Monsieur, Dijon, 28 January [1791], folder L210/2, ADCO.

48 Claudon, Dijon, to M. le procureur général, Dijon, 11 February 1791, folder L210/2, ADCO.

49 Ibid.

50 Claudon, Dijon, to M. le procureur général, Dijon, 12 February 1791, folder L210/2, ADCO.

51 "Extrait des process verbaux des séances du directoire du département de la Côte d'Or," 12 February 1791, folder L210/2, ADCO.

52 Giraud, "Volfius," 26. Bouillote, curé of his hometown, was sixty-seven in 1791 when he lost the election to Volfius, his junior by a decade. Bouillote had been elected to represent the clergy at the Estates-General by the *bailliage* of Auxois. He took the ecclesiastical oath of 1791. See M. Prevost, "Bouillotte, (Guy)," in *Dictionnaire de biographie française*.

53 The description given in the *Journal patriotique de la Côte-d'Or* is quoted in Marc, *Biographie de Messire Chamberland*, 41.

54 Navier, *Extrait du procès-verbal de l'Assemblée électorale*, 5.

55 Volfius, "Discours de M. Volfius, élu Evêque," 8–10.

56 Fonds Reinert, "Election de Volfius," MS3882, BM Dijon.

57 Ibid.

58 [Assemblée constituante], *Décret sur la constitution civile du clergé*, 16–17.

59 Le Cardinal de Lomenie, Sens, to Directoire du département de la Côte-d'Or, Dijon, 21 February 1791, folder L1142, ADCO.

60 Delessart, Paris, to M. Guitton, Dijon, 21 February 1791, folder L1142, ADCO.

61 All letters are located in folder L1142, ADCO. One response from the *procureur-général* of the Haute-Saône, as well as letters from the *procureurs-générals* of the Haut-Rhin and the Haute-Marne are cited below. Other responses came from Vigneron, Procureur general syndic du department de la Haute-Saône, to Procureur général syndic du département de la Côte-d'Or, Dijon, 22 march 1791; Voullainfont, Pr. Gen. Syndic du départ. du Vosges, to Procureur général Côte-d'Or, Dijon, 25 February 1791; Ebrares, Procureur général syndic du département du Jura, to M. Guyton, Proc. Gen. de Côte-d'Or, Dijon, 23 February 1791.

62 Procureur général syndic du département de la Haute-Saône, Vesoul, to Procureur général Côte-d'Or, Dijon, 21 February [1791], folder L1142, ADCO. Séguin's delay in accepting the position was perhaps due to his effort to get the archbishop of Besançon, M. de Durfort, to take the oath. De Durfort refused, and Séguin, doctor of theology and formerly canon of Sainte-Madeleine of Besançon, was consecrated as metropolitan of the Metropole of the East on 27 March 1791 by the Gobel in Paris.

63 Procureur general syndic du département du Haut Rhin, Colmar, to Procureur général syndic du département de la Côte-d'Or, Dijon, 26 February 1791, folder L1142, ADCO.

64 Procureur general Syndic du département de la Haute Marne, Chaumont, to Procureur Général Côte-d'Or, Dijon, 29 March 1791, folder L1142, ADCO.

65 Marc, *Biographie de Messire Chamberland*, 41; "Extrait des proces verbaux des séances du directoire du département de la Côte-d'Or," 21 March 1791, folder L1793, ADCO. Jean-Baptiste Massieu and Jean-Baptiste Aubry, respectively.

66 Description given in the *Journal patriotique de la Côte-d'Or*, quoted in Marc, *Biographie de Messire Chamberland*, 41.

67 "Extrait des proces verbaux," 21 March 1791.

68 J.B. Volfius, Dijon, to Messieurs les administrateurs composanat le directoire du district d'issurtille, Is-sur-Tille, 12 April 1791, folder L1945, ADCO.

69 A succursal church was one that was dependent on another, larger parish. Administratively, it was a branch or auxiliary of the larger parish.

70 Volfius to to Messieurs les administrateurs, 12 April 1791. Les membres composant le Directoire du district d'Il-sur-tilles, to M. l'Evêque, Dijon, 15 April 1791, folder L1945, ADCO.

71 Volfius, Dijon, to Messieurs les administrateurs composant le directoire du département de la Côte-d'Or à Dijon, 19 April 1791, folder L1793, ADCO.

72 J.S.D. Gillotte, "Extrait du procès verbal des séances du directoire du district de Dijon, Département de la Côte-d'Or," 20 April 1791, folder L1793, ADCO.

73 Volfius, *Lettre pastorale de M. L'évêque*, 2–4. This pastoral letter is also discussed in chapter 2.

74 Ibid., 4, 6–7, 11–15.

75 Upon arriving in the diocese in 1787, Des Monstiers de Mérinville named Dillon vicar-general and dean of Sainte-Chapelle in Dijon. Dillon had been vicar-general to the bishop of Nevers. An ardent opponent of the Constituent Assembly's religious legislation, in 1790 he published the pamphlet *Protestation contre les décrets relatifs au clergé*. He followed this in 1791 with his letter to Volfius. Once the constitutional church was established in Dijon, he went into exile in London. Dillon was not popular with the revolutionaries in Dijon, and his effigy and pamphlets were burned in a public square by members of Dijon's Société des amis de la constitution. See Jacques de Terrefort, "Dillon, Roger-Henry," in *Dictionnaire de biographie française*.

76 Des Monstiers de Mérinville, "Ordonnance de M. l'évêque de Dijon,", 8.

77 Ibid., 9–13, 15–16.

78 Dillon, *Lettre de M. l'abbé Henri Dillon*, 2–3.

79 Ibid., 5–7.

80 Ibid., 15–19, 23–7, 29–30.

81 La Due, *The Chair of Saint Peter*, 33–9; McBrien, *Lives of the Popes*, 404.

82 For this insight into the difference between the imagined Roman Republic of the revolutionaries and their projected image of the early church, I am indebted to David P. Jordan.

83 For a full discussion of the pope's two briefs, see Mathiez, *Rome et le clergé français*, 490–8, 510–11.

84 Des Monstiers de Mérinville, *Instruction pastorale de M. l'Évêque de Dijon*.

85 Ibid., 4.

86 Ibid., 6–7. Again, Des Monstiers de Mérinville's use of St. Cyprian is selective. Cyprian supported two Spanish bishops selected by the people of

their dioceses after they had deposed their predecessors as *lapsi* during the persecution of Decius. Despite Pope Stephen's decision to support the reinstatement of the deposed bishops (Basilides and Martialis), Cyprian praised the Spanish churches and encouraged them to remain faithful to their new bishops. La Due, *The Chair of Saint Peter*, 36–7.

87 Des Monstiers de Mérinville, *Instruction pastorale*, 8.

88 Ibid., 9–10.

89 Citation of [Pope Innocent XII], *Sermon sur l'unité*, in Des Monstiers de Mérinville, "Ordonnance de M. l'évêque de Dijon," 63. The Gallican liberties asserted that the pope held a supreme spiritual, but not secular, power and was subject to the rulings of church councils. In matters concerning the French church, including the appointment of bishops, France had the right to abide by its own traditions. Pope Alexander VIII, Innocent's predecessor, condemned the four Gallican articles. Innocent continued the campaign against them convincing Louis XIV to repeal the French Assembly of the Clergy's Declaration of 1682.

CHAPTER FOUR

1 Tackett, *Religion, Revolution and Regional Culture*, 41–4, 320. Nationally about 6 per cent of priests retracted their oaths.

2 Bernard Cousin, Monique Cubells, and René Moulinas provide an overview of the problems faced by constitutional bishops as they organized their dioceses. The experience of the Côte-d'Or mirrors many of the issues they highlight: a lack of cooperation among priests, resistance from nuns, and the continuing presence of non-juring clergy. See *La pique et la croix*, 145–8.

3 Quoted in Jarrot, *Le clergé constitutionnel dans la Côte-d'Or*, 4.

4 Letter from district of Arnay-le-Duc's *procureur-syndic* to the department's *procureur-general-syndic*, 28 March 1792, folder L1144, Archives départementales de la Côte-d'Or (hereafter ADCO). Abbé Reinart, an early twentieth-century ecclesiastic who devoted a lifetime to studying the clergy of northern Burgundy in the revolutionary era, provides brief biographies of eleven of the seventeen individuals elected to parishes in Arnay-le-Duc in the spring of 1791. See Appendix A for an overview of their careers following their election.

5 Information on nominations to the district of Dijon's parishes comes from "Résultat du procès verbal de nominatons aux cures," n.d., in folder L1795, ADCO.

6 Jarrot, *Le clergé constitutionnel dans la Côte-d'Or*, 4–5.

7 J. Musard, and J.F.D. Gittotte, untitled handwritten report, 3 December 1790, folder L1141, ADCO.

8 "Extrait des procès verbaux des séances du directoire du district d'Arnay le Duc," 24 March 1791, folder L1140, ADCO. A good comparative study is Françoise Panhaleux's "La circonscription des paroisses dans le Morbihan.".

9 [Assemblée constituante], *Décret sur la constituion civile*, 19.

10 Tackett, *Religion, Revolution and Regional Culture*, 320. Fifty-nine per cent of Arnay-le-Duc's clergy took the oath in the spring of 1791. This figure had dropped by two percentage points by autumn 1792.

11 Potier, "Lettre écrite par la Garde nationale de Flavigny; à MM les administrateurs du département de la Côte d'Or; le 26 avril 1791," *Journal patriotique du département de la Côte d'Or*, no. 22 (31 May 1791): 191–2.

12 *Journal patriotique du department de la Côte d'Or*, no. 22 (31 May 1791): 194.

13 "Loi relative a la circonscription des paroisses de Dijon. Donnée à Paris, le quinze mai mil sept cent quatre-vingt-onze," poster, folder L1141, ADCO.

14 Oratories were chapels used for masses on Sundays and other feast days.

15 In 1171, Hugh III, duke of Burgundy, pledged to raise a chapel to the Holy Virgin and St. Jean the Baptist if he survived his voyage to crusade in the Holy Land. On his return to Burgundy, he presented his pledge to Pope Alexander III, who issued a brief placing the chapel and its administration directly under the Holy See. In 1433, the duke Philip the Good made the chapel the seat of his new order of knights, the Toison d'Or.

16 "Loi relative a la circonscription des paroisse de Dijon." These petitions are referred to on the department's poster printed, at the earliest, in September 1791 to publish the law of 15 May in the department. Further reference to these early petitions is made by Volfius in letters dated 12 and 25 July 1791, noted below.

17 Volfius, Dijon, to Messieurs du Directoire du department de la Côte d'or, Dijon, 12 July 1791, folder L1141, ADCO.

18 Volfius, Dijon, to Messieurs (of the Comité ecclesiastique), Paris, 25 July 1791, folder L1140, ADCO.

19 "Loi relative a la circonscription des paroisses de Dijon." Printed below the law on this poster is the order of the department of the Côte d'Or providing for its publication. This order includes a discussion of the correspondence of the department with the minister of the interior.

20 Comité ecclésiastique de l'Assemblée nationale, Paris, to Messieurs (directoire du département de la Côte d'Or), Dijon, 7 September 1791, folder L1140, ADCO.

21 Ibid. A draft of the department's response is indicated in a note dated 22 September 1791, written in the margins of the Ecclesiastical Committee's letter.

22 Handwritten petition, [Parishioners of Saint-Nicolas], Dijon, to Messieurs les Députes de la Côte d'or a la premiere Législature, 10 September (1791), folder L 1141, ADCO.

23 For an important discussion of the co-optation of revolutionary rhetoric by France's catholic laity, see Desan, *Reclaiming the Sacred*, 135–48.

24 The petitioners were almost correct in the ratio of an episcopal vicar's salary in relation to a simple vicar's, but their absolute figures are quite a bit off. The Civil Constitution of the Clergy provided that, in cities with fewer than 50,000 inhabitants, the first vicar (the highest-paid episcopal vicar) would receive 1,200 *livres* and simple vicars 700 *livres*. [Assemblée constituent], *Décret sur la Constitution civil du clergé*, 25.

25 Petition, Dijon, to Messieurs les Administrateur[s] du Département de la Cotte Doré [*sic*] le 8bre [October] l'an trois de la Libertté francoise [*sic*] 1791, folder L1141, ADCO.

26 Citoyens actifs, Dijon, Petition to Messieurs les Administrateurs composant le directoire du departement de la Côte D'or, n.d., noted as registered by the department 15, 9br [November] 1791, folder L1141, ADCO. One hundred fifty individuals signed this petition. Active citizens were those who could vote in electoral assemblies. The Constituent Assembly established this division of France's citizenry into "active" and "passive" catagories with the law of 22 December 1789. Active citizens were male and at least twenty-five years old, and paid direct taxes equalling at least three days labour. The value of this tax depended on local conditions and could vary from ten to twenty *sous*. In Burgundy, the provision excluded about one-third of the male population twenty-five or older. As Jean Bart notes, this standard effectively disenfranchised those "elements judged the most dangerous": Bart, *La Révolution française en Bourgogne*, 150.

27 Sr. Françoise de St. Antoine, Sr. Marie-Anne de Ste. Claire, and Sr. Michele de St. Augustin to Messieurs, les Administrateurs du directoire du département de la Côte d'Or, n.d., received 23 8bre [October] 1791, folder 1141, ADCO. Les dames Bernardines de Tart à Dijon (Cistercians) were an early seventeenth-century reform of the Abbey Notre-Dame de Tart initiated by Bishop Zamet. The revolutionaries closed the convent and church in Dijon

at the end of September 1792. See Marilier, "Le monastère et l'église des Bernardines," 256–9, 288.

28 Parishioners of St –Pierre, Dijon, Petition to Messieurs les Administrateures du département de la Côte D'or, n.d., received 22, 9bre [November] 1791, rsolder L1141, ADCO.

29 Volfius, to Arnoult, Procureur-général-syndic, Dijon, 23 9bre [Novembee] 1791, folder 1141, ADCO.

30 Evidence of Volfius's support for the petitioning parishioners is found in the archives. In addition to his correspondence supporting the parishioners of Saint-Nicolas and Saint-Pierre during the summer months, he also wrote in early November to the president of the department's directory in support of the demands of these parishioners that their suburbs receive succursals. J.B. Volfius, Dijon, to Monsieur le president, 6 9bre [November] 1791, folder L1141, ADCO.

31 In addition to the Ecclesiastical Committee's letter of 7 September, Delenart, the minister of the interior, sent a form letter in late October instructing departments to carry out the laws related to the clergy and the redistricting of parishes. Delenart, Paris, to the Département de la Côte d'Or, Dijon, 31 October 1791, folder L1140, ADCO.

32 *Loi relative à la circonscription des paroisses des ville & faubourgs de Dijon, 9 mai 1792* (Paris: Imprimerie royale, 1792), folder L1141, ADCO.

33 Volfius, to Monsieur le president, 6 9bre [November] 1791.

34 The bishop of Langres had built Saint-Étienne to serve as his cathedral when he was resident in Dijon. With the creation of the diocese of Dijon in 1731, it became the bishop's cathedral. Saint-Bénigne was built in the sixth century over a large sarcophagus located in a cave that locals believed produced miracles. Grégoire, bishop of Langres, judged it a pagan tomb, but the cult of St. Bénigne persisted. By the time Grégory of Tours, grandson of the bishop, wrote *Liber in gloria martyrum* in the late sixth century, St. Bénigne had a *vita* and chapel consecrated to him. P. Gras, "Dijon," in *Dictionnaire d'histoire et de géographie ecclésiastiques*.

35 Volfius, Dijon, to Messieurs, Dijon, 6 June 1792, folder L1141, ADCO.

36 J.B. Volfius, Dijon, to Monsieur le president (of the department), Dijon, 27 June 1792, folder L1141, ADCO.

CHAPTER FIVE

1 Volfius, *Mandement de M. l'évêque de la Côte-d'Or* [6 February 1792], 3.

2 Five hundred *livres* was roughly the income of a priest in the pre-revolutionary period working on the *portion congrue*. The *portion congrue* was

a national minimum set for priests in areas where they received a salary rather than support from tithes, or other payments from parishioners, lands attached to the parish, or other type of endowment. The income of some priests was a mix of the *portion congrue* and one or more of these other sources of income. Other types of income supported some priests who did not receive the *portion congrue.*

3 Marc, *Biographie de Messire Chamberland* , 34–7.

4 Baker, "Politics, Privilege, and Political Culture," 156–7, 163, 169–72. Over the course of the revolution, Dijon lost 1,781 citizens to emigration.

5 "Arrêté du directoire de Département de la Côte d'Or, Pour le rétablissement de la tranquillité," 11 March 1792, folder L1439, Archives départementales de la Côte-d'Or (hereafter ADCO).

6 Guérin, "Une épisode de la persécution religieuse," 211.

7 Henriot, "La deportation des prêtres," 490.

8 Ibid., 492.

9 Sutherland, *The French Revolution and Empire*, 127.

10 Chauvot and Dubard et al., membres composant le Directoire du District d'Ilsurtille, Ilsurtille, to MM les administrateurs du Département, Dijon, 13 March 1792, folder L1144, ADCO.

11 Latreille and Rémond, *Histoire du catholicisme en France*, 101–3. Jean Leflon, *Histoire de l'église*, 99–102. Latreille, Rémond, and Leflon focus on the national level and discuss the September Massacres and the decree ordering the deportation of refractory clergy, both of which occurred after the fall of the monarchy in August 1792. The departmental repression in the Côte-d'Or demonstrates that the Terror against the refractory clergy actually began earlier and was first initiated on the local level.

12 J.B. Volfius, Dijon, to Messieurs du Directoire du Departement, 28 April 1792, folder L1091, ADCO.

13 "Extrait du registre des délibérations de la muncipalité d'Arnay sur Perroux," 7 May 1792, folder L1180, ADCO.

14 See Guérin, "Une épisode de la persécution religieuse"; Dijon's municipal library holds Leprince's papers, including his account of the revolutionary period in the city.

15 In the Côte-d'Or, the mobilization of a battalion of volunteers followed the Declaration of Pillnitz on 27 August 1791. Jean Bart notes that this was the department's first patriotic response to the growing threat of war. See *La Révolution française en Bourgogne*, 200. See also, Guérin, "Une épisode de la persécution religieuse," 212n1. While fighting with General Lafayette's Army of the North, Cazotte and his men engaged in a minor skirmish at Gliswelle. Although the action was ancillary to the Army of

the North's objectives, one writer later celebrated it as revealing the heroic spirit of France's revolutionary volunteer soldiers and styled it France's Thermopylae. See Z.J. Pierart, who dedicated an appendix to the fighting at Gliswelle in *La grande épopée de l'an II*.

16 The franc was not in use as a currency in 1792, being introduced in 1795. Guerin gives this figure in his notes.

17 "Extrait des register des deliberations de la municipalité de Dijon," 18 June 1792, folder L1181, ADCO. In a letter to the National Assembly read by Guyton de Morveau, a deputy from the Côte-d'Or, the department wrote that it was the "affaire de Mons" that agitated the crowd. The department's letter does not survive, only the account of it in the Archives parlémentaire. The *affaire de Mons* involved the accusations of treason and subsequent court martial of the officers and dragoons of the fifth and sixth regiments of the Army of the North who, when ordered into battle at Jemappes, had abandoned their posts and in their flight disrupted others. They were under the command of Lieutenant General Biron. The National Assembly ordered the men to face court martial in mid-May 1792, and the affair was not resolved until mid-summer. It is possible, that the *affaire de Mons* was also a topic of concern for the Jacobins of Dijon in mid-June. The immediate report of the club's meeting, provided by the city's commissioners, however, names the death of Cazotte at Gliswelle as the war news that agitated the crowds that evening. Madival and Laurent et al., eds. *Archives parlémentaire*, 43: 248 ff. There is discussion of this affair in volumes 44–6 as well. Baudot also recorded that it was the death of Cazotte that agitated the Jacobins at the meeting on 17 June. See Guerin, "Une épisode de la persécution religieuse."

18 For a recent reconsideration of the Girondin and Jacobin politics leading up to the Terror, see Linton, *Choosing Terror*, 120–33.

19 Ibid.

20 Leprince provides the fullest account of these attempted arrests. Efforts to arrest nuns in these disturbances in Dijon are also noted by Guyton de Morveau in his report to the legislative assembly. See *Archives parliamentaires*.

21 Ibid., 216.

22 Leprince reprinted the petition with the department's response in his account. See ibid., 217–18. See also *Pétition des membres du conseil épiscopal*, available in Bibliothèque nationale (France), *The French Revolution Research Collection*.

23 Volfius, letter to the department directory, 19 June 1792, folder L1181, ADCO.

24 Municipalité de Dijon, "Tranquillité publique" (1792). The poster's date is
    21 June 1792.

25 *Archives parliamentaire.*

26 Letter from Terrier, minister of the interior, to the directory and *pro-
    cureur-générale* of the Côte-d'Or, 23 June 1792 and 26 June 26, 1792,
    folder L1181, ADCO.

27 "Extrait des registres de la municipalité de Dijon, 3 juillet 1792" and
    "Extrait de régistre des déliberations de la municipalité de Dijon, 4 juillet
    1792," folder L1181, ADCO.

28 Giroux, "Les femmes clubistes à Dijon," 23.

29 One example is Suzanne Desan's study of lay religious activism in the
    department of the Yonne, adjacent to the Côte-d'Or. See *Reclaiming the
    Sacred.*

30 Chauvin, *Le clergé à l'épreuve de la Révolution,* 71.

31 Albert Mathiez discussed the various pieces of legislation concerning
    the clergy and the churches that followed the fall of the monarchy on
    10 August. See *Les conséquences religieuses,* 10–13.

32 Henriot, "La deportation des prêtres"; Mathiez, *Les conséquences
    religieuses,* 3–4.

33 Henriot, "La deportation des prêtres," 490. Districts in each department
    carried out these deportation orders; the lists of forty to fifty districts
    survive.

34 Ibid., 490–1.

35 Sutherland, *The French Revolution and Empire,* 140. For a discussion of
    the widespread arrests that took place in late August, see Schama, *Citizens,*
    624–7, and Latreille and Rémond, *Histoire du catholicisme,* 102.

36 Henriot, "La deportation des prêtres," 491.

37 Ibid., 495.

38 Ibid., 496.

39 Ibid., 497.

40 Ibid.

41 Mathiez, *Les conséquences religieuses,* 8.

42 See Latreille and Rémond, *Histoire du catholicisme,* 101–3; Jean Leflon,
    Histoire de l'église, 99–102.

43 Volfius, *Mandement de M. L'Évêque de la Côte-d'Or* [20 September
    1792], 12.

44 Ibid., 2–8.

45 Ibid.

46 Volfius, *Instruction pastorale de M. l'Évêque.*

47 Ibid., 5–6.

48 Ibid., 7.
49 Ibid., 15–16.
50 Volfius, *Mandement du Citoyen Évêque*, 2.
51 Ibid., 3.
52 Ibid., 3–4, 5–6.
53 Mathiez, *Les consequences religieuses*, 13–21.
54 Sciout's analysis is given in, *Histoire de la Constitution civile du clergé*, vol. 3, *L'église sous la Terreur et le directoire*, 362. Cited by Mathiez in *Les consequences religieuses*, 21.
55 Volfius, *Mandement du Citoyen Évêque*, 8.
56 Ibid., 8–9.
57 Ibid., 10.
58 Ibid., 11–12, 14.
59 "Le directoire du department de la Côte-d'Or, aux officiers municipaux de son ressort" (Dijon, 1792), microform copy in Bibliothèque nationale, *French Revolution Research Collection*, 8/361.
60 Cheveneau et al. "Arrête," 6 April 1793, folder L1142, ADCO, which references the convention's decree of September 1792.
61 Order reprinted in Ledeuil, *La Révolution à Dijon*, 37.

CHAPTER SIX

1 A study of the role of religion in this conflict is Woell, *Small-town Martyrs and Murderers*, 143–53.
2 The tensions between the Girondin deputies and the Jacobins grew after the fall of the monarchy and the establishment of the National Convention. See Linton, *Choosing Terror*, 148–58 and 170–3.
3 Aston, *Religion and Revolution in France*, 215; Latreille and Rémond, *Historie du Catholicism*, 114–15.
4 Latrielle and Rémond, *Historie du Catholicism*, 115.
5 After 9 *thermidor*, Louis Guyardin (1758–1816) successfully defended himself against the charge of being a Terrorist and went on to have a career under the Directory and Empire. See Lesueur, "Guyardin (Louis)," in Hoefer, ed., *Nouvelle biographie générale*, 926. Following the Terror, Jean-Baptiste Milhaud (1766–1833) escaped prosecution despite his arrest on 12 *germinal l'an* 3 [1 April 1795]. Too young to serve in the new legislative body, he returned to military service and played an important role in the events of 18 *brumaire*. In 1800 he was made a brigadier general. Following Napoleon's defeat in 1815, he retreated to the Loire with his cavalry corps. He was among the first of Napoleon's generals to surrender to Louis XVIII. See the

entry "Milhaud (le comte Jean-Baptiste)" in J Michaud, Michaud, and Desplaces, eds., *Biographie universelle ancienne et moderne*.

6 *Arrêté des représentans du Peuple près l'armée du Rhin* (Dijon: P. Causse, l'an 2 [1793–4]), older L1153, Archives départementales de la Côte-d'Or (hereafter ADCO).

7 "Arrêté du conseil général du département de la Côte-d'Or, relatif à l'exercice des cultes religieux," printed with *Arrêté des représentans du Peuple près l'armée du Rhin*, 2–4, folder L1153, ADCO.

8 Green, "Dechristianization at Dijon," 31.

9 La société populaire, Beaune, to Directoire du département de la Côte-d'Or, Dijon, 28 *brumaire l'an 2* [18 November 1793], folder L1153, ADCO.

10 *Arrêté du conseil général du département de la Côte-d'Or, qui ordonne la suppression de l'oblation du pain-béni, dans tous les temples du culte catholique de son ressort, du 27 brumaire l'an second de la république française, une et indivisible* (Dijon: P. Causse, 2), folder L1153, ADCO.

11 *Procès-verbal dressé par le conseil général du département de la Côte-d'Or, relativement à la renonciation faite par les citoyens Jean-Augustin Alteyrac, demeurant à Châtillon-sur-Seine, et Charles Chaisneau, de Plombières, de leur caractère de prêtre. Séance du 22 brumaire, l'an 2* (Dijon: P. Causse, *l'an 2*).

12 Ibid., 2.

13 "Du régistre des délibérations de la municipalité de Brion sur ource a été extrait ce qui Sivr," 2 July 1791, folder L1502 128 (Rebourceau (Edme)), ADCO.

14 *Procès-verbal dressé par le conseil général*, 3.

15 By November 1793, Chaisneau had two published pamphlets in support of the revolution: *Pastorales dédiées à la Nation* (Dijon: Bidault, 1791) and *Le Panthéon français, ou discourse sur les honneurs publics décernés par la nation à la mémoire des grands hommes* (Dijon: P. Causse, 1792). Before the revolution, Chaisneau had published pastorales, including *Palémon, pastorale* (Paris: Chez Lesclapart, 1787) and *Acras, pastorale sur les assemblées provincials* (Sens: Chez la veuve Tarbé, 1788). After his resignation, Chaisneau continued to write in support of the revolution, publishing *Éloge de Michel Lepelletier, prononce dans le temple de la Raison, à Auxerre, le 20 pluv. an II* (Auxerre: L. Fournier, n.d.) and *Couplets sur la reprise de Toulon, dont la ville sera rasée & le port conservé sous le nom Port de la Montagne* (Auxerre: L. Fournier, 1794), as well as an edited collection of patriotic speeches, *Recueil de pièces*

patriotiques, à l'occasion de la reconnaissance de l'Être suprême & de l'immoralité de l'âme, & de la fête qui a eu lieu à Paris & à Auxerre à ce sujet, le 20 prairial, seconde année républicaine (Auxerre: L. Fournier, 1794). During the empire, Chaisneau continued to write, publishing a work on natural history and a book on rhetoric. For a brief study of Chaisneau, see Durandeau, *Un curé sans-culotte.*

16 *Procès-verbal dressé par le conseil général,* 3.

17 Ibid., 5.

18 *Procès-verbal dressé par le conseil général,* 6–7. The popularity of printing as a career for ex-priests is suggested by the report of one ex-curé, Géruzez, of the department of the Marne. Writing to the editor of the widely circulated journal, *La feuille villageoise,* in April 1794, he explained that he had left the priesthood to become a printer. His decision to take up a career in printing, he continued, was influenced by Rousseau's argument in the novel *Émile* for the nobility of artisanal labour. See Géruzez, "Ex-curé Imprimeur," *La feuille villageoise* (5 floréal l'an 2 [24 April 1794]), 73–9.

19 Like Alteyrac and Chaisneau, priests across France submitted their letters of abdication to the National Convention. Today these documents fill twenty-one cartons in the Archives nationales F19 872-93, *Lettres de prêtres classes, démissions données devant diverses administrations.* From November 1793 to April 1794, most publicly functioning priests resigned their positions and submitted their *lettres de prêtrise* to departmental or other civil officials. See Byrnes, *Priests of the French Revolution,* 142–9, 281.

20 Jean Leflon, *Histoire de l'église,* 117–19; Schama, *Citizens,* 778.

21 Most of the anti-religious violence was directed against France's Catholic majority, but Protestant and Jews were targeted in locations where they held prominent social positions. For example, in Nîmes, Catholic artisans attacked rich Protestant bankers, and, in eastern France, economic grievance inspired violence against the local Jewish population. See Cobb, "Les débuts de la déchristianisation," 194–5nn14–15.

22 The term *dechristianization* was first used by Monseigneur Dupanloup, the bishop of Orléans, who after 1854 applied it to the drift away from the Christian Church in the nineteenth century. It was applied to the revolution by Aulard and Mathiez, who, writing at the beginning of the twentieth century, were working in the climate of "a Republican and secularized France," following the separation of church and state of 1905. In their analysis of the events of year 2, Aulard and Mathiez owe a debt to the nineteenth-century French historian Jules Michelet, who had written

about the "dechristianization of the Latin races." See Plongeron and
Argyriou, *Les défis de la modernité*, 366. Michel Vovelle also discusses the
role of Mgr. Dupanloup in developing the term *dechristianization*: see *The
Revolution against the Church*, 5.

23 Marissa Linton provides a helpful discussion of the historiography of the
Terror in *Choosing Terror*, 4–20.

24 Sutherland, *The French Revolution and Empire*, 175.

25 Jordan, *The Revolutionary Career of Maximilien Robespierre*, 174–5.

26 Furet, "Terror," in Furet and Ozouf, eds., *A Critical Dictionary of the
French Revolution*, 148–9; Furet, *Revolutionary France*, 136, 140.

27 Sutherland, *The French Revolution and Empire*, 177.

28 Linton, *Choosing Terror*, 3–8, 23–5.

29 Sutherland, *The French Revolution and Empire*, 177, 197.

30 An excellent discussion of the involvement of these citizen armies in the
dechristianization movement of year 2 is found in Cobb, *The People's
Armies*, 442–79.

31 Van Kley "Christianity as Casualty and Chrysalis."

32 Vovelle, *Religion et revolution*.

33 Vovelle, *The Revolution against the Church*, 6.

34 Cobb, *People's Armies*, 477–78.

35 Sutherland, *The French Revolution and Empire*, 188–90.

36 Plongeron and Argyriou, *Les défis de la modernité*, 363–4.

37 Péronnet and Lochot, *La Révolution dans le département de la Côte-d'Or*,
116. The first issue of *Le Nécessaire* appeared 5 *pluviôse l'an* 2
(24 January 1794). This new journal continued the effort of an earlier
weekly, *Le Journal patriotique de la Côte d'Or*, which had folded at the
end of 1791.

38 These departments were the Ain, Jura, Doubs, Côte-d'Or, Mont Terrible,
and Haute-Saône.

39 Kuściński, *Dictionnaire des conventionnels*, 50–1.

40 Named to the Committee of General security in January 1793, Bernard de
Saintes first went on mission in March 1793 to help recruit troops to meet
the goal of conscripting 300,000 men. On that mission, he went, with Jean
Guimbertau, to the departments of Charente and Charente-Inférieure.
Kuściński, *Dictionnaire des conventionnels*, 50–1. Additional discussions
of Bernard de Saintes' work in the Côte-d'Or can be found in "Bernard de
Saintes (Adrien-Antoine)," in Michaud et al., eds., *Biographie universelle
ancienne et moderne*, 66–7; Péronnet and Lochot, *La Révolution dans le
département de la Côte-d'Or*, 114–17; and Baker, "Politics, Privilege, and
Political Culture," 213–15, 217. It should be noted that the biographical

note in Michaud's volume contains some inaccurate information that is corrected by Kuściński.

41 John McManners provides a brief overview of the cult of reason in *The French Revolution and the Church*, 98–105. Longer studies include Aulard, *Le culte de la raison* and Vovelle, *The Revolution against the Church*.

42 Ledeuil, *La Révolution à Dijon*, 40. The department named Devosges as a special commissioner to assess and conserve the art from the city's churches; his acquisitions became the foundation for Dijon's museum of fine arts; see Péronnet and Lochot, *La Révolution dans le département de la Côte-d'Or*, 123.

43 *Discours destine à être prononcé au temple de la raison.*

44 Ibid., 1, citing Pierre Corneille's *Polyeucte*, IV, 6.

45 Ibid., 1–2.

46 Ibid., 9. For the author's deistic description of God, see, 3–10.

47 Ibid., 7, 10–11, 13–15, 17, and 20–1.

48 Ibid., 22, 29–30, 26–7; the quote is on 27.

49 Ibid., 33–8, 41–3.

50 Ledeuil, *La Révolution à Dijon*, 48; Baker, "Politics, Privilege, and Political Culture," 216.

51 Fondard's death was one of the executions carried out in the spring of 1793 after the arrival of Léonard Bourdon. It was offered as an example of the crimes of Bourdon and Pioche-Fer Bernard de Saintes in a pamphlet written by the sections of Dijon denouncing the two men in May 1795. See *Dénonciation faite par les six sections de la commune de Dijon à la Convention nationale, des crimes commis par les représentans du peuple Léonard Bourdon et Pioche-Fer-Bernard de Saintes, pendans leur mission dans le département de la Côte-d'Or* (Dijon: Imprimerie de Frantin, *l'an* 3), 6. Baker names Fondard as the instigator of the March riot, and states that it is not clear whether Bourdon brought Fondard before the revolutionary tribunal in Dijon or whether the tribunal acted on its own; see Baker, "Politics, Privilege, and Political Culture," 209–10. Péronnet and Lochot are more confident of the influence of Bourdon and of Claude-Charles Prost, a second representative on mission travelling with Bourdon, on the execution of Fondard. They write that the arrest of Fondard was the first action of the representatives in their visit to the department; see Péronnet and Lochot, *La Révolution dans le département de la Côte-d'Or*, 113. A recent biography of Bourdon, by Michael J. Sydenham, provides more detail on the incident and casts a sceptical eye toward Bourdon's later detractors in the Côte-d'Or. The authors of the *Dénonciation* were,

according to Sydenham, substantial citizens who were shut out of the political process in Dijon during the Terror. On Fondard's execution, Sydenham concludes that Bourdon's presence in Dijon and inspection of its prisons moved the local tribunal, which had been "dilatory," to act in Fondard's case. See Sydenham, *Léonard Bourdon*, 119–25; the discussion of Fondard's case begins on 123.

52 Joly, *Le Nécessaire*, no. 8 (10 *ventôse l'an 2* / 28 February 1794), 31. *Le Nécessaire* first appeared 5 *pluviôse l'an 2* (24 January 1794), about a month before Joly's article. It appeared twice each *décade*, the ten-day week of the revolutionary calendar, and cost nine *livres* per year. In 1796, Vivant Carion, a former constitutional priest, took over the paper. Carion kept the newspaper publishing under various titles until his death in 1834, when it passed to his son-in-law. See Milsand, *Périodiques publiés à Dijon*, 4–10; Hugueney, *Les clubs Dijonnais*, 158.

53 *Le Nécessaire*, no. 9 (15 *ventôse l'an 2* / 5 March 1794), 35. The original quotation is as follows: "O vous qui croyez *par ce qu'on vous dit*, devenez hommes! faites, enfin, usage de votre raison; cherchez, par son secours, à connoître avec nous si ce qu'on vous a appris du culte porte une empreinte sacrée, ou si l'on n'y découvre que des absurdités avancées sans fondement."

54 The Archives départementales de la Côte-d'Or has thirteen different posters signed by Albitte that list the names of priests from various districts in the departments of Ain and Mont-Blanc who had resigned their positions. The earliest of these posters was dated 20 *pluviôse l'an 2* (8 February 1794) and did not include the *Acte d'Abdication de Prêtrise*. It provided a table listing the name, age, place of birth, year of ordination, and title of the priests who had resigned. Later posters included the text of the statement the priests had signed. The last of these posters was dated 27 *ventôse l'an 2* (17 March 1794). Another poster with the same date did not list the names of abdicating priests but instead explained that Albitte's purpose in creating and distributing these posters was to encourage priests in other departments to also resign. Only the poster of 4 *ventôse l'an 2* (22 February 1794) included a speech by an abdicating priest. See folder L1144, ADCO. Albitte was elected to both the Legislative Assembly and the National Convention. During his tenure in the Legislative Assembly, he was especially occupied with military affairs. In the National Convention, his expertise in this area was utilized in 1793, when he was sent on mission with the Army of the Alps. In January 1794, he undertook the task of organizing the revolutionary governments in the departments of the Ain and Montblanc. For a brief biography of Albitte, see Kuściński, *Dictionnaire des conventionne*, 2–3.

55 Albitte, "Tableau des ci-devant prêtres du district de Belley, département de l'Ain," 4 *ventôse l'an* 2 (22 February 1794), 3, folder L1144, ADCO.

56 The tables of priests abdicating in the districts of Cluse, Thonon, and Arc in the department of Mont-Blanc were placed together on one poster.

57 *Le Nécessaire*, no. 11 (25 *ventôse l'an* 2 / 15 March 1794), 42–3.

58 In the previous issue of *Le Nécessaire*, the journal had printed a copy of the department's letter to the minister of the interior that established four classes among the priests who were renouncing their positions. Only the first class, those who had declared in writing that they renounced both their state (*état*) and functions as priests and had submitted their letters of ordination, were judged to be entitled to receive the annual aid the law provided. The second class included individuals who had declared in writing that they were leaving both their state and functions as priests and who affirmed that they had intended to do so since the passage of the Civil Constitution. In contrast to the first class of priests, this second class had not submitted their letters of ordination. Volfius's declaration fell into the third class. He had renounced his state and functions in writing but had not argued that this resignation reflected a long held disdain for Christianity. Like the second class, he also had not submitted his letters of ordination immediately. The department indicated that it doubted that individuals in the second and third classes were deserving of the annual aid being offered by the state. The final class of priests resigning were those who only resigned their functions. For this last group, the department recommended without reservation that they be denied any state aid. See *Le Nécessaire*, no. 10 (20 *ventôse l'an* 2 / 10 March 1794), 40.

59 Petetin et al., Dijon, to Comité d'instruction publique de la Convention nationale, 17 *germinal l'an* 2 (6 April 1794), folder L1144, ADCO.

60 Volfius, "Discours de J. B. Volfius, au directoire du département," *Affiches de Dijon ou Journal du Département de la Côte-d'or*, no. 17 (7 *ventôse l'an* 2 / 25 February 1794), 66–7. Enclosure in letter of Volfius, Dijon, to the abbé Grégoire, Paris, 22 *germinal l'an* 3 (11 April 1795), Lettres de Volfius, évêque de la Côte-d'Or, Dossier Côte-d'Or, Collection Grégoire, Bibliothèque de la Société de Port-Royal (hereafter PR). A manuscript copy of Volfius's letter of resignation can be found in folder L1142, ADCO. An older periodical than *Le Nécessaire*, the *Affiches de Dijon* began publication in 1783. It appeared on Tuesdays and cost six *livres* per year. Unlike *Le Necéssaire*, it did not have a long revolutionary career, ceasing publication in 1795.

61 Volfius related his account of the Terror in the Côte-d'Or and his resignation of his position as bishop in two letters to the abbé Grégoire, written a
   year after the events described. Volfius, Dijon, to the abbé Grégoire, Paris,
   1 *germinal l'an* 3 (21 March 1795) and 22 *germinal l'an* 3 (11 April
   1795), in Lettres de Volfius, évêque de la Côte-d'Or, Dossier Côte-d'or,
   Collection Grégoire, PR. He also published, in March 1795, an explanation of his resignation and the events surrounding it. See Volfius, "Lettre
   de J.B. Volfius, au Rédacteur."

62 Volfius, Dijon, to the abbé Grégoire, Paris, 22 *germinal l'an* 3 (11 April
   1795), Lettres de Volfius, évêque de la Côte-d'Or, Dossier Côte-d'Or,
   Collection Grégoire (PR).

63 At this point of reversal in his career, Volfius identified with Fénelon, the
   bishop of Cambrai, who lived from 1651 to 1715. As the preceptor of the
   Duc de Bourgogne and Louis XIV's grandson and presumed heir, Fénelon
   had been a rising star in the court of Louis XIV until he was undone in
   1697 by his association with the Quietist controversy. Banished from Paris
   and Versailles, Fénelon spent the remainder of his career at Cambrai, a
   bishopric he was awarded by the king during friendlier times. A brief biography of Fénelon's life as well as discussions of his major works can be
   found in Davis, *Fénelon*. In the eighteenth century, Fénelon enjoyed
   unusual popularity for a churchman among the *philosophes*. Celebrated
   as an "*âme sensible*," as well as a hero and a martyr, *Fénelon* was depicted
   as "a sort of earlier edition of the Vicaire Savoyard," Rousseau's good
   priest in the novel Émile who teaches a simple faith that is in harmony
   with nature. For a discussion of the eighteenth-century's re-creation of
   Fénelon, see Jones, "Fénelon," in Hearnshaw, ed., *Social and Political Ideas
   of Some Great French Thinkers of the Age of Reason*, F.J.C., 70–103; the
   phrases quoted above on 72.

64 Volfius, "Discours de J.B. Volfius, au directoire du département."

65 Petition, "Au Nom du Peuple Française," Velard le Trivy, 2 décade de 2
   mois de 1793, 2eme de la République française, folder L1164/10, ADCO.

66 Arrête, Directoire de la department de la Côte-d'Or, 18 *brumaire l'an* 2 (8
   November 1793), folder L1164/10, ADCO.

67 Chauvot, Dubard, Muteau, et al., Procès verbal, comité de suveillance
   d'Is-sur-Tille, 14 *nivôse l'an* 2 (3 January 1794), folder L1948/14, ADCO.
   The office of national agent is another development of this era.
   Replacing the locally elected *procureur*'s, the national agents, who were
   appointed by the convention or its representatives on mission, were
   established in December 1793. The departmental councils were suspect

after the Federalist revolts of 1793, and the National Convention side-lined them with the creation of national agents. R.R. Palmer judged the creation of the national agents the foundation of revolutionary dictatorship; François Furet offered a more measured assessment, arguing that eighteenth-century conditions (e.g., slow communication, ingrained habits, local attitudes) mitigated somewhat the centralization of authority envisioned with this new office. See Palmer, *Twelve Who Ruled*, 127, and Furet, "Revolutionary Government" in Furet and Ozouf, eds., *A Critical Dictionary of the French Revolution*, 552.

68 Arrête, Pioche-Fer Bernard, représentant du people, Dijon, 18 *pluviôse l'an* 2 (6 February 1794), folder L1948/14, ADCO.
69 Arrête, Bernard, représentant de people, 11 *ventôse l'an* 2; copy made by A. Lombard, 5 *brumaire l'an* 3 (26 October 1793), folder L1949/9, ADCO.
70 J.B. Grosdidier, manuscript statement resigning his ecclesiastical functions, 20 *ventôse l'an* 2 (10 March 1794), folder L1949/9, ADCO.
71 Letter from J.B. Grosdidier, de la maison d'arrestation d'Is-sur-Til[le], to citoyens administrateurs, 20 *ventôse l'an* 2 (10 March 1794), folder L1949/9, ADCO.
72 Gouget, Chauvot, Muteau, et al., declaration by directory of Is-sur-Tille, not dated, inserted between Grosdidier's statement resigning his functions, 20 *ventôse l'an* 2 (10 March 1794) and a letter by Grosdidier, from the prison at Is-sur-Tille, to citoyens administrateurs, 20 *ventôse l'an* 2, folder L1949/9, ADCO. Grosdidier's position as president of the local Société des sans-culottes républicains is noted in a certificate of civism issued to him in January 1794 by that society, see Grosdidier, Boudet, Barlet, and Goulard, "Société des Sans-Culottes Républicains, séante à Champagne-sur-Vingeanne," 30 *nivôse l'an* 2 (19 January 1794), folder L1949/9, ADCO.
73 "Extrait du tableau rempli par le comité de surveillance de la muncipalité de Champagne," 5 *germinal l'an* 2 (25 March 1794), folder L1949 /9, ADCO.
74 Letter from the administration of the department of the Côte-d'Or, Dijon, to the district of Is-sur-Tille, 4 *germinal l'an* 2 (24 March 1794), folder L1167/13, ADCO.
75 "Extrait du register des déliberations du conséil général permanent de la commune de Dijon," 1 July 1793, Folder L 1949/9, ADCO.
76 Comité de surveillance, Champagne, 24 *prairial l'an* 2 (12 June 1794), folder L1949/9, ADCO.

77 Letter, J.B. Grosdidier, Gray, to "le citoyen représentant du peuple rélégué de la convention nationale près le département de la Côte-d'Or" [Jean-Marie Calès], ca. November 1794, folder L1949/9, ADCO.

78 Grosdidier explained the difficulties he had been facing in a letter. See J.B. Grosdidier, Gray, to le citoyen Burard, sécrétaire greffier du bureau de conciliation, Dijon, 16 *brumaire l'an* 3 (6 November 1794), folder L1949/9, ADCO.

79 "Extrait du register des deliberations du conseil général de la commune de Champagne," 22 *vendémiaire l'an* 3 (13 October 1794), folder L1949/9, ADCO.

80 "Bernard de Saintes," in Michaud et al., eds., *Biographie universelle ancienne et modern.*

81 Letter, J.B. Grosdidier, Gray, to "le citoyen représentant du peuple," n.d., ca. November 1794, folder L1949/9, ADCO.

82 Letter, J.B. Grosdidier, Gray, to Citizen Burard, Dijon, 16 *brumaire* l'an 3 (6 November 1794), folderL1949/9, ADCO.

83 "Extrait des régistres du sécretariat du district de Gray département de la Haute Saône, Convention Nationale, " 7 *pluviôse l'an* 3 (26 January 1795), folder L1949/9, ADCO.

84 Judgment of Procureur Syndic, 2 *brumaire l'an* 4 (23 October 1795), folder L1949/9, ADCO.

85 Baker, "Politics, Privilege, and Political Culture," 201, 216–17.

86 Péronnet and Lochot, *La Révolution dans le département de la Côte-d'Or,* 123, 125.

87 This number is based upon an analysis byXavier Maréchaux, "Prêtres mariés de la Révolution à l'Empire." Maréchaux's principal source is Eugène Reinert, who had wide-ranging interests as he collected data, and his tables on married clergy include every married priest with any connection to the department. The analysis in this paragraph is based upon Maréchaux's biographical entries.

88 In Appendix 2 in *Noces révolutionnaire,* 169–71, Maréchaux gives a total for married priests from the Côte-d'Or. This figure includes all priests with a relationship to the department, not only those that were clearly constitutional clergy in the department. However, the Côte-d'Or was a region with a large number of priestly marriages, as Maréchaux's study reveals.

89 Sauvageot, *Discours prononce le 10 germinal.*

90 Ibid., 2–6.

91 "Instruction républicaine," *Le Nécessaire,* no. 14 (10 *germinal l'an* 2 / 30 March 1794), 56: "Le premier miracle que ce suaire ait fait, est de

rammener à la raison ceux qui sembloient condamnés a ne jamais l'entendre."

92 "Instruction républicaine," *Le Nécessaire*, no. 15 (15 *germinal l'an 2* / 4 April 1794), 59.

93 Ibid., 60: "O citoyens quand ferez vous donc hommes, quand connoîtrez-vous toute la grandeur de votre être?"

94 Ibid.: "fuiez, fuiez vous tous qui demandez des prêtres; allez habiter un séjour où règne le dèshonneur, l'esclavage, la tyrannie, la superstition, vous n'êtes pas dignes d'être républicains."

95 [Villemin], "Instruction républicaine," *Le Nécessaire*, no. 16 (20 *germinal l'an 2* / 9 April 1794), 63.

96 "Les déprêtrisés," *Le Nécessaire*, no. 18 (30 *germinal l'an 2* / 19 April 1794), 71.

97 The first instalment of this article was in *Le Nécessaire* issue 17 (25 *germinal l'an 2* / 14 April 1794). Later instalments appeared in issue 18 (30 *germinal l'an 2* / 19 April 1794, issue 19 (5 *floréal l'an 2* / 24 April 1794), and issue 21 (15 *floréal l'an 2* / 4 May 1794).

98 "Instruction républicaine," *Le Nécessaire*, no. 17 (25 *germinal l'an 2* / 17 April 1794), 67–8.

99 "Instruction républicaine," *Le Nécessaire*, no. 18 (30 *germinal l'an 2* / 19 April 1794), 71–2.

100 "Instruction républicaine," *Le Nécessaire*, no. 19 (5 *floréal l'an 2* / 24 April 1794), 75–6.

101 "Instruction républicaine," *Le Nécessaire*, no. 21 (15 *floréal l'an 2* / 4 May 1794), 82–3; "Instruction républicaine," *Le Nécessaire*, no. 36 (9 *messidor l'an 2* / 27 June 1794), 143–4.

102 These columns appeared in numbers 42, 44, and 46 of *Le Nécessaire* in year 2, and numbers 2, 4, and 6 in year 3.

CHAPTER SEVEN

1 *La société populaire régénérée de Dijon*, French Revolution Pamphlet Collection, Newberry Library (hereafter NB).

2 Kennedy, *The Jacobin Clubs in the French Revolution*, 243–4.

3 Calès's mission in the Côte-d'Or was brief. He remained in the department until early January 1795. The National Convention passed a decree on 5 *nivôse l'an 3* (25 December 1794) instructing him to move to Besançon in the department of the Doubs. Biard, *Missionnaires de la République*, 473. Calès's mission in the Côte-d'Or is also discussed in Peronnet and Lochot, *La Révolution dans le département de la Côte-d'Or*, 126.

4   "Jean Marie Calès," in Michaud et al., eds., *Biographie universelle ancienne et moderne*, 392–3, cites a speech by Calès, "Discours du citoyen Calès, représentant du peuple à l'armée des Ardennes, prononcé au champ de Mars de Sedan, le 10 août, l'an 2ᵉ de la république françoise, une et indivisible" (Sedan: De l'imprimerie de C. Baudin, 1794).

5   Peronnet and Lochot, *La Révolution dans le département de la Côte-d'Or*, 127–8; Baker, "Politics, Privilege, and Political Culture," 175–6, 241–4.

6   Baker, "Politics, Privilege, and Political Culture," 175–6, 241–4.

7   A copy of Calès's order was printed in *Le Nécessaire, ou journal du department de la Côte-d'Or, par Carion*. See "Administration: Arrêtés du représentant du people, 26 frimaire," no. 19 (5 *nivôse l'an 3 / 25 December 1794), 75.

8   "Administration: Arrêtés du représentant du people, 3 nivôse," *Le Nécessaire*, no. 21 (15 *nivôse l'an 3 / 4* January 1795), 83–4.

9   Lamarre, *Petites villes et fait urbain*, 121, 130.

10   "Extrait des procès verbaux des séances du directoire du district d'Arnay le Duc," 24 March 1791, folder L1140, Archives départementales de la Côte-d'Or (hereafter ADCO).

11   "Citoyens administrateurs du directoire du district de Dijon," [December 1794], folder L1806/9, ADCO.

12   "Aux officiers municipaux de la commune de Prâlon, canton de Fleurey, district de Dijon," 4 *nivos* [*sic*], *l'an* 3 (24 December 1794), folder L1806/9, ADCO.

13   "Déclaration de Jean Jerôme Quillot faite a Dijon par devant les Citoÿens administrateurs, composant Le directoire du district de dijon, conformément à L'arreté du Citoÿen Cales représentant du peuple francois dans le département de la Côte d or," 11 *nivos* [*sic*] *l'an* 3 (31 December 1794), folder L1176/29, ADCO.

14   Manuscript declaration signed by Marinet, n.d., folder L1176/29, ADCO.

15   The local journal, *Le Nécessaire*, reported on the provisions of this law in early March, see "Legislation," *Le Nécessaire* 33 (15 *ventôse l'an* 3 / 5 March 1795): 130.

16   Suratteau, "Le Directoire ," 79.

17   Dean notes that Grégoire first attended a meeting of the Évêques réunis on 13 December 1794. He submitted to the group a draft of his speech to the Convention. See Dean, *L'abbé Grégoire*, 11–21.

18   Ibid.

19   Grégoire, *Discours sur la liberté des cultes*, 5, French Revolution Pamphlet Collection, NB.

20   Ibid., 7–8, 11–13.

21 Ibid., 15–16.

22 Ibid., 3.

23 Dean, *L'abbé Grégoire*, 18–21. Jean Leflon also discusses the efforts of Durand de Maillane and Baudin in *Histoire de l'église*, 131.

24 Desan, *Reclaiming the Sacred*, 202.

25 Augustin Gazier, Études sur l'histoire religieuse, 249–51.

26 Guezno's surname is spelled at times as Guesno. Kuściński, *Dictionnaire de Conventionnels*, 314–15.

27 Cited in Dean, *L'abbé Grégoire*, 22.

28 Gazier, Études *sur l'histoire religieuse*, 252–3.

29 Cited in Jean Leflon, *Histoire de l'église*, 131–2.

30 Dean, *L'abbé Grégoire*, 24–5.

31 Plongeron and Argyriou, *Les défis de la modernité*, 454.

32 Suratteau, "Le Directoire," 80.

33 *Lettre encyclique ... Avec leur déclaration de foi* , French Revolution Pamphlet Collection, NB.

34 Ibid., 2–4. The prophet Ezra led a group of Israelites from exile back to Jerusalem during the reign of Artaxerxes I (464–423 BCE). Although given a free hand by Artaxerexes to reconstitute the Israelite community in Jerusalem. Ezra's task was complicated by the intermarriage of the Israelites with the peoples in the lands where they had been exiled. In the book of Ezra, this intermarriage is presented as a violation of the commandment of the Israelite's god that they not marry the people of the lands of Canaan. See Ezra 7–9, especially 9:1–12.

35 *Lettre encyclique ... Avec leur déclaration de foi*, 5–6.

36 Ibid., 9–11.

37 Ibid., 12.

38 Ibid., 15–20.

39 Ibid., 20–1, 23–5.

40 Van Kley, "The Abbé Grégoire," 101, 103. *Richerism* was a set of ideas built from the writings of the early seventeenth-century French priest Edmond Richer. He argued for the priority of parish priests, claiming that they were the direct descendants of the seventy-two disciples that Jesus sent forth to preach the good news. According to Richer, priests, bishops, and the pope were the only church positions sanctioned in the gospels; therefore, they should have priority over canons, abbots, and priors, which were later innovations of the church. See Tackett, *Priest and Parish*, 242–3. Alyssa Sepinwall also concluded that the United Bishops sought to implement Richerist ideals as they reorganized the constitutional church as the Gallican church. See *The Abbé Grégoire and the French Revolution*, 145.

41 Administration du département de la Côte-d'Or, "Arrêté," 8 *germinal l'an* 3 (28 March 1795), folder L1161/19, ADCO.

42 Chauchot's letters to the pope and unidentified "messieurs" are located in Lettres de prêtres du department de la Côte d'Or, Lettres de Chauchot, curé de Is-sur-Tille, Dossier Côte d'Or, Collection Grégoire, Bibliothèque de la Société de Port-Royal (hereafter PR).

43 Directoire du département de la Côte-d'Or, "Arrêté," 3 *prairial l'an* 3 (22 May 1795), folder L1161/19, ADCO.

44 Directoire du district d'Issurtille, "Procès verbal," 6 *prairial l'an* 3 (25 May 1795) (Copy made by the departmental directory of the district directory's minutes), folder L1161/19, ADCO.

45 Conseil général of Is-sur-Tille, 6 *prairial l'an* 3 (25 May 1795), folder L1161/19, ADCO.

46 The district's denunciation is related in the department's order of 3 *prairial l'an* 3 (22 May 1795); see Directoire du département de la Côte-d'Or, "Arrêté," folder L1161/19, ADCO.

47 Directoire du department de la Côte-d'Or, "Arrêté," 12 *messidor l'an* 3 (30 June 1795), folder L1180, ADCO.

48 Suratteau, "Le Directoire," 80–1.

49 Louis Bitouzel, Beaune, to Grégoire, Paris, 1 *thermidor l'an* 3 (19 July 1795), and Grosdidier, Champagne sur Vingeanne, to Grégoire, Paris, 18 July 1795, both located in Lettres de prêtres de la Côte-d'Or, Collection Grégoire, Dossier Côte-d'Or, PR.

50 Volfius, "Lettre de J.B. Volfius, au rédacteur," 221–4, Bibliothèque municipale de Dijon. The editor of *L'Original* was Claude Legoux, a political moderate who supported the work of Calès and the moderate republicans he appointed to power in the department. See Péronnet and Lochet, *La Révolution dans le département de la Côte-d'Or*, 128.

51 Bitouzel to Grégoire, 1 *thermidor l'an* 3 (19 July 1795); Grosdidier to Grégoire, 18 July 1795, Lettres de prêtres de la Côte-d'Or, Collection Grégoire, Dossier Côte-d'Or (PR).

52 Volfius, "Lettre de J.B. Volfius, au rédacteur," 222.

53 Volfius, Dijon, to Grégoire, Paris, 1 *germinal l'an* 3 (21 March 1795), Lettres de Volfius, évêque de la Côte-d'Or, Collection Grégoire, Dossier Côte-d'Or, PR.

54 Ibid.

55 Volfius, Dijon, to Grégoire, Paris, 22 *germinal l'an* 3 (11 April 1795), Lettres de Volfius, évêque de la Côte-d'Or, Collection Grégoire, Dossier Côte-d'Or, PR; "Discours de J.B. Volfius, au directoire du département,"

*Affiches de Dijon ou Journal du Dé*partement de la Côte-d'Or, no. 17
(*7 ventôse l'an 2 / 25* February 1794).

56 Volfius, "Lettre de J.B. Volfius, au rédacteur."

57 Ibid., 221–2.

58 Ibid., 223.

59 Ibid., 224.

60 Volfius et al., "Les prêtres assermentés de Dijon.". The other signers of this
letter were André Brès, episcopal vicar; Nicolas-Sulpice Gelot, epsicopal
vicar; Jean-Hervé-Nicolas Simon, priest of Notre-Dame; Pierre Heulte,
vicar of Notre-Dame; Antoine Pasteur, vicar of Notre-Dame; Claude-
René Merceret, priest of Fontaine; Etienne-Bernard Delamarre, priest of
Trouhans; Antoine Semetier, priest of Beyre; Jean-Jérome Quillot, priest of
Saint-Julien; Jean-Joseph Genret, priest of Marsannay; Claude Marchand,
priest of Souffrans; Troigros, priest of Chenôve; Jean-Baptiste Pierret,
priest; Pierre-Thomas Rousselot, priest.

61 Ibid., 422–3, 425–6.

62 Ibid., 425.

63 Volfius, Dijon, to Grégoire, Paris, 27 *thermidor l'an* 3 (14 August 1795),
Lettres de Volfius, évêque de la Côte-d'Or, Collection Grégoire, Dossier
Côte-d'Or, PR.

64 Volfius, Dijon, to Grégoire, Paris, 21 *thermidor l'an* 3 (8 August 1795),
Lettres de Volfius, évêque de la Côte-d'Or, Collection Grégoire, Dossier
Côte-d'Or, PR.

65 Ibid.

66 *Lettre encyclique de plusieurs évêques de France* (1795), 26, French
Revolution Pamphlet Collection, NB.

67 Volfius to Grégoire, 27 *thermidor l'an* 3 (14 August 1795), Lettres de
Volfius, évêque de la Côte-d'Or, Collection Grégoire, Dossier Côte-d'Or,
PR.

68 Volfius, Dijon, to Grégoire, Paris, 27 *fructidor l'an* 3 (13 September 1795),
Lettres de Volfius, évêque de la Côte-d'Or, Collection Grégoire, Dossier
Côte-d'Or, PR.

CHAPTER EIGHT

1 Champagnac, *Quiberon*, 12. The fleet included three ships of the line, each
carrying seventy-four cannons; six frigates, two with forty-four cannons
and the others carrying from thirty-three to thirty-six cannons; and a cor-
vet with twenty-six cannons and fourteen smaller armed vessels.

2 Ibid., 11–14.

3 Champagnac offers a summary of Hoche's forces, ibid., 40. The Chouans counted several groups among their numbers: remnants of the forces that fought a civil war in the Vendée in 1793 and 1794; draft dodgers who resisted the *levées* of March and August 1793; deserters from the revolutionary army sent to suppress the insurgency in the Vendée; and former soldiers from the royal army; see Dupuy, *Les Chouans*, 36–7.
4 Champagnac, *Quiberon*, 32–3.
5 Martin, *La Vendée*, 268–9; see also Martin's article, "Sur le traité de paix."
6 Martin, *La Vendée*, 274–5.
7 Fournier, *Les derniers martyrs de la Vendée*, 135–6, 141–4. Baraud, *Le clergé vendéen*, 433–41."
8 Suratteau, "Le Directoire," 81–2.
9 J.B. Volfius, oath, 2 *brumaire l'an* 4 (23 October 1795), folder L1142, Archives départementales de la Côte-d'Or (hereafter ADCO).
10 Suratteau, "Le Directoire," 81–2.
11 Plongeron and Argyriou, *Les défis de la modernité*, 428.
12 "Dijon," *Le Nécessaire*, no. 20 (10 *nivôse l'an* 4 / 31 December 1795), 81–2.
13 Ibid., 81.
14 Ibid., 82.
15 François Sivry, Combertaut, to presidents and administrators of the department of the Côte-d'Or, Dijon, 30 *nivôse l'an* 4 (19 January 1796), folder L1178/17, ADCO.
16 *Le Nécessaire*, no. 37 (5 *germinal l'an* 4 / 25 March 1796), 178.
17 "Administration départemental," *Le Nécessaire*, no. 38 (10 *germinal l'an* 4 / 30 March 1796), 187.
18 "Arrêté," Administration départementale de la Côte-d'Or, 7 *pluviôse l'an* 4 (26 January 1796), folder L1167/13, ADCO.
19 "Notice des lois," *Le Nécessaire*, no. 45 (15 *floréal l'an* 4 / 4 May 1796), 242–3. On 22 *germinal* (11April), the national government reiterated its support of the law of 3 *ventôse*.
20 "Arrêtés des administration départementale," *Le nécessaire*, no. 53 (25 *prairial l'an* 4 / 13 June 1796), 305. The provisions against bell ringing in the law of 3 *ventôse* had been subverted by some Catholics. Thus in the early spring of 1796, the Directory returned to the issue, passing a clarifying law through the Council of Ancients on 11 April 1796 (22 *germinal l'an* 4). See Dean, *L'abbé Grégoire*, 200.
21 Dean, *L'abbé Grégoire*, 201.
22 [Jean-Baptiste Arnoux], Beaune, to [Directory of the Côte-d'Or], Dijon, 14 *floréal l'an* 4 (3 May 1796), folder L1154/13, ADCO.

23 "Arrêté," Directoire du department de la Côte-d'Or, 24 *messidor l'an* 3 (12 July 1795), folder L1154/13, ADCO.

24 District de Beaune, Beaune, to Directoire du département de la Côte-d'Or, Dijon, second note at bottom of letter, 23 *thermidor l'an* 8 (10 August 1800), folder L1154/13, ADCO.

25 [Arnoux].

26 "Dijon," *Le Nécessaire*, no. 56 (10 *messidor l'an* 4 / 28 June 1796), 327–8.

27 "Dijon," *Le Nécessaire*, no. 57 (15 *messidor l'an* 4 / 3 July 1796), 336.

28 Volfius, Dijon, to Grégoire, Paris, 15 July l'an 4, Lettres de Volfius, évêque de la Côte-d'Or, Collection Grégoire, Dossier, Côte-d'Or, Bibliothèque de la Société de Port Royale (hereafter PR).

29 *Seconde lettre encyclique*, French Revolution Pamphlet Collection, Newberry Library.

30 Volfius is included in a list of twelve bishops and two presbyteries that had signed the *Seconde lettre encyclique*; see *Annales de la religion* 2, no. 21 (6 *germinal l'an* 4 / 26 March 1796): 503. For Volfius's critique of the letter, expressed in his correspondence with Grégoire, see Volfius, Dijon, to Grégoire, Paris, 27 *ventôse l'an* 4 (17 March 1796)], Lettres de Volfius, évêque de la Côte-d'Or, Collection Grégoire, Dossier Côte-d'Or, PR.

31 See *Seconde lettre encyclique*, 29–44.

32 James of Soissons, born François of Fitz-James, was the son of a Scottish noble who came to France with James II. He became bishop of Soissons in 1739. A supporter of the Jansenist critique of *Unigenitus*, he commissioned his secretary Gourlin to write a study of the ideas of Hardouin and Berruyer, publishing it as a four-volume pastoral instruction in the early 1760s. This work was important in the campaign to expel the Jesuits from France. See Palmer, *Catholics and Unbelievers*, 43, 75; and John M'clintock and James Strong, *Cyclopædia*, 12: 393. Dale Van Kley notes that Fitz-James expressed his Jansenist convictions only after his appointment as bishop. See *The Religious Origins of the French Revolution*, 140. Joachim Colbert, bishop of Montpellier from 1696 to 1739, was the nephew of Jean-Baptiste Colbert, adviser to Louis XIV. The catechism of Montpellier produced during his episcopacy was a favourite of Jansenists until the revolution. He was one of four Jansenist bishops who went to the Sorbonne in March 1717 and formally appealed the papal bull *Unigenitus*. See Van Kley, *Religious Origins of the French Revolution*, 86, 177, 228.

33 Volfius may have been wrong about the national origins of the "two Lamis" intended by the Évêques réunis. They were two seventeenth-century French monks, Dom François Lami, a Benedictine monk of the

congregation of St. Maur, and Bernard Lami, a monk of the Oratory. Dom François published writings debating the ideas of Malebranche until his order silenced him, after which he continued his dispute with the famous theologian in private correspondence. See, Michaud et al., eds., *Biographie universelle ancienne et moderne*, 23: 81–90. Bernard Lami joined the Oratians at eighteen and pursued an academic career, studying *belles lettres* and philosophy. His attraction to the philosophy of Descartes got him in trouble with the professors at the University of Angers, who arranged to have him detained by a *lettre de cachet*. In 1675 an *arrêt de conseil* condemned his ideas and ordered him to leave Angers. After a short exile to Saint-Martin-de-Misère in the Dauphiné, he went to the seminary of Saint-Magloire in Paris, where he completed his career, publishing in 1689 *Harmonie évangelique*. See Michaud, *Biographie universelle ancienne et moderne*, 23: 90–1.

34 Samuel Clarke was an English philosopher, rationalist theologian, and Anglican clergyman. He defended Isaac Newton's physics. While many suspected Newton of having a Unitarian theology, Clarke presented his anti-Trinitarian beliefs in *Scripture Doctrine of the Trinity* (1712). Although charged with heresy, he successfully defended himself and retained his position as rector of St. James Westminster. *Socinianism* refers to the anti-Trinitarian theology first expounded by Laelius Socinus (Lelio Sozzini), a sixteenth-century resident of Siena, and his nephew, Faustus Socinus (Faustus Sozzini). Socinus argued that Christ was divine not by nature but by office. He was a man, born of the Virgin, whom God resurrected from the dead as a reward for his obedience.

35 Rodney J. Dean characterized the second encyclical letter as going beyond Jansenism to represent a fusion of the United Bishops' Gallican and revolutionary ideas. See *L'abbé Grégoire*, 92. Jean Dubray underscored Grégoire's stronger embrace of Jansenism after the Terror in his study *La pensée de l'abbé Grégoire*, 27–34.

36 Volfius, Dijon, to Grégoire, Paris, 15 March, l'an 5 (1797), Lettres de Volfius, évêque de la Côte-d'Or, Collection Grégoire, Dossier Côte-d'Or, PR.

37 Déré, accusateur public, Is-sur-Tille, to Administration municipale, Dijon, 27 *nivôse l'an* 5 (16 January 1797), folder L1948/14, ADCO.

38 Carion abandoned his vows and married. His father-in-law aided his entry into journalism. Carion edited and published the *Journal de la Côte-d'Or* under various titles until his death in 1834. Milsand, *Périodiques publiés à Dijon*, 4–10.

39 "Dijon," *Journal de la Côte-d'Or* 4, no. 30 (30 *pluviôse l'an* 5 / 18 February 1797), 234.

40 *Journal de la Côte-d'Or* 4, no. 56 (10 *messidor l'an* 5 / 28 June 1797): 442. Here the writer references the sixteenth-century St. Bartholomew's Day massacre of Huguenots in Paris.

41 "Lettre au rédacteur, Dijon," *Journal de la Côte-d'Or* 4, no. 57 (15 *messidor l'an* 5 / 3 July 1797), 453–5. For information on *La Glaneuse*, see Péronnet and Lochot, *La Révolution dans le département de la Côte-d'Or*, 132. In mid-September, the *Journal* recorded the death of *La Glaneuse*'s editor, identified only as "Le valet de pique." See *Le Journal* 4, no. 72 (30 *fructidor l'an* 5 / 16 September 1797): 572.

42 Plongeron and Argyriou, *Les défis de la modernité*, 432–3.

43 *Journal de la Côte-d'Or* 4, no. 31 (5 *ventôse l'an* 5 / 23 February 1797), 243–4.

44 This is most probably General Louis-Antoine Pille, who in year 4 was given the command of the twenty-two departments of the Midi with the grade of division general. He began his revolutionary career in Dijon as the organizer of the volunteers of the Côte-d'Or, leading their first battalion in 1791. See Hoefer, "Pille (Louis-Antoine, comte)," in *Nouvelle biographie générale*, 237.

45 *Journal de la Côte-d'Or* 4, no. 57 (15 *messidor l'an* 5 / 3 July 1797), 452–3.

CHAPTER NINE

1 J.B. Volfius, Dijon, to Grégoire, Paris, 10 May *an* 5 (1797), Lettres de Volfius, évêque de la Côte-d'Or, Collection Grégoire, Dossier Côte-d'Or, Bibliothèque de la Société de Port Royale (hereafter PR).

2 The royalist journal, *La Glaneuse*, heralded Robert as "le pieux Robert," an anomalous epithet for a former departmental administrator during the Terror. Robert began his career as a professor of philosophy and mathematics at the college de Chalon-sur-Saône, but in 1780 he became an engineer and geographer of the king. Jean Bart explains that, despite his scepticism about religion, Robert had become convinced of its utility for the people. See Bart, *La Révolution française en Bourgogne*, 287–88.

3 Bouillotte, Arney-sur-Aroux, to Grégoire, Paris, 8 *prairial l'an* 5 (27 May 1797), Lettres de prêtres du département de la Côte-d'Or, Dossier Côte-d'Or, PR.

4 Furet, *Revolutionary France*, 182; Bart, *La Révolution française en Bourgogne*, 288–90.

5 "Arrêté de l'administration centrale du département de la Côte-d'Or, relatif aux ministres de culte," 21 *brumaire l'an* 6 (11 November 1797), folder

L1152, Archives départementales de la Côte-d'Or (hereafter ADCO); see also Suratteau, "Le Directoire," 86–7.

6 "État des prêtres résidans dans le Département de la Côte d'Or admis à prêter le serment décrété le 19 fructidor 5," folder L1152, ADCO.

7 For a list of the constitutional clergy attending the diocesan synod see, *Actes du synode diocésain*, 32–3, Fonds Delmasse, Bibliothèque municipale de Dijon.

8 The taking of this oath is well documented in the ADCO. A few representative examples of the documentation generated can be found in the following folders: "Chauchot (Denis) an III-an VII," folder L1161/19; "Babeau (Philippe) an VI," folder L1155/1; and "Distely (François-Joseph), 1791–an VI," folder 1163/39.

9 Sotin, "Le minister de la police générale de la République, aux administrations centrales et municipales de la République," Paris, 29 *frimaire l'an* 6 (19 December 1797), folder L1153, ADCO. Sotin was minister of police for about six months, from July 1797 until January 1798. He was particularly diligent in his efforts to enforce the law of 19 *fructidor*, see Michaud et al., eds., *Biographie universelle, ancienne et modern*, 43: 142–3.

10 Presevot, Fremyet, Jouvelot, and Musard, "Arrêté de l'administration centrale de la Côte-d'Or relatif aux cloches," 19 *nivôse l'an* 6 (8 January 1798), folder L1153, ADCO.

11 Jean-Baptiste Grosdidier, to les citoyens composans l'administration centrale de la Côte-d'Or, Dijon, received 11 *pluviôse l'an* 7 (30 January 1799), folder L1167/13, ADCO.

12 Grosdidier identified this author only as Jouffrey. There are several church leaders in eastern France in the early modern period with that surname.

13 Plongeron and Argyriou, *Les défis de la modernité*, 570–4. For a description of the educational reforms proposed in year 2 and those enacted by the Thermidoreans, see Lefebvre, *The French Revolution*, 287–90.

14 Plongeron and Argyriou, *Les défis de la modernité*, 544–5.

15 François de Neufchateau, Ministre de l'Intérieur, Paris, to Commission exécutif, administration centrale de la Côte-d'Or, 27 *ventôse l'an* 7 (17 March 1799), folder L1152, ADCO.

16 Fouché, Ministre de la Police générale, Paris, to Commissaires du Directoire exécutif, administration centrale de la Côte-d'Or, Dijon, an 7 (1799), folder L1152, ADCO. The letter from the Côte-d'Or was dated 15 *thermidor* (1 August).

17 Fouché, Ministre de la Police générale, Paris, to Commissaire du gouvernement, administration centrale, Côte-d'Or, commissaire superintendent [police], 23 *pluviôse l'an* 8 (11 February 1800), folder L1152, ADCO.

18 Mathiez, *La théophilanthropie et la culte décadaire*, 26.

19 Ibid., 27. The Convention approved the *fétes décadaire* on 18 *floréal*.

20 Ibid., 28.

21 Ibid., 29.

22 Ibid., 28.

23 These reasons for the failure of the civil religion were outlined by Ginguené, formerly the editor of *La feuille villageoise* who was the official in the Ministry of the Interior in charge of overseeing the national festivals. Ibid., 34.

24 Ibid., 34–5.

25 Surrateau, "Le Directoire," 88.

26 Ibid., 91.

27 Plongeron and Argyriou, *Les défis de la modernité*, 430; Surrateau, "Le Directoire," 88.

28 Plongeron and Argyriou, *Les défis de la modernité*, 429.

29 Mathiez, *La théophilanthropie et la culte décadaire*, 401–3.

30 Ibid., 415, 445.

31 Ibid., 424–6.

32 Ibid., 443–5, 448–51.

33 Posters published in Beaune and Dijon provide two examples. See "Arrêté de l'administration municipale de la commune de Beaune, relative aux réunions décadaires" (Beaune: Imprimerie de Bernard, fils, l'an 7), folder L476, ADCO, and "Arrêté de l'administration municipale de la commune de Dijon" (Dijon: Imprimerie de la Veuve Defay, n.d. [l'an 7]), folder L476, ADCO. Discussion in the text is of the poster published in Beaune. The poster from Dijon differs in only a few small details: fiancées of public officials were not permitted to sit in the reserved seating area in Beaune, but could do so in Dijon if they were at least twenty-one; Children were also required to be accompanied by their teachers in Dijon; those without a seat in Dijon were permitted to stand in the back.

34 Péronnet and Lochot, *La Révolution dans le département de la Côte-d'Or*, 134.

35 "Extrait du registres des séances de l'administration municipale du canton d'Issurtille, séance du 21 ventôse an 7," (11 March 1799), folder L1161/19, ADCO.

36 Balanche, Arnay sur Arroux, to Grégoire, Paris, 13 *pluviôose l'an* 10 (1 February 1802), Lettres de prêtres du département de la Côte-d'Or, Collection Grégoire, Dossier Côte-d'Or, PR.

37 Volfius, Dijon, to Desbois, Paris, 14 *prairial l'an* 7 (2 June 1799), Lettres de Volfius, évêque de la Côte-d'Or, Collection Grégoire, Dossier Côte-d'Or,

PR. General Mack resigned his position in the face of a popular insurrection in Naples. Entering into a treaty with the French commander, General Championnet, he received passports for himself and his officers to return to Germany. On his journey northward, the Directory ordered his arrest at Bologna. His journey to Paris took him through Dijon, where he was held for a time. In all, Mack spent two years in French custody, escaping in disguise in 1800. In 1805, he commanded Austrian forces against Napoleon at the battles of Ulm and Austerlitz. "Campaign of 1805," 408–9.

38 Latreille and Rémond, *Histoire du catholicisme*, 151–2.
39 Volfius, Dijon, to Desbois, Paris, 13 *thermidor l'an* 7 (31 July 1799), Lettres de Volfius, évêque de la Côte-d'Or, Collection Grégoire, Dossier Côte-d'Or, PR.
40 Volfius, Dijon, to Desbois, Paris, 3 *fructidor l'an* 7 (20 August 1799), Lettres de Volfius, évêque de la Côte-d'Or, Collection Grégoire, Dossier Côte-d'Or, PR.

CHAPTER TEN

1 Van Kley, "Catholic Conciliar Reform."
2 Dean, *L'abbé Grégoire*, 280.
3 Tuffery-Audrieu, *Le council national*, 256.
4 Plongeron and Argyriou, *Les défis de la modernité*, 454–5.
5 Tuffery-Andrieu, *Le council national*, 27–30, 38–9, 137–42.
6 Ibid., 137–47.
7 Volfius, "Mandement de l'éveque diocésain," i–ii.
8 Ibid., ii–iii.
9 *Actes du synode diocésain*, 1–33.
10 Ibid., 2–4.
11 Ibid., 4–6.
12 Ibid., 7–11.
13 Ibid., 11–15.
14 Tuffery-Audrieu, *Le council national*, 151–2.
15 Ibid., 179–90. Tuffery-Audrieu provides a long discussion of this development in the Gallican church.
16 *Actes du synode diocesain*, 20–3.
17 Ibid., 1–2.
18 Ibid., 23–6.
19 Ibid., 27–8.
20 Ibid., 29–31.
21 "Prières," in *Actes du synode diocésain*, 34–5.

216 Notes to pages 147–52

22 Volfius, Dijon, to Citoyen Prefet, 9 *fructidor l'an* 8 (27 August 1801), folder L1142, Archives départementales de la Côte-d'Or (hereafter ADCO).

23 Volfius, "Mandement de l'évêque," i.

24 Volfius, Dijon, to Grégoire, Paris, 3 *messidor l'an* 8 (22 June 1801), Lettres de Volfius, évêque de Côte-d'Or, Collection Grégoire, Dossier Côte-d'Or, Bibliothèque de la Société Port Royal (hereafter PR).

25 Dean, *L'église constitutionnelle*, 262–77.

26 *Le Concordat de 1801*, 11–23.

27 Plongeron, "Hypothèques sur le Concordat," 57–8.

28 Plongeron, "Face au Concordat," 5–6. There were two versions of this brief. The harsher version, demanding a retraction of their revolutionary careers, was presented to the constituional clergy in 1801 and 1802. A more paternal version, requiring only a statement of submission and obedience to the Holy See, was discovered by Henri Grégoire in 1810, when French troops gained possession of the Vatican archives.

29 Tuffery-Andrieu, *Le council national*, 325–329.

30 Plongeron, "Hypothéques sur le Concordat," 64.

31 Plongeron, "Face au Concordat," 3, 5.

32 Plongeron, "Hypothèques sur le Concordat," 69.

33 Plongeron, "Face au Concordat," 2.

34 Van Kley, "Catholic Conciliar Reform," 105–6.

35 Dean, *L'église constitutionnelle*, 460–2. Dean expresses some scepticism about Caprara's ignorance of these articles, given that similar regulations were imposed on clergy in the French-controlled Italian Republic (formerly the Cisalpine Republic) in January, but he grants that the cardinal was consumed by the task of trying to obtain the retractions of the former constitutional bishops in March 1802.

36 Boudon, *L'épiscopat français*, 298–301.

37 Plongeron, "Hypothèques sur le Concordat," 75–7, 81, 87–90.

38 Plongeron, "Face au Concordat," 12.

39 Ibid., 12–13.

40 Ibid., 13.

41 J. B. Volfius, "Déclaration de M. Volfius," 71–2. Volfius's original retraction has not survived in the departmental or diocesan archives in Dijon. In this article published in 1816, he quotes his earlier letter and gives its date.

42 Latreille and Rémond, *Histoire du catholicisme*, 164–5.

43 Ibid., 166–7.

CONCLUSION

1 McManners, *Church and Society*, 214. In 1790, Jean-Baptiste Asseline, bishop of Boulogne, was the last member of the Third Estate elevated to the France's old regime episcopacy. The author of an influential pamphlet against the Civil Constitution of the Clergy, *Instruction pastorale de M. l'évêque de Boulogne* (1790), he refused the ecclesiastical oath of 1791.

2 Chomton, *Histoire de l'Église Saint-Bénigne*, 304. Chomton discussed the various forays of the district authorities into the relics at Saint-Bénigne.

EPILOGUE

1 J. B. Volfius, "Déclaration de M. Volfius," 71–2.

2 Ibid., 72.

3 "Nouvelles ecclésiastiques … Dijon," *L'ami de la religion et du roi: Journal ecclésiastique, politique, et littéraire* 7, no. 164 (6 March 1816): 109–10.

4 In his second letter of retraction sent to the Pope in April 1816, Volfius named Collin as the individual who prevailed upon him to see the error of his ways. Volfius, Dijon, to Pope Pius VII, Rome, n.d., folder 1D5bis Volfius, Archives diocésaines, Archevêché de Dijon, Dijon, France (hereafter AD).

5 Jean Collin, Dijon, to Pius VII, Rome, 24 mars 1816, AD, folder 1D5bis, Volfius, AD.

6 "Au rédacteur. Dijon, 25 avril 1816," *L'ami de la religion et du roi* 8, no. 190 (5 June 1816): 111–12.

7 "Tres Saint Pere [sic]," n.d. folder 1D5bis, Volfius, AD.

8 "Nouvelles ecclésiastiques," *L'ami de la religion et du roi* 8, no. 203 (20 July 1816): 313–14.

9 J.B. Volfius, "Rétraction de M. Jean Baptiste Volfius," 25 mai 1816, folder 1D5bis, Volfius, AD.

10 "Tres Saint Pere."

11 The Latin original along with a French translation of Pope Pius VII's declaration concerning Volfius can be found in folder 1D5bis, Volfius, AD.

12 "Discours pronounce en chaire à la cathédrale lors de la réintégration du Sr. Volfius ancien évêque constitutionnel," n.d., folder 1D5bis, Volfius, AD.

13 "Reymond (Henri)," in *Biographie universelle*, ed. J.Fr. Michaud et al., vol. 35 (1968), 505–6.

14 "Retractions des prêtres assermenter," folder 9D1.liasse2, 9D1/2, AD. Twenty-three statements are found in this file, which also contains a letter reporting on various individuals.

15 Ladey and Foisset, *Consultation pour les héritiers légitimes*, 1–68.
16 Ibid., 6–8, 35–6, 65.
17 "Notice sur Volfius, évêque constitutionnel," *L'ami de la religion et du roi* 31, no. 785 (16 February 1822), 23.
18 J.P. Abel Jeandet, "Volfius (Jean-Baptiste)," *Nouvelle biographie générale*, ed. Hoefer, 46:347.

APPENDIX A

1 "Arnay le Duc," folder L1144, Archives départementales de la Côte-d'Or (ADCO); Fonds Reinert, MS 3238 (1–4), Bibliothèque Municipal de Dijon (BM Dijon).
2 Fonds Reinert, MS 3238 (1–4), BM Dijon. For a biography of Reinert and an overview of the collection, see Sébastien Langlois, "Un fonds d'archives."
3 Éric Wenzel, *Curés des lumières*, 52–3

APPENDIX B

1 Fonds Reinert, "Serments par ordre de dates," MS 3846, Bibliothèque Municipal de Dijon (BM Dijon).

Bibliography

ARCHIVAL AND MANUSCRIPT COLLECTIONS

Archives départementales de la Côte-d'Or (ADCO)

G1 Evéche de Dijon, Erection de l'Évéché

L178 Municipalités, 1790 – l'an 3

L210 Documents related to nomination, election, and installation of
Volfius as constitutional bishop

L429 Suspects, étrangers, détenus, émigrés et déportés, Dossiers
personnels, 1790 – l'an 8. Melchior-Mutin (dossiers 1–40)

L476 Fêtes décadaires

L1080 Beaune

L1091 Lycée

L1108

L1140 Conscriptions paroissiales

L1141 Affaires spéciales, par commune, ... 1790 –2

L1142–52 Personnel: affaires générales et collectives, ... 1790 – l'an 10

l1153 Police du culte, contraventions, troubles religieux

L1154–5, 61–8, 70, 72, 75–8, 80 Personnel et police du culte: affaires
spéciales, ... 1790 – l'an 8

L1181 Administration et tribunaux révolutionnaires

L1317 District d'Arnay-le-Duc: Affaires générale et collectives,
1791 – l'an 3

L1319 District d'Arnay-le-Duc: Dossiers individuels des ecclésiastiques,
1790 – l'an 4: M–V

L1439 District de Beaune: Personnel

L1441 District de Beaune: Culte catholique, Dossiers individuels des
ecclésiastiques, 1790 – l'an 4

L1501 District de Châtillon-sur-Seine: Affaires générales et collective, l'an 2

L1502 District de Châtillon-sur-Seine: Dossiers individuels des ecclésiastiques, 1791 – l'an 3

L1648

L1791 District de Dijon: Constitution civile du clergé, 1790–1

l1793–4 District de Dijon: Peronnel et police du culte, affaires générales et collectives, Évêques constitutionnel, Ancien séminaire

L1795 District de Dijon: Serments, abdications, déclarations du soumission aux lois, 1791 – l'an 3

L1806, L1808 District de Dijon: Personnel et police du culte, affaires spéciales

L1945 District d'Is-sur-Tille: Culte catholique, Lettre pastorale de l'évêque Volfius

L1948-50 District d'Is-sur-Tille: Dossiers individuels des ecclésiastiques, 1790 – l'an 4

Archives diocésaines, Archevêché de Dijon (AD)

1D5bis Volfius

5bis Portrait de J.B. Volfius

9D1.liasse 2, 9D1/2 Retractions des prêtres assermenter

9D1/1 Certificats de civisme

Archives municipales de Dijon (AMD)

Série D1-68 Affaires religieuses, 1216–1789

Sous-Série 5 P Cultes, 1789 – l'an 14

Sous-Série 1 P Culte catholique, 1790–3

Archives nationales de France, Paris (ANP)

Microfilm E1b "Arrêt autorisant l'érection d'un évêché à Dijon," 2, 3, 5 July 1597

Archives nationales de France, Pierrefitte-sur-Seine (AN)

D/XIX/93 Lettres, addresses, suppliques, délibérations des municipalités envoyées au Comité ecclésiastiques

Bibliothèque municipale de Dijon (BM Dijon)

Fonds Delmasse

Fonds Milsand

Fonds Reinert MS 3238, *Dic. d'écclesiastiques*; MS 3806, *Fichier des clergé*; MS 3846, *Serments entre 1790 et 1821*; MS 3813, *Répertoire alphabétique de clergé côte-d'orien*; MS 3845, *Vie politique et religieuse sous la Révolution et l'Empire*; MS 3882, Jean-Baptiste Volfius

MS 685 *Mémoires d'état de Messieur Jean de Marvilliers, évêque d'Orléans*

MS 988-71 *Collection de manuscrits de Pierre-Louis Baudot,* Fol. 132–8, *Mémoire du chapitre de Langres contenant les raisons qui semblent devoir engager le roi de ne pas permettre l'érection d'un évéché à Dijon*

Bibliothèque de la Société de Port-Royal, Paris (PR)

Collection Grégoire, Dossier Côte-d'Or

Newberry Library, Chicago (NB)

French Revolution Collection, French Pamphlets

JOURNALS AND PERIODICALS

Affiches de Dijon ou Journal du Département de la Côte-d'Or
Ami de la religion et du roi: journal ecclésiastique, politique, et littéraire
Annales de la religion
Feuille villageoise, la
Journal de la Côte-d'Or, par Carion
Journal patriotique de la Côte-d'Or
Nécessaire, le
L'original, ou Journal du département de la Côte-d'Or

PRINTED PRIMARY AND SECONDARY SOURCES

Actes du synode diocésain, tenu à Dijon le 8 juillet 1800 de Notre Seigneur (19 messidor de l'an 8 de la République française), et jours suivans. Dijon: Imprimerie de Carion, *l'an* 8 [1800].

Adresse des électeurs du département de la Seine Inférieure, à l'Assemblée Nationale; Imprimée par son ordre, 8 février 1791. Paris: L'imprimerie nationale, [1791].

Amanton, Claude-Nicolas. *Notice sur J.B. Volfius, prêtre du diocese de Dijon.* Dijon: Frantin, 1824.

Arbaumont, Jules d'. *Essai historique sur la Sainte-Chapelle de Dijon.* Dijon: Lamarche, 1863.

Archives parlémentaires de 1787 à 1860. Paris: Librairie administrative de P. Dupont, 1860.

Archives parlémentaires de 1787 à 1860. Première série (1789 à 1800). 1883; Nendeln, LI: Kraus Reprint, 1969.

Asseline, Jean René. *Instruction pastorale de M. l'évêque de Boulogne sur l'autorité spirtuelle.* Boulogne: Dolet, 1790.

[Assemblée constituante.] *Décret de l'Assemblée nationale, concernant le serment à prêter par les évêques, curés & autres Ecclésiastiques fonctionnaires publiques; precedé du rapport fait par M. Voidel, au nom des comités ecclésiastiques, des rapports, d'aliénation & de recherches, réunis, sur la ligue d'une partie du clergé, contre l'état & contre la religion.* Paris: Chez Baudouin, 1790.

– *Décret sur la Constitution civile du clergé du 12 juillet 1790.* Paris: Chez Baudouin, 1790.

Aston, Nigel. *Christianity in Revolutionary Europe, 1750–1830.* Cambridge: Cambridge University Press, 2002.

– *The End of an Elite: The French Bishops and the Coming of the Revolution, 1786–1790.* Oxford: Oxford University Press 1992.

– *Religion and Revolution in France, 1780–1804.* Washington, DC: Catholic University of America Press, 2000.

Aubert, R., ed. *Dictionnaire d'histoire et de géographie ecclésiastiques.* Paris: Letouzay et Ané, 1977.

Aulard, Aphonse. *Le culte de la raison et le culte de l'être suprême, 1793–1794: Essai historique.* Paris: Félix Alcan, 1892.

Baker, Larry Lee, Jr. "Politics, Privilege, and Political Culture: Dijon during the French Revolution." PhD diss., University of Illinois at Chicago, 2002.

Baker, Lee. "Survival Strategies of Widows in Dijon during the French Revolution." *Women's Studies* 31, no. 1 (January/February 2002): 53–65.

Baraud, Armand. *Le clergé vendéen, victim de la Révolution françaises: notices biographiques, 1790–1801.* Luçon: Imprimerie M. Bideaux, 1904.

Bart, Jean. *La Révolution française en Bourgogne.* Clermont-Ferraud: La Française d'Éditions et d'Imprimerie, 1996.

Bergin, Joseph. *Church, Society and Religious Change in France, 1580–1730.* New Haven, CT: Yale University Press, 2009.

– *The Making of the French Episcopate, 1589–1661.* New Haven, CT: Yale University Press, 1996.

Biard, Michel. *Missionnaires de la République*. Paris: CTHS, 2002.

Bibliothèque nationale (France). *The French Revolution Research Collection: Les archives de la Revolution française*. Oxford: Pergamon Press, 1989–95.

Billot, Claudine. "Les saintes-chapelles (XIIIe au XVIe siècle): Approche comparée de fondations dynastiques." *Revue d'histoire de l'église de France* 73, no. 191 (1987): 229–48.

Bonin, Serge, and Claude Langlois. *Atlas de la Révolution française*. Paris: Éditions de l'École des hautes études en sciences sociales, 1987.

Bonnel, Roland G. "Ecclesiological Insights at the 1790 National Assembly: An Assessment of the Contribution of Catholic Thought to the French Revolution." In *The French Revolution in Culture and Society*, edited by David G. Troyansky, Alfred Cismaru, and Norwood Andrew, 45–56. New York: Greenwood Press, 1991.

Boudon, Jacques-Olivier, ed. *Le Concordat et le retour de la paix religieuse: Actes du colloque organisé par l'institut Napoléon et la bibliothèque Marmotten le 13 octobre 2001*. Paris: Éditions SPM, 2008.

– *L'épiscopat français à l'époque concordataire, 1802–1805*. Paris: Les Éditions du Cerf, 1996.

Bourdin, Philippe, and Philippe Boutry, "L'Église catholique en Révolution: L'historiographie récente." *Annales historiques de la Révolution française*, no. 355 (January–March 2009): 3–23.

Burson, Jeffrey D., and Jonathan Wright. *The Jesuit Suppression in Global Context: Causes, Events, and Consequences*. Cambridge: Cambridge University Press, 2015.

Byrnes, Joseph F. *Priests of the French Revolution: Saints and Renegades in a New Political Era*. University Park: Pennsylvania State University Press, 2014.

"Campaign of 1805: Surrender of Ulm: Particulars of General Mack." *Edinburgh Magazine and Literary Miscellany* 11 (October 1822): 401–9.

Chaisneau, Charles. *Acras, pastorale sur les assemblées provincials*. Sens: Chez la veuve Tarbé, 1788.

– *Couplets sur la reprise de Toulon, dont la ville sera rasée et le port conservé sous le nom Port de la Montagne*. Auxerre: L. Fournier, 1794.

– *Éloge de Michel Lepelletier, prononce dans le temple de la Raison, à Auxerre, le 20 pluv. an II*. Auxerre: L. Fournier, n.d.

– *Palémon, pastorale*. Paris: Chez Lesclapart, 1787.

– *Le Panthéon français, ou discourse sur les honneurs publics décernés par la nation à la mémoire des grands hommes*. Dijon: P. Causse, 1792.

– *Pastorales dédiées à la Nation*. Dijon: Bidault, 1791.

– *Recueil de pièces patriotiques, à l'occasion de la reconnaissance de l'Être suprême et de l'immoralité de l'âme, et de la fête qui a eu lieu à Paris et à Auxerre à ce sujet, le 20 prairial, seconde année républicaine*. Auxerre: L. Fournier, 1794.

Champagnac, Jacques-Philippe. *Quiberon: La répression et la vengeance*. Paris: Perrin, 1989.

Chantin, Jean-Pierre. *Le Jansénisme*. Paris: Les Éditions du Cerf, 1996.

Charrier de la Roche, Louis. *Examen des principes sur les droits de la religion, la juridiction et le régime de l'Église catholique relativement à l'influence de l'autorité séculière dans la Constitution Civile du Clergé*. Paris: Leclère, 1790.

Chauvin, Charles. *Le clergé à l'épreuve de la Révolution, 1789–1799*. Paris: Desclée de Brouwer, 1989.

Chidjou, Abdoul Karime. "Le clergé constitutionnel de Dijon, 1789–1792." Mémoire DEA [Master's thesis], Université de Bourgogne, 1994.

Chomton, Louis, abbé. *Histoire de l'Église Saint-Bénigne*. Dijon: Jobard, 1900.

Chopelin, Caroline, and Paul Chopelin. *L'obscurantisme et les Lumières: Itinéraire de l'abbé Grégoire, évêque révolutionnaire*. Paris: Vendémiaire, 2013.

Chopelin, Paul, ed. *Gouverner une église en révolution: histoires et mémoires de l'épiscopat constitutionnel*. Lyon: LARHRA, 2017.

– *Ville patriote et ville martyre: Lyon, l'église, et la Révolution, 1788–1805*. Paris: Letouzey et Ané, 2010.

Chopelin-Blanc, Caroline. *De l'apologétique à l'église constitutionnelle: Adrien Lamourette, 1724–94*. Paris: Champion, 2009.

Cobb, Richard. "Les débuts de la déchristianisation à Dieppe." *Annales historiques de la Révolution française* no. 28 (1956): 191–209.

– *The People's Armies*. Translated by Marianne Elliot. New Haven, CT: Yale University Press, 1987.

Colas, [Antoine], and Ph. Voillery. "Les premier évêques de Dijon." *Bulletin d'histoire et d'archéologie religieuses du diocèse de Dijon* 1 (1883): 15–22.

– "Les premier évêques de Dijon. (Suite)." *Bulletin d'histoire et d'archéologie religieuses du diocèse de Dijon* 2 (1884): 63–71.

Le Concordat de 1801 et les articles organiques du culte catholique avec toutes les modifications jusqu'à nos jours: Textes officiels annotés avec les protestations du Pape Pie VII. Marseilles: Librairie de l'Œuvre de Dom Bosco, 1894.

Cottret, Monique. *Histoire du jansénisme, XVIIe au XIXe siècle*. Paris: Perrin, 2016.

Courtépée, Claude, and M. Béguillet. *Description générale et particulière du duché de Bourgogne*. Dijon: V. Lagier, 1847–8.

Cousin, Bernard, Monique Cubells, and René Moulinas. *La pique et la croix: Histoire religieuse de la Révolution française*. Paris: Centurion, 1989.

Davis, James Herbert, Jr. *Fénelon*. Boston: Twayne, 1979.

Dean, Rodney J. *L'Abbé Grégoire et l'église constitutionnelle après le Terreur, 1794–1797*. Paris: Author, 2008.

– *L'Assemblée constituante et la réforme ecclésiastique, 1790: La Constitution civile du clergé du 12 juillet et le serment ecclésiastique du 27 novembre*. Paris: Author, 201.

– *L'église constitutionnel: Napoléon et le concordat de 1801*. Paris: Author, 2004.

Delattre, Pierre, ed. *Les établissements de Jésuites en France depuis quatre siècles*. Vol. 4. Enghiem, BE: Institute supérieur de théologie, 1956.

Délissey, Joseph. *Le Vieux Beaune:* Étude d'histoire locale. 1941. Marseille: Laffitte reprints, 1980.

Delumeau, Jean. *Catholicism between Luther and Voltaire: A New View of the Counter-Reformation*. London: Burns and Oates, 1977.

Desan, Suzanne. *Reclaiming the Sacred: Lay Religion and Popular Politics in Revolutionary France*. Ithaca, NY: Cornell University Press, 1990.

Desaunais, A. "Le canal de Bourgogne et son trafic." *Géocarrefour* 4, no. 1 (1928): 115–56.

Des Marches, A.S. *Histoire du Parlement de Bourgogne de 1733 à 1790*. Chalons S[ur]-S[eine]: J. Dejussieu, 1851.

[Des Monstier de Mérinville], René. *Instruction pastorale de M. l'Évêque de Dijon, à l'occasion des lettres de N.S. Père le Pape Pie VI, sur le serment civique prêté par les Ecclésiastiques, ainsi que sur les élections et les consécrations des faux évêques de France*. Paris: L'imprimerie de Guerbart, [1791].

– *Lettre de M. l'évêque de Dijon à MM. les électeurs du département de la Côte-d'Or*. Paris, 1791.

– "Ordonnance de M. l'évêque de Dijon, au sujet des entreprises faites dans son diocèse, tendantes à y établir un chisme." In *Instruction pastorale de M. l'Évêque de Dijon, à l'occasion des lettres de N.S. Père le Pape Pie VI* ... Paris: Imprimerie de Guerbart, 1791.

Dictionnaire de biographie française. Paris: Librairie Letouzey et Ané, 1933–.

Dictionnaire d'histoire et géographie ecclésiastiques. Paris: Librairie Letouzey et Ané, 1912–.

Dictionnaire historique de la langue française. Vol. 2. Paris: Dictionnaires Le Robert, 1992.

Dijon (Bailliage), [Clergy]. *Chambre du clergé du bailliage de Dijon* [Cahier de l'ordre du clergé, du bailliage principal de Dijon, et des bailliages secondaires de Beaune, Nuits, Auxonne, et Saint-Jean-de-Lône]. N.p., n.d. [1789].

Dijon (Bailliage), Clergé. *Vœu des pasteurs du second ordre, du bailliage de Dijon, en faveur de leurs paroisses, pour faire suite au vœu de quelques curés du diocèse de Dijon.* N.p., n.d. [1789].

Dijon (Diocèse), Curés. *Vœu de quelques curés de campagne, du diocèse de Dijon.* N.p., [1789].

Dillon, Henri. *Lettre de M. l'abbé Henri Dillon, à M. Volfius, évêque du département de la Côte d'Or.* N.p., n.d. [1791].

Dinet, Dominique. *Religion et société: Les réguliers et la vie régionale dans les diocèses d'Auxerre, Langres et Dijon (fin XVIe–fin XVIIIe siècles).* 2 Vols. Paris: Publications de la Sorbonne, 1999.

Discours destine à être prononcé au temple de la raison, et qui été à la société populaire et républicaine de Dijon, par un de ses membres, le 15 pluviôse, l'an second de la république. [Dijon]: P. Causse, n.d.

Discours pronounce par l'un de MM. Les secretaires de la noblesse, au nom de son ordre, à l'assemblée des deputes du clergé de la Sainte-Chapelle de Dijon, et de ceux des corps et communautés du tiers-etat de cette ville, qu'elle y avoit invites le 27 décembre 1788. N.p., n.d. [1788?].

Doyle, William. *Jansenism: Catholic Resistance to Authority: from the Reformation to the French Revolution.* New York: St. Martin's Press, 2000.

– *The Oxford History of the French Revolution.* Oxford: Clarendon Press, 1989.

Dubray, Jean. *La pensée de l'Abbé Grégoire: despotisme et liberté.* Oxford: Voltaire Foundation, 2008.

Dumay, Gabriel. *Les Évêques de Dijon (1731–1889).* Dijon: Jobard, 1889.

Dupuy, Roger. *Les Chouans.* Paris: Hachette Littératures, 1997.

Durand de Maillane, [Pierre-Toussaint]. *Histoire apologétique du comité ecclésiastique de l'assemblée nationale.* Paris: F. Buisson, 1791.

– *Plan du rapport à faire à l'Assemblée nationale par son comité ecclésiastique où il a été lu par M. Durand de Maillane, membre de ce comité, dans une de ses séances, le 23 novembre 1789.* Paris: Imprimerie nationale, 1789.

Durandeau, J. *Un curé sans-culotte, member de l'Académie de Dijon, 1790 à 1794*. Dijon, 1913.

Encyclopedia of the Middle Ages. Edited by André Vauchez with Barrie Dobson and Michael Lapidge. Translated by Adrian Walford. 2 vols. Chicago: Fitzroy Dearborn, 2000.

Évêques, deputés à l'Assemblée nationale. *Exposition des principes sur la Constitution du Clergé*. Paris: Ve. Herissant, 1790.

Farr, James. "Consumers, Commerce, and the Craftsmen of Dijon: The Changing Social and Economic Structure of a Provincial Capital, 1450–1750." In *Cities and Social Change in Early Modern France*, ed. Philip Benedict, 134–73. London: Unwin Hyman, 1989.

Flament, Pierre. *Deux milles prêtres normands face à la Révolution, 1789–1801*. Paris: Perrin, 1989.

Fournier, Élie. *Les derniers martyrs de la Vendée: Histoire des frères Brumauld de Beauregard*. Paris: Pierre Téqui, 1995.

Furet, François. *La Révolution de Turgot à Jules Ferry (1770–1880)*. Paris: Hachette, 1988.

– *Revolutionary France, 1770–1880*. Translated by Antonia Nevill. Oxford: Blackwell, 1992.

Furet, François, and Mona Ozouf, eds. *A Critical Dictionary of the French Revolution*. Translated by Arthur Goldhammer. Cambridge, MA: Belknap Press, 1989.

Gazier, Augustin. *Études sur l'histoire religieuse de la Révolution française*. Paris: Armand Colin, 1887.

Gazier, Georges. *Les Évêques constitutionnels du Doubs*. Besançon: Dodivers, 1906.

Giraud, Françoise. "Volfius, évêque constitutionnel de la Côte-d'Or." MA thesis, Université de Dijon, 1969.

Giroux, Henri. "Les femmes clubistes à Dijon (1791–1793)." *Annales de Bourgogne* 57 (1985): 23–45.

Gouttes, [Jean-Louis]. *Lettre de M. Gouttes, curé d'Argilliers, nommé à l'évêché du département de Saône et Loire, à MM. les curés de ce département & autres fonctionnaires publiques*. Beaune: Chez F. Bernard, 1791.

Gras, Pierre, Jean Marilier, and Pierre Quarré. *Le diocèse de Dijon: histoire et art*. Dijon: Musée de Dijon, 1957.

Grateau, Philippe. *Les cahiers de doléances: Une relecture culturelle*. Rennes: Presse Universitaire de Rennes, 2001.

Green, Andrea Jane. "Dechristianization at Dijon during Year II of the First French Republic (22 September 1793–21 September 1794)." MA thesis, University of Waikato, New Zealand, 1998.

Grégoire, Henri. *Discours sur la liberté des cultes*. N.p., *l'an* 3 [1794/5].

– *Légitimité du serment civique exigé des fonctionnaires ecclésiastiques.* Paris: Imprimerie nationale, 1791.

Guérin, A. "Une épisode de la persécution religieuse pendant la Révolution." *Bulletin d'histoire et d'archéologie religieuses du diocèse de Dijon* 2 (1884): 209–28.

Guittienne-Mürger, Valérie, and Jean Lesaulnier, eds., *L'abbé Grégoire et Port-Royal*. Paris: Nolin, 2010.

Hearnshaw, F.J.C., ed. *Social and Political Ideas of Some Great French Thinkers of the Age of Reason*. London: George G. Harrap, 1930.

Henriot, Marcel. "La deportation des prêtres en Côte-d'Or." *Annales historiques de la Révolution française* no. 129 (1952): 489–97.

Hermon-Belot, Rita. *L'abbé Grégoire: La politique et la vérité*. Paris: Seuil, 2000.

Hoefer, [Jean-Chrétien Ferdinand], ed. *Nouvelle biographie générale depuis les temps les plus reculés jusqu'à nos jours*. Paris: Firmin Didot, 1862–70.

Hood, James N. "Permanence des conflits traditionnels sous la Révolution: L'exemple du Gard." *Revue d'histoire moderne et contemporaine* 24 (July–September 1977): 602–40.

– "Protestant-Catholic Relations and the Roots of the First Popular Counterrevolutionary Movement in France." *Journal of Modern History* 43, no. 2 (June 1971): 245–75.

– "The Riots in Nîmes in 1790 and the Origins of a Popular Counterrevolutionary Movement." PhD diss., Princeton University, 1968.

Hugueney, Louis: *Les clubs dijonnais sous la Révolution*. Dijon: J. Nourry, 1905.

Hutt, M.G. "The Role of the Curés in the Estates-General of 1789." *Journal of Ecclesiastical History* 6 (1955): 190–220.

Jannon, et al. *Déclaration unanime des doyen, dignités, chanoines et chapitre de l'église cathédrale de Dijon*. N.p., n.d. [1790].

Jarrot, L. *Le clergé constitutionnel dans la Côte-d'Or*. Dijon, 1898.

Jedin, Hubert, and John Dolan, eds. *The Handbook of Church History*. Translated by Anselm Biggs. New York: Herder and Herder, 1970.

Jones, R.A. "Fénelon." In *Social and Political Ideas of Some Great French Thinkers of the Age of Reason*. Edited by F.J.C. Hearnshaw, 70–103. London: George G. Harrap, 1930.

Jordan, David P. *The Revolutionary Career of Maximilien Robespierre*. Chicago: University of Chicago Press, 1989.

Kennedy, Michael L. *The Jacobin Clubs in the French Revolution, 1793–1795*. New York: Berghahn Books, 2000.

Kus´cin´ski, Auguste. *Dictionnaire des conventionnels.* 1916. Breuil-en-Vexin, Yvelines: Éditions du Vexin Français, 1973.

Ladey, L.R. Morelot, and Th. Foisset. *Consultation pour les héritiers légitimes de M. Volfius, appelans; contre le sieur Esprit Sylvestre, Marie et Rose-Edmée Guedeney, intimés, se disant donataires et légataires de mondit sieur Volfius.* Dijon: Douillier, 1824.

La Due, William J. *The Chair of Saint Peter: A History of the Papacy.* Maryknoll, NY: Orbis Books, 1999.

la Gorce, Pierre (de), *Histoire religieuse de la Révolution française.* Volume 1. 1912–23. New York: AMS Press, 1969.

Lamarre, Christine. *Petites villes et fait urbain en France au XVIIIème siècle: Le cas bourguignon.* Dijon: Éditions universitaires de Dijon, 1993.

Lamarre, Christine, Claude Farenc, and Frank Laidié. *Religion et Révolution en Côte-d'Or.* Cahier du comité pour l'histoire de la Révolution en Côte-d'Or, nouvelle série n° 4. Dijon, Archives départementales de la Côte-d'Or, 2012.

Langlois, Claude, Timothy Tackett, and Michel Vovelle, eds. *Atlas de la Révolution française.* Volume 9. Religion. Paris: Éditions de l'école des hautes études en sciences sociales, 1996.

Langlois, Sébastien, "Un fonds d'archives inédit à la bibliothèque municipale de Dijon: Les papiers de l'abbé Reinert." Bibliothèque Municipal de Dijon, accessed 30 May 2018. http://patrimoine.bm dijon.fr/pleade/ead. html?id=FR212316101_etat_fonds#!{%22content%22:[%22FR 212316101_etat_fonds_BMDIJON44952T%22,false,%22%22]}.

Latreille, A. *L'Église catholique et la Révolution française.* 2 vols. Paris: Hachette, 1946.

Latreille, A., and R. Rémond. *Histoire du catholicisme en France: La périod contemporaine.* Paris: Éditions Spès, 1962.

Laurent, Jacques. "Fragments de la correspondance de Volfius à la Bibliothèque de Dijon." *Mémoires de l'académie des sciences, arts et belles-lettres de Dijon,* 1914.

Ledeuil, Justin. *La Révolution à Dijon.* Paris: J.-B. Dumoulin, 1872.

Ledré, Charles. *Une controverse sur la Constitution Civile du Clergé: Charrier de la Roche, métropolitain des Côtes de la Manche, et le chanoine Baston.* Lyon: Librairie Emmanuel Vitte, 1943.

Lefebvre, Georges. *The French Revolution from 1793 to 1799.* Translated by John Hall Stewart and James Friguglietti. London: Routledge and Kegan Paul, 1964.

Leflon, Jacques. *Les prêtres, les fidèles et l'état: Le ménage à trois du XIXe siècle*. Paris: Beauchesne, 1987.

Leflon, Jean. *Histoire de l'église depuis les origines jusqu'à nos jours: La crise révolutionnaire, 1789–1846*. Vol. 20. Paris: Bloud et Gay, 1949.

Lettre encyclique de plusieurs évêques de France, à leur frères les autres évêques et aux églises vacantes. Avec leur déclaration de foi. Paris: Leclère, n.d.

Lettre encyclique de plusieurs évêques de France, à leur frères les autres évêques et aux églises vacantes. 4th ed. Paris: L'imprimerie-librairie Chrétienne, 1795, *l'an 3*.

Ligou, Daniel. "De Louis XIV à la Révolution." In *Histoire de Dijon: Univers de la France*, edited by Pierre Gras, 143–94. Toulouse: Privat, 1987.

– *Montauban à la fin de l'Ancien Régime et aux débuts de la Révolution, 1787–1794*. Paris: Librairie M. Rivière, 1958.

Linton, Marisa. *Choosing Terror: Virtue, Friendship, and Authenticity in the French Revolution*. Oxford: Oxford University Press, 2013.

Liste des évêques, députés à l'Assemblée nationale qui ont signé l'Exposition des principes sur la Constitution du Clergé; des autres ecclésiastiques députés qui y ont adhéré, et des évêques qui ont envoyé leur adhésion. Paris: Laurens, n.d. [1790].

M'clintock, John, and James Strong, *Cyclopædia of Biblical, Theological and Ecclesiastical Literature*. Vol. 12. New York: Harper and Brothers, 1891.

Madival J., E. Laurent, et al., eds. *Archives parlementaires de 1787 à 1860: Recueil complet des débats législatifs et politiques des Chambres françaises*. Paris: Librairie administrative de P. Dupont, 1862–1914. French Revolution Digital Archive, Stanford University Libraries and the Bibliothèque nationale de France. http://purlstanford.edu/mc666yy3026.

Marc, Henri. *Biographie de Messire Chamberland, curé constitutionnel de Longchamp (de 1769 à 1825)*. Dijon: Darantiere, 1897.

Maréchaux, Xavier. *Noces révolutionnaire: Le mariage des prêtres en France, 1789–1815*. Paris: Vendémiaire, 2017.

– "Prêtres mariés de la Révolution à l'Empire: Répertoire biographique." Vol. 2. Doctoral diss., Université de Paris, 1995.

Marilier, Jean. "Le diocèse de Dijon: Histoire et art." In *Le diocèse de Dijon: Histoire et art*. Dijon: Musée de Dijon, 1957.

– "Le monastère et l'église des Bernardines de Tart à Dijon." *Mémoires de la commission des antiquités du département de la Côte-d'Or* 33 (1982–3): 255–90.

Martin, Jean-Clément. "Sur la traité de paix de La Jaunaye, février 1795, conditions d'une compromise." *Annales de Bretagne et de pays de l'Ouest* 104, no. 1 (1997): 73–88.

– *La Vendée et la France.* Paris: Éditions du Seuil, 1987.

Mathiez, Albert. *Les conséquences religieuses de la journée du 10 août 1792: La déportation des prêtres et la sécularisation de l'état civil.* Paris: E. Leroux, 1911.

– *Le culte de la raison et le culte de l'être suprême, 1793–1794: Essai historique.* Paris: Félix Alcan, 1892.

– *La Révolution française.* Vol. 1. *La chute de la royauté (1787–1792).* Paris: Librairie Armand Colin, 1922.

– *Rome et le clergé français sous la constituante: La Constitution civile du clergé et l'affaire d'Avignon.* Paris: Armand Colin, 1911.

– *La théophilanthropie et le culte décadaire: Essai sur l'histoire religieuse de la Révolution, 1796–1801.* 1903. Geneva: Slatkine-Megariotis reprints, 1975.

McBrien, Richard P. *Lives of the Popes: The Pontiffs from St. Peter to John Paul II.* San Francisco: HarperSanFrancisco, 1997.

McManners, John. *Church and Society in Eighteenth Century France.* Volume 1. *The Clerical Establishment and Its Social Ramifications.* Oxford: Oxford University Press, 1998.

– *The French Revolution and the Church.* Westport, CT: Greenwood Press, 1969.

Michaud, J. Fr. [Joseph François], Louis Gabriel Michaud, and Eugène Ernest Desplaces, eds. *Biographie universelle ancienne et moderne.* New ed. Paris: Madame C. Desplaces, 1854. Reprint Graz, AT: Akademische Druck-u. Verlagsanstalt, 1966–70.

Milbach, Sylvain. *Prêtres historiens et pèlerinages du diocèse de Dijon, 1860–1914.* Dijon: Éditions universitaires de Dijon, 2000.

Milsand, Ph[ilibert]. *Bibliographie bourguignonne.* Dijon: Gustave Lamarche, 1885.

– *Périodiques publiés à Dijon, depuis leur origine jusqu'au 31 décembre 1860.* Paris: Auguste Aubry Libraire, 1861.

Monnot, Annie. "Le clergé beaunnois pendant la Révolution, 1789–1795." Mémoire D.E.A. [master's thesis], Faculté de droit et de science politique de Dijon. 1988.

Moyse, Gérard. *Joyaux d'archives, jalons d'histoire: Les archives départementales de la Côte-d'Or à l'aube du troisième millénaire: onze siècles d'histoire.* Dijon: Archives départementales de la Côte-d'Or, 2001.

Muller, Claude, "La Croix et la cocarde: Les évêques constitutionnels

Alsaciens." In *Gouverner une église en revolution: Histoires et mémoires de l'épiscopat constitutionnel*, edited by Paul Chopelin, 99–123. Lyon: Laboratoire de recherche historique Rhônes-Alpes, 2017.

Navier. *Extrait du procès-verbal de l'Assemblée électorale du département de la Côte d'Or*. Dijon: Imprimerie de P. Causse, 1791.

Necheles, Ruth, F. "The Curés of the Estates General of 1789." *Journal of Modern History* 46 (1974): 425–44.

Palliot, Pierre. *Le parlement de Bourgogne, son origine, son établissement et son progrés …* Dijon: Chés ledit Palliot, 1649.

Palmer, R.R. *Catholics and Unbelievers in Eighteenth Century France*. Princeton, NJ: Princeton University Press, 1939.

– *Twelve Who Ruled: The Year of the Terror in the French Revolution*. Princeton, NJ: Princeton University Press, 1941.

Panhaleux, Françoise. "La circonscription des paroisses dans le Morbihan de 1790 au 10 août 1792." In *Pratiques religieuses, mentalités et spiritualités dans l'Europe révolutionnaire, 1770–1820: Actes du colloque de Chantilly, 27–29 novembre 1986*, edited by Bernard Plongeron, 225–9. Turnhout, BE: Brepols, 1988.

Peignot, Gabriel. *Notice exacte de toutes les personnes nées ou domiciliées dans le département de la Côte-d'Or qui ont peri sur l'échafaud pendant le régime révolutionnaire, 1793–1794*. Paris: Aug. Aubry, 1865.

Pelletier, Gérard. *Rome et la Révolution française: La théologie et la politique du saint siège pendant la Révolution française, 1789–1799*. Rome: École française de Rome, 2004.

Péronnet, Michel, and Serge Lochot. *La Révolution dans le département de la Côte-d'Or, 1789–1799*. Le Coteau: Horvath, 1988.

Perrouas, Louis, and Paul d'Hollander. *La Révolution française, une rupture dans le Christianisme? Le cas du Limousin (1775–1822)*. Treignac: Éditions "les Monedières," 1988.

Pétition des membres du conseil épiscopal du département de la Côte d'Or, extraordinairement assemblé, le mardi matin 19 juin 1792, l'an quatrième de la liberté, au directoire du même département. Dijon: P. Causse, 1792.

Phillips, Henry. *Church and Culture in Seventeenth Century France*. 2nd ed. Cambridge: Cambridge University Press, 2002.

Pierart, Z.J. *La grande épopée de l'an II: Souvenirs, rapprochements, rectifications et faits inédits relatifs aux Batailles de Wattignies, de Fleurus, et au Passages de la Sambre en 1793 et 1794*. Paris: A. Ferrould, Libraire-éditeur, 1887.

Pisani, Paul. *L'Église de Paris et la Révolution*. Paris: Alphonse Picard et Fils, 1908.

– *Répertoire biographique de l'épiscopat constitutionnel, 1791–1802.* Paris: Alphonse Picard et Fils, 1907.

Plongeron, Bernard. *L'Abbé Grégoire (1750–1831), ou, L'Arche de la fraternité.* Paris: Letouzey et Ané, 1989.

– *Conscience religieuse en révolution: Regards sur l'historiographie religieuse de la Révolution française.* Paris: A. et J. Picard, 1969.

– "L'église constitutionnelle [gallicane] à l'épreuve du Directoire: Réorganisation, liberté des cultes et Concile national de 1797." In *Du Directoire au Consulat,* edited by Hervé Leuwers. 1: 149–64. Lille: Université de Lille III, 2000.

– "L'exercise de la démocratie dans l'Église constitutionnelle de France, 1790–1801." *Concilium: Revue internationale de théologie* 77 (1972): 125–32.

– "Face au Concordat (1801): Résistances au évêques anciens constitutionnels." *Annales historiques de la Révolution française* no. 337 (July–September 2004): 85–115.

– "Hypothèques sur le Concordat: Lecture Gallicane des anciens évêques constitutionnels." In *Le Concordat et le retour de la paix religieuse: Actes du colloque organisé par l'Institut Napoléon et la Bibliothèque Marmotten le 13 octobre 2001.* Edited by Jacques-Oliver Boudon, 57–93. Paris: Éditions SPM, 2008.

– *Les réguliers de Paris devant le serment constitutionnel, sens et conséquences d'une option 1789–1801.* Paris: J. Vrin, 1964.

– "Théologie et applications de la collégialité dans l'église constitutionnelle de France, 1790–1801)." *Annales historiques de la Révolution française,* no. 211 (1973): 71–84.

– *Théologie et politique au siècle des lumières, 1770–1820.* Geneva: Librairie Droz, 1973.

– *La vie quotidienne du clergé français au XVIII siècle.* Paris: Librarie Hachette, 1974.

Plongeron, Bernard, and Astérious Argyriou. *Les défis de la modernité, 1750–1840.* Volume 10. *Histoire du christianisme des origins à nos jours.* Paris: Desclée, 1997.

Plongeron, Bernard, and Paule Lerou. *La piété populaire en France: Répertoire bibliographique.* Volume 3. *Bourgogne, Franche-Comté, Massif central, Rhône-Alpes.* Turnhout, BE: Brepols; Paris: GRECO no. 2, 1985.

Plongeron, Bernard, Paule Lerou, and Raymond Dartevelle, eds. *Pratiques religieuses, mentalités et spiritualités dans l'Europe révolutionnaire, 1720–1820: Actes du Colloque de Chantilly, 27–29 novembre 1986.* Turnhout, BE: Brepols, 1988.

Popkin, Jeremy D., and Richard H. Popkin, eds. *The Abbé Grégoire and His World*. Dordrecht, NL: Kluwer Publishers, 2000.

Pressensé, E. de. *The Church and the French Revolution: A History of Church and State, from 1789 to 1802*. Translated by John Stroyan. London: Unzin Brothers, 1869.

Procès-verbal dressé par le conseil général du département de la Côte-d'Or, relativement à la renonciation faite par les citoyens Jean-Augustin Alteyrac, demeurant à Châtillon-sur-Seine, et Charles Chaisneau, de Plombières, de leur caractère de prêtre. Séance du 22 brumaire, l'an 2. Dijon: P. Causse, l'an 2 [1793].

Prunel, Louis. *Sébastien Zamet, Évêque de Langres, Pair de France, 1588–1655: Sa vie et ses œuvres. Les origines du Jansénisme*. Paris: Picard, 1912.

Quérard, Joseph-Marie. *La France littéraire, ou dictionnaire bibliographique*. Paris: Chez Firmin Didot, Père et Fils, 1827.

Rémond, René. *Religion and Society in Modern Europe*. Translated by Antonia Nevill. Oxford: Blackwell Publishers, 1999.

Ribas, Paul. "Les prêtres fonctionnaires publiques et les serments dans le district de Dijon (décembre 1790 – prairial an III)." *Annales de Bourgogne* 54 (1982): 82–8.

Richard, Jean, ed. *Histoire de la Bourgogne*. Toulouse Cedex: Editions Privat, 1978.

Robert, Adophe, Edgar Bourloton, and Gaston Cougny, eds. *Dictionnaire des parlementaires français*. 3 vols. Paris: Bourloton, 1891.

Roserot, Alphonse. *Dictionnaire topographique du département de la Côte-d'Or*. Paris: Imprimerie nationale, 1924.

Sautereau, Philibert-Bernard, *L'Évêché de Dijon et ses Évêques*. Cîteaux, 1885.

Sauvageot, [Pierre]. *Discours prononce le 10 germinal, l'an second de la république français, au temple de la raison de la commune de Dijon, par Sauvageot, maire & président de la société populaire régénérée de la même commune*. Dijon: Imprimerie nationale, n.d.

Schama, Simon. *Citizens: A Chronicle of the French Revolution*. New York: Alfred A. Knopf, 1989.

Sciout, Ludovic. *Histoire de la Constitution civile du clergé, 1790–1801*. 4 vols. Paris: Firman-Didot, 1881.

Seconde letter encyclique de plusieurs évêques de France, réunis à Paris à leurs frères les autres évêques et aux églises veuves. Paris: Imprimerie-Librairie Chrétienne, 1795.

Sepinwall, Alyssa Goldstein. *The Abbé Grégoire and the French*

Revolution: The Making of Modern Universalism. Berkeley: University of California Press, 2005.

La Société populaire régénérée de Dijon, a la Convention nationale. Paris: G.F. Galletti, n.d.

Sottocasa, Valérie. *Mémoires affrontées: Protestants et Catholics face à la Révolution dans les montagnes de Languedoc*. Rennes: Presse universitaires de Rennes, 2004.

Spang, Rebecca. *Stuff and Money in the Time of the French Revolution*. Cambridge, MA: Harvard University Press, 2015.

Suratteau, J.R. "Le Directoire avait-il une politique religieuse?" *Annales historique de la Révolution française*, no. 283 (January–March 1991): 79–92.

Sutherland, D.M.G. *The French Revolution and Empire: A Quest for a Civic Order*. Oxford: Blackwell, 2000.

Sydenham, Michael J. *Léonard Bourdon: The Career of a Revolutionary, 1754–1807*. Waterloo, ON: Wilfrid Laurier University Press, 1999.

Tackett, Timothy. *Becoming a Revolutionary: The Deputies of the French National Assembly and the Emergence of a Revolutionary Culture, 1789–1790*. University Park, PA: Penn State University Press, 2006.

– *Priest and Parish in Eighteenth-Century France: A Social and Political Study of the Curés in a Diocese of Dauphiné, 1750–1791*. Princeton, NJ: Princeton University Press, 1977.

– *Religion, Revolution, and Regional Culture in Eighteenth-Century France: The Ecclesiastical Oath of 1791*. Princeton, NJ: Princeton University Press, 1986.

Tackett, Timothy, and Claude Langlois. "Ecclesiastical Structures and Clerical Geography on the Eve of the French Revolution." *French Historical Studies* 11, no. 3 (Spring 1980): 352–70.

Thompson, D. Gillian, "French Jesuits, 1756–1814." In *Jesuit Suppression in Global Context, Causes, Events, and Consequences*, edited by Jeffrey Burson and Jonathan Wright, 181–99. Cambridge: Cambridge University Press, 2015.

Tuffery-Audrieu, Jeanne-Marie. *Le council national en 1797 et en 1801 à Paris: L'abbé Grégoire et l'utopie d'un Église républicaine*. Bern: Peter Lang, 2007.

Van Kley, Dale. "The Abbé Grégoire and the Quest for a Catholic Republic." In *The Abbé Grégoire and His World*, edited by Jeremy Popkin, 71–107. Dordrecht, NE: Kluwer, 2000.

– "The *Ancien Régime*, Catholic Europe, and the Revolution's Religious Schism." In *A Companion to the French Revolution*, edited by Peter

McPhee, 123–44. Chichester, UK: Blackwell, 2013.

– "Catholic Conciliar Reform in an Age of Anti-Catholic Revolution: France, Italy, and the Netherlands, 1758–1801." In *Religion and Politics in Enlightenment Europe*, edited by James E. Bradley and Dale K. Van Kley, 46–118. Notre Dame, IN: University of Notre Dame Press, 2001.

– "Christianity as Casualty and Chrysalis of Modernity: The Problem of Dechristianization in the French Revolution." *American Historical Review* 108, no. 4 (October 2003): 1081–104.

– *The Jansenists and the Expulsion of the Jesuits from France, 1757–1765*. New Haven, CT: Yale University Press, 1975.

– "Plots and Rumors of Plots: The Role of Conspiracy in the International Campaign against the Society of Jesus, 1758–1768." In *The Jesuit Suppression in Global Context: Causes, Events, and Consequences*, edited by Jeffrey D. Burson and Jonathan Wright, 13–39. Cambridge: Cambridge University Press, 2015.

– *The Religious Origins of the French Revolution: From Calvin to the Civil Constitution, 1560–1791*. New Haven, CT: Yale University Press, 1996.

Varry, Dominique, and Claude Muller. *Hommes de Dieu et Révolution en Alsace*. Turnhout, BE: Brepols, 1993.

Vauchez, André, with Barrie Dobson and Michael Lapidge, eds. *Encyclopedia of the Middle Ages*. Translated by Adrian Walford. 2 vols. Chicago: Fitzroy Dearborn, 2000.

Vignier, F. "Tentative d'érection d'un siège épiscopal à la Sainte-Chapelle de Dijon en 1630." *Mémoires de la société pour l'histoire du droit et des institutions des anciens pays bourguignons, comtois et romands* no. 24 (1963): 299–303.

Volfius, Jean-Baptiste. "Déclaration de M. Volfius, ancien évêque constitutionnel de Dijon." *Journal de la Côte-d'Or*, 2 March 1816.

– "Discours de J.B. Volfius, au directoire du département." *Affiches de Dijon ou Journal du Département de la Côte-d'or*, no. 17 (7 *ventôse l'an* 2 [25 February 1794]), 66–7.

– *Discours de M. l'Abbé Volfius, Président de l'Assemblée électorale du District de Dijon, prononcé à la clôture des séances, le 1er juin 1790*. Dijon: Defay, n.d. [1790].

– "Discours de M. Volfius, élu Evêque du département de la Côte-d'Or, après sa proclamation." In *Extrait du procès-verbal de l'Assemblée électorale du département de la Côte-d'Or*. Dijon: Imprimerie de P. Causse, 1791.

– *Discours pour l'ouverture du cours d'histoire, prononcé dans la grand salle du collège Godrans du Dijon, le 19 novembre 1777*.

– *Discours prononcé à la bénédiction des drapeaux de messieurs les volontaires-artilleurs de la garde nationale de Dijon, dans l'église Saint-Bénigne, le 4 décembre 1789*. Dijon: De l'imprimerie de Jean-Baptiste Capel, 1789.

– *Discours prononcé à la bénédiction des drapeaux patriotiques de la milice citoyenne de Dijon, dans l'église paroissiale Saint-Michel, le 27 août 1789*. Dijon: Capel, 1789.

– *Discours prononcé le 18 mai 1790 à la cérémonie du serment fédératif prêté sous les murs de Dijon par MM. Les députés des départemens ci-devant province de Bourgogne*. Dijon: Causse, 1790.

– *Instruction pastorale de M. l'Évêque de la Côte-d'or*. [27 January 1793]. Dijon: P. Causse, 1793.

– "Lettre de J.B. Volfius, au Rédacteur du Journal du département de la Côte-d'Or." *L'original, ou Journal du département de la Côte-d'Or*, 1re année, no. 28 (18 *messidor l'an 3* [6 July 1795]): 221–4.

– *Lettre pastorale de M. l'évêque de la Côte-d'Or*. Dijon: Capel, 1791.

– "Mandement de l'évêque diocésain, pour la publication du synode." In *Actes du synode diocésain, tenu à Dijon le 8 Juillet 1800, de Notre Seigneur (19 mesidor de l'an 8 de la République française), et jours suivans*. Dijon: Imprimerie de Carion, *l'an 8* [1800].

– *Mandement de M. l'évêque de la Côte-d'Or*. [6 February 1792]. Dijon: P. Causse, 1792.

– *Mandement de M. l'évêque de la Côte-d'Or*. [20 September 1792]. Dijon: P. Causse, 1792.

– *Mandement du Citoyen Évêque de la Côte-d'Or*. [29 January 1793]. [Dijon]: P. Causse, 1793.

– *Rhétorique françoise à l'usage des collèges, dans laquelle on a recueille les observations sur l'art de bien dire, répandues dans les meilleurs auteurs*. 2nd ed. Dijon: L.N. Frantin, 1781.

Volfius, J-B, et al., "Les prêtres assermentés de Dijon, aux prêtres insermentés, Dijon, 19 thermidor an 3, 6 août 1795." *Annales de la religion* 1, no. 18 (12 *fructidor l'an 3* [29 August 1795]): 420–7.

Vovelle, Michel. *Piété baroque et dechristianisation en Provence au XVIII siècle: Les attitudes devant la mort d'après les clauses des testaments*. Paris: Plon, 1973.

– *Religion et révolution: La déchristianisation de l'an II dans le Sud-Est*. Paris: Hachette, 1976.

– *The Revolution against the Church: From Reason to the Supreme Being*. Translated by Alan José. Columbus: Ohio State University Press, 1991.

Wenzel, Éric. *Curés des lumières: Dijon et son diocèse*. Dijon: Éditions universitaire de Dijon, 2006.

Woell, Edward J. "The Origins and Outcomes of Religious Schism, 1790–99." In *A Companion to the French Revolution*, edited by Peter McPhee, 145–60. Chichester, UK: Blackwell, 2013.

– *Small-town Martyrs and Murderers: Religious Revolution and Counterrevolution in Western France, 1779–1914*. Milwaukee, WI: Marquette University Press, 2006.

Yolton, John W, ed. *The Blackwell Companion to the Enlightenment*. London: Blackwell, 1991.

Young, Arthur. *Arthur Young's Travels in France: During the Years 1787, 1788, and 1789*. Ed. Miss Betham-Edwards. 4th ed. London: George Bell and Sons, 1892.

Index

143; historiography, 8; imprisonment in Dijon, 11, 66–72; and
law of 11 *prairial*, 113; and marriage, 98; and oath of liberty and
equality, 74; and Pius VII, 140–1;
and religious liberty, 118, 131–4;
reports of activities, 58, 106, 112,
114, 122, 124–6, 128–30, 134–6,
154, 162; and synod of the Côte-
d'Or, 144–6; and theophilanthropy, 137; and United Bishops,
110–12; and Vendée, 82; and
Volfius, 66–7, 70, 72, 77–8, 81,
116–18, 126, 128, 131, 134,
140–1, 144–6. *See also* oath of 19
fructidor
regular clergy, 24, 98
Reinert, Eugène, 43, 45, 47, 161–8
relics, 99, 154
religious liberty, 9, 103–4, 107–9,
118, 120; law of 3 *ventôse*, 93,
107, 109–10, 112–13, 115, 118,
120, 124; and Volfius, 9, 115–18.
See also Hoche, Grégoire; Vendée
representatives on mission, 83, 86,
88–9, 92, 94, 98, 104, 109
Reubell, Jean-François, 138
revolutionary addresses of Volfius,
29–32, 34–7
Reymond, Henri, 152, 159
Richelieu, Cardinal Armand Jean du
Plessis, duke de, 127
Robert, François, 131
Robespierre, Maximilien, 12, 69, 73,
87–8, 97, 103, 120
Rohan, Cardinal Louis René
Édouard de, 22
Roland, Jean-Marie, 69, 80
Roman Republic, 53
royalists, 74, 119–22, 132, 135, 138,
140. See also *Glaneuse, La*
Royer, Jean-Baptiste, 7, 9–10,
107–8. *See also* United Bishops

Saillant, Charles, 7, 107. *See also*
United Bishops
Saint-Bénigne, abbey of, 16, 18–19,
154; cathedral, 90; crypt of 42;
and parish reduction in Dijon,
59–64; use as artillery park, 126.
See also church organs
Saint-Chapelle: and closing of
churches, 57, 59; and diocese of
Dijon, 18–19; and diocese of
Langres, 15–17; and Henri Dillon,
51; and Leprince, 68; and meeting
of second estate, 27
Saint-Claude, diocese of, 13
St. Cyprian, 50–3, 111
Saint-Étienne: and diocese of Dijon,
16, 18–19, 46; and parish closing
in Dijon, 59, 61–2, 64
Saint-Jean: arrest of refractories, 69;
church of, 55; closing of Dijon's
parishes, 57, 59, 64
Saint-Jean-de-Losne, 22, 43, 56, 65
Saint-Médard, 46, 59
Saint-Michel, 29, 31, 55, 90; and
closing of Dijon's parishes, 59, 61,
62–3. *See also* church organs;
temples of reason
Saint-Nicolas, 58; and closing of
Dijon's parishes, 59–63
Saint-Pierre, 42, 55; and closing
Dijon's parishes, 59–63;
faubourg of, 84
Saurine, Jean-Pierre, 107, 145, 150.
See also United Bishops
Saussay, André de, 17
Sauvageot, Pierre, 99, 104
Second National Council of the
Gallican Church, 144, 147–9, 152
Séguin, Philippe-Charles-François,
48
Ségur, Philippe de, 53
September massacres, 75–7
Sivry, François, 44, 122–3